*f*P

Also by Martin Mayer

The Bankers: The Next Generation
Nightmare on Wall Street
Stealing the Market
Whatever Happened to Madison Avenue?
The Greatest-Ever Bank Robbery
Markets: Who Plays, Who Risks, Who Gains, Who Loses
Making News
The Money Bazaars
The Fate of the Dollar
Conflicts of Interest: The Broker/Dealer Nexus
The Builders
The Bankers
About Television
New Breed on Wall Street
The Lawyers
Madison Avenue, USA
Wall Street: Men and Money

THE
FED

The Inside Story of How the World's Most Powerful Financial Institution Drives the Markets

MARTIN MAYER

THE FREE PRESS
New York   London   Toronto   Sydney   Singapore

THE FREE PRESS
A Division of Simon & Schuster Inc.
1230 Avenue of the Americas
New York, NY 10020

THE FREE PRESS and colophon are trademarks
of Simon & Schuster Inc.

Designed by Deirdre C. Amthor

Manufactured in the United States of America

10   9   8   7   6   5   4   3   2   1

Library of Congress Cataloging-in-Publication Data

Mayer, Martin, 1928–
    The Fed: the inside story of how the world's most powerful financial
institution drives the markets / Martin Mayer.
      p. cm.
    Includes bibliographical references and index.
    1. Board of Governors of the Federal Reserve System (U.S.) 2. Monetary
policy–United States. 3. Stock exchanges–United States.

HG2563 .M293   2001   2001023250
332.1'1'0973–dc21

ISBN 0-684-84740-X

For Karin with love
And for those who served with her at the IMF,
with affection and respect

Contents

Preface   *ix*

PART ONE: MAGIC TRICKS   1

Chapter 1: The Magician on the World Stage   *3*
Chapter 2: The Magician at Home   *28*

PART TWO: CENTRAL BANKS   53

Chapter 3: What Is a Central Bank?   *55*
Chapter 4: The Question of Independence   *80*

PART THREE: AVOIDING CATASTROPHE   99

Chapter 5: The System and Its Risks   *101*
Chapter 6: The American Lender of Last Resort   *120*

PART FOUR: MAKING MONEY   141

Chapter 7: The Age of Invention   *143*

CONTENTS

Chapter 8: Monetary Policy in the Maelstrom   164

Chapter 9: Disaster Time   181

Chapter 10: Greenspan and the Markets   205

Chapter 11: Internationally   226

PART FIVE: THE DAY JOBS   245

Chapter 12: The Payments Franchise   247

Chapter 13: Supervisions   264

Chapter 14: The Fed and the Poor   285

PART SIX: WHAT'S NEXT?   299

Chapter 15: The Fed in Our Future   301

Notes   323

Index   339

Preface

This is a book about how our central bank got to be what it is, why it does what it does, and why it must become something else.

The Federal Reserve System is the most forceful participant in American economic governance, but it is so today by custom and belief, and by the power of theater. The publicity element is new and largely misleading. When the Fed's actions directly and strongly influenced the course of the economy–roughly in the 1951–69 period when William McChesney Martin was chairman–the Fed was much less in the news. The most important single event in its history, the "Accord" with Harry Truman's Treasury Department that first asserted the independent authority of the Board of Governors to determine the price of short-term Treasury securities, does not rate a mention in the standard college history texts. (The full story is here.)

Now the Fed is always in the news. Its chairman, Alan Greenspan, appears at least four times a year, by statute, before congressional committees, and each appearance sends a *frisson* through the markets and then the media. Greenspan also makes several dozen speeches a year, widely, sometimes frenetically, reported. His views about what is happening in the U.S. economy are by universal agreement the most authoritative and thus predictive. The decisions to raise or lower short-term interest rates taken by the Federal Open Market Committee, which Greenspan chairs, are presumed to determine the nation's product, employment, and price levels looking forward six months to a year.

Only nobody knows anymore *why* very small changes in short-term rates, clearly unimportant in themselves, should have such a great influence on the economy. Long-term rates are by general agreement more significant than short-term rates, because investment decisions are made on a higher time horizon. In the 1950s, the conventional wisdom was that long-term rates were inevitably higher than short-term rates because the longer term is more uncertain and interest rates are the payment savers receive for accepting uncertainty. Talk at the Fed was of a kind of pegboard, where the movement of the short-term peg moved all the others, too. But today, with sophisticated theories and even more sophisticated instruments, long-term rates can move down when short-term rates go up, as they did in the spring of 2000—or can jump in response to a very small tightening, as they did in February 1994.

When Chairman Martin raised rates in the 1950s, he directly restricted lending by banks. In those days, banks could fund new loans only by selling investments—and these dropped in price, meaning the banks had to take a loss to sell them. Following the Fed's guidance, banks were the makers of interest rates: the "prime rate" that banks charged their best customers was the key to what borrowers at all maturities would have to pay.

Because more than three-fifths of all the financing required by American commerce and industry was mediated through the banks, the decrease in lending showed up fairly quickly in economic activity, and the constriction was felt by and in the markets. On the other side of the Fed's coin, a reduction in short-term rates gave banks a profit when they sold investments, and thus an incentive to make loans that could be funded by those sales. They said in the 1950s that Bill Martin could regulate by lifted eyebrow, and it was true.

Today, the department store charge accounts, the auto sales, the credit card debt, and the mortgages are all funded directly out of the market. Indeed, the working capital of large corporations that once borrowed from banks comes predominantly from the sale of commercial paper directly to investors. Only one-fifth of the nation's commercial and industrial financing now comes from the banks. Banks now take interest rates from the market instead of imposing them on borrowers. And the proprietors of the "new economy" companies don't borrow at all; they raise their money from venture capitalists and initial public offerings of common stock. Small movements of interest rates at the banks cannot any longer generate dramatic changes in businessmen's behavior.

Lifted eyebrows don't do much for Fed chairmen these days: to stop inflation in 1981–82, Paul Volcker had to jam his foot on the brakes so hard that interest rates rose above 20 percent per year; to rouse the economy ten years later, Alan Greenspan had to buy so much Treasury paper with Federal Reserve money that the nation's immediate money supply—cash plus balances in checking accounts—rose by more than 12 percent in a single year. And then Greenspan got lucky: the liquidity he pumped into the economy in 1991–92, and again in fall 1998, and again in late 1999 when fear of Y2K malfunctions dominated Fed actions, flowed into higher prices for assets, a stock-market boom, rather than into higher prices for goods and services. The eruption of Y2K money created a giant spike in the prices of technology stocks leading up to spring 2000. But it did not, to say the least, create a spike in the demand for the products of the companies that had issued the stock.

In the Martin and Volcker and early Greenspan days, the Fed moved in secrecy and expected that observers would draw their own conclusions about what the central bank was doing from observing price changes in the market. Paul Samuelson in his classic economics textbook suggested that announcements of the lifting or lowering of the Fed's discount rate usually *followed* the market, which had already been pushed, secretly, in the direction the Fed wished. Today the Fed announces its changed targets for overnight interest rates in the light of day *while the market is still open*, to maximize the immediate impact on stock and bond prices. This book opens with the tale of the near-disaster in October 1998, and Greenspan's triumph in staunching the blood with a single unanticipated interest rate cut of one quarter of one percent. The markets jumped up and never looked back. October 1998 was a psychological problem that could be solved by theatrical means. When he tried it again in January 2001, though the cut was deeper and the immediate reaction was the largest one-day rise in the history of the NASDAQ market, stock prices rather quickly fell back. Growth in the national product had slowed, and corporate profits were declining because the market boom had financed investment that didn't earn its carrying costs. This was a real difficulty that would take time to overcome.

The Fed's tools in this new millennium deal with psychology and the financial markets, which have been separated by technology and technique from the reality of employment and output. The rules have changed. Hence this book.

We live in a market-dominated world, and we have no road map to tell us the role of banks, bank regulators, and central banks in a market-dominated world. For those who believe that markets solve their own problems, and they were clearly dominant in the Bush administration in its early months, the disconnect between the Federal Reserve and the desired effects of its actions is not a matter of great concern. All they wanted from Alan Greenspan was his endorsement of a large tax cut, and he gave it to them. For those of us who agree with Walter Bagehot that "money will not manage itself," there is a great deal of work to be done—and it is not getting done.

Among the many who have been helpful to me over the years I have written about the Fed, I wish especially to acknowledge William McChesney Martin, Arthur Burns, Paul Volcker, Alan Greenspan, Henry Wallich, George Mitchell, Robert Holland, Roger Ferguson, Laurence Meyer, Alan Blinder, Janet Yellen, Robert Litan, Barry Bosworth, Hyman Minsky, Bernard Shull, Bruce Summers, Henry Kaufman, Elliott McEntee, Paul Connolly, Preston Martin, David Humphrey, Walker Todd, Scott Pardee, Maurice Mann, Gerald Dunne, Allan Sproul, Gerald Corrigan, George White, Frank Morris, William McCullough, Fred Deming, Tom Waage, Ernest Patrikis, John Heimann, William Isaac, George Martin, Jerry Hawke, Eugene Ludwig, Peter Fisher, Carter Golembe, "Adam Smith," Peter Bakstansky, Christine Cumming, Patrick Parkinson, Lynne Fox, and Timothy Dickinson. Also my grandson Lewis, who taught me that most of our currency no longer carries a letter identifying the Federal Reserve Bank that issued it; and, of course, Karin Lissakers.

Martin Mayer
Washington, February 2001

THE
FED

PART ONE

Magic Tricks

Chapter 1

The Magician
on the World Stage

Since the last great universal crisis of 1867 many profound changes have taken place. The colossal extension of the means of transportation and communication—seagoing steamers, railroads, electric telegraphs, the Suez Canal—have made the real world market a fact. . . . Infinitely greater and varied fields have been opened in all parts of the world for the investment of superfluous European capitals, so that it is far more distributed, and local overspeculation may be more easily overcome. By means of these things, the old breeding grounds of crises and opportunities for the growth of crises have been eliminated or strongly reduced.

—Friedrich Engels (1894)[1]

As THE MILLENNIUM TURNS, central banks are in apotheosis. Never has their prestige, their authority, or their independence—indeed, their mystique—been greater. But the appearances are deceptive. The volcano rumbles under Olympus and fissures are visible on the slopes. The unprecedented volatility in the markets—stock markets, bond markets, foreign exchange markets—demonstrates that instead of settling down, the postmodern financial system is acting up. Central banking in the twentieth century, especially as practiced by the Federal Reserve System in the United States, is one of the great stories in economic history, and no one can understand the present policy dilemma worldwide (the need, as former Treasury Secretary Robert Rubin put it, for a new financial architecture) without understanding that story. In a world where tiny changes in interest rates can produce rapid and vast change in the prices of financial instruments and the viability of national economic policies, the decisions the central banks must make are exquisitely important. They had better know what they're doing. We had better know what they're doing.

The touchstone has to be October 1998. It very nearly all came apart in October 1998.

As they do in two of every three years, bankers and central bankers, financiers and finance ministers came to Washington by the thousands in the first week of October 1998 for the annual meetings of the International Monetary Fund and the World Bank. It turned out to be an experience they will never forget as long as they live, a weekend of pure terror, as though an asteroid were descending on Earth, much worse than the riotous and riotously publicized protests at the smaller Interim Committee meeting eighteen months later. David Komansky, CEO of Merrill Lynch, the prototype of the jolly fat man, said that he woke up on Saturday morning an optimist, and that night he wanted to crawl under the bed to hide.

This was far from a normal experience at the Bank/Fund meetings, which have usually been a kind of reward for their participants, divided by age. Seniors enjoy their importance in various caucuses formed for self-congratulation and finger-pointing at others outside the caucus. They eat and drink the very best, decorously, at parties in venues like the Corcoran Gallery and the Folger Library. Juniors, drafted during the day to provide an audience for the big shots at the plenary sessions in the enormous ballroom of the Sheraton Park Hotel near the National Zoo, party vigorously late into the night at the expense of various publications and suppliers to the finance community. All the 182 countries that belong to the Bank and the Fund are represented, usually by both finance minister and central bank chairman (all expenses paid by the Bank or the Fund), and all the world's two hundred largest banks are there (at their own expense), sometimes with delegations of thirty and forty people.

Not much work is required. Some of the pleasantries in the corridors will turn into deals, and everybody's Rolodex grows larger. But the closing communiqués are in large part ritual, and where in fact real decisions must be made, the terms if not the details are arranged before the first limousine takes the first delegate from Dulles Airport to his or her hotel. "The deputies" have already met, in Paris or Tokyo or Rome, and written the draft of the communiqué, which will be presented in Washington to selected representatives of the outliers of globalism, noblesse oblige, before the public meetings begin on Monday. If disagreements persist, they are resolved on Saturday, when the finance ministers of the seven big financial powers (the list includes Canada, but not China or Russia) meet as a group.

The official meetings are only part of the show. Perhaps the most important side event is a Monday morning conference sponsored by the Group of Thirty, a think tank established in the late 1970s with help from the Rockefeller Foundation. The anointed Thirty in 1998 included active executives of the Bank for International Settlements in Basle, the Banque de France, the European Central Bank, the Bank of England, and the Bank of Israel, plus former chief executives of the Federal Reserve, the Bank of Japan, Danmarks Nationalbank, the International Monetary Fund, and the Federal Reserve Bank of New York; half a dozen academics; and present or recently retired senior executives of Citibank, Dresdner Bank, Deutsche Bank, Goldman, Sachs, Industrial Bank of Japan, Merrill Lynch, J. P. Morgan, and Morgan Stanley. When the Bank/Fund meeting is in Washington, the Group of Thirty affair occurs at the Pan-American Union or in the top-floor meeting room of the Federal Reserve's Martin Building.

Beneath the practiced mallet of Paul Volcker, a former Fed chairman, the conference proceeds in an orderly fashion for three hours through presentations by a dozen speakers (it always, miraculously, ends on time). Private bankers, finance ministers, and central bankers–since 1987, the list has always included Federal Reserve chairman Alan Greenspan, early in the proceedings–present their views on the world's financial situation and respond to a few questions from the audience. In 1998, the usual list of the great and the good–the finance minister of Italy, the chairman of the Bank of Japan, a senior executive from Deutsche Bank, and so on–was supplemented by George Soros, who had just lost $2 billion in Russia.

But for once the context of the meeting had been set not by its own eminent speakers but at another meeting two days before, when Deutsche Bank, the largest by some margin of the German banks, presented the report of its Global Markets Group. Volcker also chaired this meeting, which was held in the downstairs ballroom of the Omni Hotel near the Sheraton. Each member of the audience was presented with an 83-page large-format coated-paper pamphlet on *Global Emerging Markets,* tastefully illustrated on the cover with a drawing of the *Titanic* sinking in an iceberg field and a bunch of lifeboats seeking to escape. Next to the illustration was the sentence: "The real problems lie below the waterline."

Lumping together the five nations devastated by the Asian financial crisis, the Deutsche Bank researchers concluded that "While it is difficult to argue that governments are insolvent . . . under most scenarios, the ability of the government to service its debt in the short run is questionable."[2] Turning attention to Russia, the German bank's experts argue that "there is a very high risk that Russia will not be able or willing to repay its foreign debt"[3]–ever. Latin America might have a chance because most countries had large enough reserves to ride out a long storm, but "failing to stay on course might have very costly and lasting consequences."[4] And the main speaker in the Latin American part of the program, Professor Guillermo Calvo of the University of Maryland, thought it would be wisest to abandon hope. Then David Folkerts-Landau, "Global Head" of Emerging Markets Research, formerly director of capital markets research for the International Monetary Fund, presented his paper on why the current behavior patterns of the international banks *and their supervisors,* especially in the creation and valuation of derivatives, made crises worse. Volcker called everybody's attention to Folkerts-Landau's paper, both at the Deutsche Bank meeting and at the Group of Thirty conference the following Monday.

Russia had defaulted in August, telling foreign investors in its government debt that they could go whistle for their money. Long Term Capital Management (LTCM) of Greenwich, Connecticut, the biggest of the "hedge funds"–the engines of great wealth that only the rich could ride–had collapsed ten days before the Deutsche Bank presentation. The second biggest such fund, Julian Robertson's Tiger, was bleeding money in the billions of dollars from a wrong bet on what would happen to the Japanese yen. The old market-savvy trading firms made their money in times of high volatility, because they had antennae all over the market and felt the shifts in sentiment. But the new computer-oriented trading firms relied on statistical distributions and normal curves, and advertised that they didn't take risks in the market because they understood the probabilities of all the price movements and placed their bets scientifically. Volatility meant that the probabilities did not hold, and destroyed them. Because they had said they weren't risky, they had been able to borrow 98, 99, 100 percent of the money they bet, some of it from banks, some from securities houses. They were incorporated in places like the Cayman Islands, and nobody in any financial center, including the Federal Reserve System, knew what they were doing. But if they really smashed and defaulted on their borrowings, a lot of big institutions might be ruined.

Secondary effects hit harshly in the world of borrowers. In September 1997, Brazil had been able to borrow money on the international market for the rates on U.S. Treasury paper plus about 4 percentage points; in September 1998, Brazil could borrow money internationally only by paying the U.S. Treasury rate plus 22 percentage points. Japan was mired in recession, longing to export its way out of trouble but constrained by the knowledge that such a policy would devastate the rest of Asia, unable to think of anything

7

else to do. In the United States itself, bonds issued by companies without a large asset base were selling to yield three times as much as bonds issued by the best corporations, and the market for initial public offerings–first issues of stocks (or bonds) by new businesses– had dried up completely. Though the publicized indices had not been so hard hit, the average share in a traded American corporation was down more than a third from its early summer highs. The closer you lived to the financial world, the greater the panic. Everybody knew there was bad trouble in Asia; in Washington, bankers, central bankers, and finance ministers from around the world–especially from Europe, whence the bankers and ministers had come to the meetings interested only in themselves and their shiny new money– were learning that if they hadn't felt the pain yet, it was because they were off the beaten track.

One of the last speakers at the Group of Thirty conference was William McDonough, president of the Federal Reserve Bank of New York, a pleasant, calculating former Chicago banker, usually a rather gray man, who said that what he saw around him was the greatest fi- nancial crisis of his lifetime. Everyone here, he said, is a banker or a bank supervisor. If you're a banker, go out and lend–you don't have to dot every i and cross every t. If you're a bank supervisor, don't crit- icize your banks for making loans even if they're loans you might not have approved just a little while ago. Get the money out; the world needs the money.

Later that same week, the Federal Reserve Bank of Chicago held a symposium jointly sponsored with the International Monetary Fund (IMF) on the causes and consequences of the Asian crisis. I was among the speakers. On Friday morning, arguing that it was time for her to get away from her usual companions from universities and governments and see what real capitalism looked like, I took the U.S. executive director of the IMF across the street to the Chicago Board of Trade, where futures contracts for agricultural and financial commodities are bought and sold in open outcry markets. We went up to the upper level of the visitors' gallery and looked out on the "pit" where futures contracts for U.S. Treasury bonds are traded ($100,000 face value per contract). It is a large, dark wood, octagonal structure, with seven steps from bottom to top; almost three hundred traders were crammed onto the rings of steps, shouting and waving their trading cards in the air to get the attention of the others. Against the wall behind the pit are row on row of desks where the clerks sit at the telephones, taking the buy and sell messages from the outside world, wig-wagging them down to the brokers in the pit, who are in constant interaction with the "locals," the traders for their own account. The important traders, making the most motions, are on the top step, where they can see the whole pit and all the clerks. ("A good place to stand," the most successful bond trader of the 1980s told novices in a lecture, "is where the locals that drive the nicest cars and make the most money stand.")[5] Sealed off behind the glass, visitors can hear the roar.

And then the roar stopped. The men stopped waving their arms in the pit, and they all just stood, arms at their sides. At 11:45 in the morning, the price of the T-bond futures contract had dropped $3,000, which was the maximum move in a single day. The market had closed "lock limit down" for the first time since Saddam Hussein invaded Kuwait. The traders stayed in the pit, because any bid above the current price would reopen trading; but there was no such bid. We returned to the Federal Reserve Bank of Chicago, and in the anteroom ran into Michael Moscow, president of the bank, a tolerant economist who does one thing at a time. We told him what we had seen across the street, and he nodded soberly. "Yes," he said. "There are no bids for anything. There is no money."

On Sunday, October 11, I flew off to Geneva, where I was to be one of four "experts" to help the member states of UNCTAD–the United Nations Conference on Trade and Development–think about "standstill agreements" that might permit everybody to draw breath after a banking-cum-currency crisis left a country unable to finance its imports or pay its debts. Monday, I met with Dr. Yilmaz Akyuz,

UNCTAD's Turkish-born chief of macroeconomic and development policies, who thought the jig was probably up for economic development financed by cross-border flows of capital. As always, banks had lent short-term money for long-term purposes, and now the loans had to be rolled over, and the banks very clearly weren't willing to do it. Delegate after delegate told me he expected that his country would be in default on its obligations before the middle of 1999. To represent UNCTAD at UN headquarters in New York, Akyuz had just hired Jan Kregel, a very smart and knowledgeable young American economist with the brush mustache of a British grenadier, who taught at the University of Bologna. On Tuesday, after the conference standstill discussions, I had dinner with Kregel, a protégé of the great post-Keynesian economist Hyman Minsky, and he laid out a scenario based on an anticipated deep world recession in 1999. There was no money internationally; nobody was prepared to bid for anything.

Then, on Thursday, October 15, at 3:04 in the afternoon, a press release from the Federal Reserve Board informed the world that Chairman Alan Greenspan, acting on authority given him by the Federal Open Market Committee after a conference call with the members of that committee, had told the system's trading desk in New York to put enough new money in the banks to lower the "Fed Funds" rate, the interest banks pay each other for overnight loans, by 25 "basis points," one-quarter of 1 percentage point.

The timing was fascinating. The bond markets had closed for Thursday, eliminating the small but real danger that bond traders, seeing Greenspan's action as an abandonment of the fight against inflation, would push up long-term rates while he was pushing down short-term rates. And the next day would see the monthly expiration of a set of exchange-traded options contracts on stocks—contracts each of which gave their holder the right (but not the obligation) to purchase or sell one hundred shares of the specified stock at a preset "strike price" that might be above or below the market price. If not exercised, these contracts for this period would expire worthless at the close of trading on Friday. People who had written contracts that gave their purchaser the right to buy stocks tomorrow at yesterday's prices would have to worry that Greenspan's action would send the market soaring, and they would therefore have every reason to buy the underlying stocks as soon as possible to limit their losses on the contract. This need for the players in the options market to cover their positions immediately (because "in-the-money" options would definitely be exercised the next day) would further strengthen the upward pressure on stock prices Greenspan's announcement was sure to cause. From three o'clock Thursday afternoon to four o'clock Friday afternoon, the stock market rose more than 7 percent. Roughly $1 trillion was added to the world's wealth, on one man's say-so.

In a world where the Russians and the educated fools of Long Term Capital Management and the crony capitalists of Asia had changed everybody's estimate of the risks undertaken by investors in the capital markets, where there was a gap of 12 to 20 percentage points between the interest rates on foreign bonds or low-rated domestic bonds and the interest rates on U.S. government paper (perfectly safe by definition, because the U.S. government can print legal tender to redeem it), one-quarter of 1 percentage point was not in itself a noticeable, let alone a commanding, move by the authorities. But you had to consider—or you *thought* you had to consider—who was doing it.

In private conversation a couple of weeks before his October 15 intervention, Greenspan had noted with weary regret that the whole world seemed to believe that the Fed was in control of what happened to the economy. Of course, he said, the Fed could strangle the economy by pushing real interest rates beyond the level honest enterprise could pay—which is roughly what his predecessor Paul Volcker had done in the early 1980s—but its powers for stimulus were very limited. Nevertheless, on October 15, he went out on centerstage with his top hat and pulled a rabbit out of the hat. It wasn't Bugs Bunny or Roger Rabbit; it was a pretty scrawny little rabbit to which nobody really *had* to pay attention; and there wasn't anything else in the hat. But the magician concentrated the attention of the world on his rabbit, and the crisis eased. Someone, the magician seemed to be saying, was now in charge. The markets had desperately wanted to believe that someone was in charge; and they believed.

The reasons Alan Greenspan gave for his *coup du théâtre* explain much of how the world works today, and how the chairman of the Fed must think about it.

Greenspan said that what convinced him he had to move was the gap that had opened between the price of the current "on-the-run" 30-year U.S. Treasury bond and the price of the bond issued the year before. In October 1998, new 30-year bonds were selling to yield one-third of a percentage point less than the 1997 bond. As investments, the two are essentially identical; there is no fundamental reason why two long-dated bonds with only a year's difference in their maturity should not offer purchasers very similar yields. In October, however, the bond that had been issued in August is still mostly in the hands of dealers and hedge funds, which are busily playing all their little arbitrage games of stripping the coupons off the bonds and selling the parts, then putting the coupons back on the bonds and selling the whole. That meant that the market was liquid, and a purchaser could count on being able to get out fast at a reasonable price if it turned out that she needed cash. The bond issued in August of the year before, by contrast, had mostly disappeared into the vaults of the insurance companies and pension funds and bond mutual funds. They had acquired this paper pursuant to longer-term strategies. They're rarely in the market to add to their holdings of "seasoned" government bonds.

Thus a purchaser of a bond with twenty-nine rather than thirty years to go ran a slightly greater risk that she would have to cut her price substantially when she wanted to sell. In October 1998, there was no money and there were no bids, and a professional purchaser of a one-year-old 30-year bond had to worry that he could be locked in, paying interest to fund his holdings that might exceed his earnings on the bond. Indeed, the only way out might be to sell a futures contract on the Chicago Board of Trade, and then to deliver the bond in satisfaction of the contract when it expired. When the bond-futures pit closed lock limit down, even that chance seemed to be foreclosed.

On October 15, 1998, the world was in fact swimming in excess liquidity. The Bank of Japan was frantically pumping yen into the stagnant pools of its economy, and in the United States all the measures of money supply were rising rapidly. But as the gap between new and seasoned long-term bonds demonstrated, the appearances were deceptive. Money supplies were rising because participants in the markets wanted cash rather than securities. The banks, which could be called on to repay their depositors at any time, were keeping the liquidity for themselves, fearful that those who funded them would take their money out. Indeed, the Japanese banks, agents of a country with literally hundreds of billions of dollar-denominated reserves, were being forced to pay a "Japan premium," a higher interest rate, when they went to market to borrow dollars from other banks.

There are many discussions in many venues of what numbers central bankers should watch. The *Wall Street Journal* is fixated on the price of gold: if gold goes up, its editors believe, there are inflationary pressures abroad in the world, and if gold goes down, the danger is deflation. Milton Friedman and a rapidly diminishing band of acolytes want the central banks to create money at a steady pace of 3 percent a year, which will give the economy room to grow at stable prices—indeed, Friedman sometimes seems to believe that it will *force* the economy to grow at stable prices. The Maastricht Treaty of 1991 that wrote a framework for the European Central Bank calls for it to maintain "price stability." The "wise men" who guide the Bank of England in its new independent existence target an inflation rate, elaborately calculated. The Humphrey-Hawkins Act in the United States requires the maintenance of high employment. In the real world, Mr. Greenspan monitors the spread between the interest rates on this year's and last year's 30-year bond.

Political Washington, a junior minister in the British Foreign and Commonwealth Office once told me, is a place where information, not knowledge, is power. Alan Greenspan's Fed is devoted to information beyond the imaginings of enterprise America or, indeed, the executive branch of the federal government; he drives his staff crazy with demands for disaggregated data. When he was a consultant in private practice, he once said that what he did for a living was "statistical espionage." But he has been extraordinarily adept at finding those pieces of information that can in fact create knowledge.

One more aspect of this remarkable story should be considered. At the depth of despair in the financial world, Greenspan gave a speech to a convention of retailers in which he suggested that the best thing they could do for the next week was throw their daily newspapers into a dresser drawer, unread. Disasters are the best stories; the chairman expected a whirlpool of news attention that would suck public confidence to the depths already reached in the financial world. But in fact, with the single exception of Thomas Friedman of *The New York Times,* who wrote a column on the op-ed page incorporating an all-caps scream of "BUT HAVE WE GONE NUTS???"[6], the press ignored the crisis. The fact that the T-bond contract had closed lock limit down in the middle of the trading day, for the first time in eight years, was never reported in the *Times* or *The Washington Post,* and simply appeared as part of the usual roundup piece about financial commodities on Monday in the *Wall Street Journal.* For newspaper editors, a story about bids drying up in the bond market is what William Safire was the first to call a MEGO (for My Eyes Glaze Over); for television producers, there is absolutely no redeeming social value in trying to tell about a financial crisis that has not yet punished telegenic people.

So the news that the world was passing through the worst financial crisis since World War II never got into the papers at all. Few beliefs are so widely held as the idea that an informed public helps decision makers do the right thing, but it's not guaranteed. Greenspan's rabbit might not have been so all-absorbing if newspaper readers had known there was blood in the streets. A little learning, Alexander Pope argued, is a dangerous thing. Looking out at the world from their eagles' nests, central bankers must feel once again that a little ignorance is a necessary evil.

Central bankers have always believed, and in their hearts most of them still do believe, though their tongues say something else, that what the people don't know won't hurt them. Historically, no occupation has been more secretive. The monetary economist Karl Brunner once described central banking as "traditionally surrounded by a peculiar and protective political mystique. . . . The possession of wisdom, perception and relevant knowledge is naturally attributed to the management of Central Banks. . . . The mystique thrives on a pervasive impression that Central Banking is an esoteric art. Access to this art and its proper execution is confined to the initiated elite."[7]

In 1989, Alan Greenspan testified before Congress against the idea that the Federal Open Market Committee (FOMC) should announce its decisions to raise or lower or maintain short-term interest rates: "it would be ill-advised and perhaps virtually impossible to announce short-run targets for reserves or interest rates when markets were in flux"—and even in normal times "a public announcement requirement also could impede timely and appropriate adjustments to policy."[8] A couple of years before, the Fed had fought to the Supreme Court and won a lawsuit in which a Georgetown University law student had tried to force publication of the decisions of the FOMC. Awful things would happen if the world knew the instructions being given to the desk that traded Treasury paper for the Fed, said Governor Charles Partee and senior staffer Steven Axilrod. It would cost the government more money to sell its bonds because the primary dealers would have to protect themselves against informed speculators (Governor Partee estimated a loss of $300 million a year), and the Fed itself might lose money on its trades if speculators had this information. Verbally, all that changed in the 1990s; the watchword now is "transparency," and it is only cynics who feel that the lady doth protest too much. "The word honor in the mouth of Daniel Webster," said Senator John Randolph of Virginia (on the Senate floor, too) "is like the word love in the mouth of a whore." I have some of that feeling when I hear a central banker recommend "transparency."

The world's central bankers meet eight times a year–formerly only those from the eleven largest Western economies, now with some added starters from poorer parts–as the directors of the Bank for International Settlements (BIS), a leftover from the days of German reparations disputes a decade after World War I. Their meeting place is a handsome round tower in Basle, the highest building in the city, not in its center but at the railroad station, which was once the most convenient locus for European conclave. They rarely tell outsiders what they talk about.

The annual report does not discuss at any length what the BIS did during the year, but presents the views of the managing director (and his very talented multinational staff) on what has been happening to the world's economies and the world's monies. Written brilliantly in English by the curmudgeonly American economist Milton Gilbert in the 1960s and 1970s, then also in English by the equally brilliant multilingual Belgian Alexandre Lamfalussy in the 1980s and early 1990s (before Lamfalussy went off to put the future European Central Bank on an intellectually stable footing while it was still called the European Monetary Institute), the BIS annual report has been for decades the world's best source of information about cross-border banking and national economic policies. Lamfalussy's successor, Andrew Crockett from the Bank of England, is still trying, with help from the easygoing Canadian William White, who runs the BIS research operation, to fill those shoes.

It's not unreasonable for BIS to concentrate on its opinions rather than its actions, because the BIS has essentially no authority to act. It has some resources, especially a hoard of gold (it still keeps its own books in "gold francs"), and the stock trades on the Paris Bourse, essentially as a proxy for gold. In January 2001, the private stockholders sued to prevent BIS from forcibly buying in their stock at what they considered an inequitable price. When big-time packages are put together to rescue this country or that from the consequences of bad luck or folly (the list includes the United States in

1978 as well as Mexico in 1995 and the Asians in 1997), the BIS has an advertised part in it, though in fact its contributions are book-keeping on both sides and the bank almost never puts up any actual cash. Its most important role has been to establish forums where issues can be thrashed out among central bankers and guidelines can be set.

The most significant of these guidelines was a recommendation back in the 1980s that national central banks should set minimum "risk-adjusted capital" standards for banks headquartered in their countries that also operated elsewhere in the world. Banks notoriously buy their assets with Other People's Money; only the bank's capital is its owners' money. Obviously, a bank that has all its assets in government bonds requires less capital than a bank making real estate development loans and speculating in the derivatives markets; hence "risk adjustment." But the immediate purpose of the capital standards recommended by Basle, and imposed over the next few years by the authorities in all the major countries, was to rein in the Japanese banks, which had been rampaging around the world's markets making loans at rates others could not match, because they had essentially no equity on which they had to deliver returns.

Unfortunately, the categories of risk were poorly defined—for example, interbank loans between the banks of countries that were members of the Organization of Economic Cooperation and Development (OECD), a group that included Mexico and South Korea, were given a weighting of only 20 percent, which meant that the same capital could support loans to such banks five times as large as loans to manufacturing enterprise. Efforts to change the definitions of risk have foundered, mostly because the Germans want a special category for their housing bonds. Pending as these words are written is a proposal by which the banks could make up their own risk schedules with reference to the published ratings of Moody's and Standard & Poor's—a truly awful idea, because lending officers at banks and ratings officers at the ratings agencies tend to be optimistic or pessimistic at the same time. So the talk at BIS too is about "transparency," letting the markets know what each central bank is doing, and urging every nation's commercial banks to publish considerable though significantly incomplete information about their investments and off-balance-sheet activities.

The transparency push, originated with the world's finance ministers and the International Monetary Fund, was led by the American Susan Krause, then senior deputy comptroller for international affairs in the U.S. Office of the Comptroller of the Currency. Krause, an energetic lady in her forties, with a casual manner but square shoulders, really did believe (most of the time) that getting more information out about banks and central banks would make the regulators' job easier. But the regulators must make a credible commitment: "[I]f shareholders, creditors and the market in general believe that governments will allow non-disclosure, partial disclosure or even misleading disclosure should a bank run into difficulties," she wrote in a paper for the Basle Committee on Banking Supervision, "they are unlikely to consider publicly disclosed information credible."[9] She admits that it goes against "the gut reactions of banking supervision." But, she adds, "Asia illustrated the dangers of a lack of transparency." It works, she suggests, if you can "think separately about valuation and disclosure." There are important converts, at least in public, among them Alan Greenspan.

The symbol of the new openness is the light that now shines on the work of the Federal Open Market Committee. In the 1980s, "Fed watchers" at the Wall Street houses, like Salomon's Henry Kaufman and First Boston's Albert Woljinower, issued streams of comments on the significance of the Fed's daily purchases and sales of government paper. Now the Fed publishes *before* each FOMC meeting the "beige book" on economic conditions in each of the twelve districts, which is prepared by the staffs of the district Federal Reserve Banks and will guide the deliberations of the FOMC. And an announcement is made, during the FOMC's two-day meetings, in time for the markets to use the information on a same-day basis, to tell the world whether the Fed will be changing short-term interest rates—and if so, why; if not, why not.

There is no question that this is Greenspan's doing, though perhaps some credit should be given to Alan S. Blinder, a Princeton economist who served as vice chairman through the middle 1990s. Blinder believes completely in transparency for central banks, arguing that it makes them more effective: "A central bank which is inscrutable gives the markets little or no way to ground [its] perceptions in any underlying reality–thereby opening the door to expectational bubbles that can make the effects of its policies hard to predict. A more open central bank, by contrast, naturally conditions expectations by providing the markets with more information about its own view of the fundamental factors guiding monetary policy. This conditioning ought to make market reactions to monetary policy changes somewhat more predictable, thereby creating a virtuous circle. . . . And that makes it possible to do a better job of managing the economy."[10]

It is not clear that the Fed's staff, which has great influence on Greenspan (he says much more interesting things on the road than he does when he speaks from his office), has signed off on the values of transparency. The Fed in recent years has asked Congress to strengthen bank secrecy laws, increasing, for example, the penalties on anyone who leaks anything from an examination report that might indicate that a bank's public statements are less than full or less than honest. To protect the privacy of his colleagues, Greenspan even misled the Congress, claiming incorrectly that no transcript was made of the tape recordings of FOMC meetings, and that the tape recordings were destroyed (the tape, we were told, was recorded over for the next meeting) once they had been used to prepare the traditional ritualized summary of the meeting. On the general issue of putting out information so that "market discipline" could reinforce the supervisory work of bank examiners, the Fed staff really agrees with Lowell Bryan of McKinsey & Co. that "market discipline by depositors is another name for bank panics."[11]

A Fed staff study, "Improving Public Policy Disclosure in Banking," published in early 2000, notes that "the public policy concern is that disclosure about individual banks would trigger actions by private stakeholders that would preempt the efforts of a central bank and supervisory agencies to contain a systemic threat." The study suggested that Federal Reserve examiners could "review the public disclosures of large banking organizations as part of their evaluations of its management."[12] By the time this process was completed, the intervention of the Fed's disclosure authorities would probably reduce the quantity of information legally available to the public.

Bank secrecy is in the bones of central bankers. It goes back to a time when the knowledge banks gathered—about changes in interest rates and foreign exchange rates, the creditworthiness of borrowers, corporate investment plans—was available only to banks, which spent a good deal of money gathering it. Bank income derived not so much from maturity transformation—taking very short term money like checking account deposits and converting it to loans of some duration—as from information advantages. *Credit* in Latin means "he believes." Banks had a rational basis for belief, because they knew a lot. Direct lenders or investors, who employed their money without the intermediation of the bank, knew much less. (Remember Partee's comment that the Fed would lose $300 million a year in its trading if the speculators on the other side of its transactions were better informed.) Banks could spread the costs of gathering credit information over a number of accounts, and use the information in a number of contexts.

As late as the years right after World War II, more than three-fifths of all lending in the United States was mediated through the commercial banks. Their profits came from their exploitation of the information they had and others didn't. Of course they wanted legal protection of their secrecy.

Which left them sitting ducks for the information revolution and the development of modern finance economics. Today, for minimal expense, anyone with a computer modem can know just about everything a bank knows, certainly about conditions in the money market and probably about the quality of potential borrowers. The BIS has even suggested that the ratings agencies know more than the banks. It's Ozymandias—there's a ruined statue in the desert, with a pedestal boasting of a glorious past when banks called the tune and markets danced to it.

In the old days, the central bank worked on the economy by influencing the behavior of the banks; enterprise was dependent on banks, and responded to their response to the pressure from the central bank; and the market moved according to participants' perceptions of what would happen to the economy with the change of behavior and attitude at the banks. Now what banks do doesn't matter all that much in the United States, and soon in Europe, too (indeed, part of the problem in the world is that banks still do matter enormously in the less developed countries and it's hard for the industrial countries to understand that, especially where there are touted "emerging markets"). Where information technology has taken hold, the central bank, still charged with keeping the currency stable and the economy growing, must work its magic *through* the markets.

To abuse Isaiah Berlin's metaphor one more time, banks are hedgehogs who know the few things they know very, very well; markets are foxes that roam the world picking up snippets of fashion. Banks are stuck with their corporate customers, who owe them money; markets can sell out the stock in a twinkling. The conflict between the information systems, one deep, one shallow, could not be more striking. Banks generate and keep information; markets forage for it, publicize it, and consume it. Banks historically have been confident in their information, and set a course with it; markets are ready to turn on a dime. As markets rather than central banks set most of the interest rates that matter and markets rather than examiners value the banks' investment portfolios, and the instability of their funding multiplies their risks, banks have become less assiduous in seeking information, less confident in the information they have, more willing to go with a flow they and their supervisors only partially understand. "Do we," asked E. Gerald Corrigan, former president of the Federal Reserve Bank of New York and chairman of the executive committee of Goldman, Sachs, "really understand the long-term consequences of the technologically driven disintermediation of payment flows away from credit-sensitive financial institutions?"[13] To which the short answer is no; we don't.

The derivatives process, permitting participants to bet on the *direction* of market prices rather than on the absolute numbers, enables participants in the business of borrowing and lending to arrange their affairs so that the actions of the central bank do not greatly affect them. In the early 1990s, it was fashionable for economists at central banks to speak of a "financial accelerator" or a "credit channel effect" that multiplied the effects of the central bank's raising or lowering of short-term interest rates. Just a touch on the brakes, raising rates a smidgen, would reduce the value of the paper borrowers used to gain cash through repurchase agreements, and by increasing the costs of carrying inventory would reduce profits to damp what Keynes once called the animal high spirits of businessmen. A touch on the gas pedal would bring the economy back to speed, Paul Krugman of MIT proclaimed in his role as a columnist, because "recessionary tendencies can usually be effectively treated with cheap, over-the-counter medication: cut interest rates a couple of percentage points, provide plenty of liquidity, and call me in the morning."[14]

But it isn't so. Ingo Fender of the Bank for International Settlements notes that given the opportunities afforded by derivatives, "firms should not be expected to accept their fate . . . like lemmings. Instead, they will implement corporate risk management strategies that are likely to alter the sensitivity of the real economy to changes in interest rates." Because the hedging is necessarily imperfect, he adds, "monetary policy will be increasingly unreliable when used to affect investment spending and real activity."[15] What remains is theater, most useful when the threat to be countered is itself dramatic. Greenspan could master the threat to the world economy in 1998 because the reason for the disruption was the previously unimaginable default by Russia on its domestic debt. In January 2001, the decline in economic activity derived from several years of careless investment (especially, though not exclusively, in dot-coms and telecoms) that did not and would not pay out its carrying cost. Against this backdrop, not even the most startling announcement—half a point, between meetings of the Fed's rate-setting committee, while President-elect George W. Bush was meeting with the big businessmen who had financed his campaign—could do much more than give a temporary goose to the stock market.

Theory has not yet confronted fact. Theory still says that the effects of changes in the interest rate play through the attitudes of the banks. The central bank cares about the real economy and the prices for goods and services, costs of production and costs of living. Too much "money" in the system generates higher prices for goods and services and the cost of living. Too little money denies funds to producers and reduces national product. But the central bank can't decree how much "money" will be in the economy. It needs "intermediate targets" that more closely impact the real economy. Those targets are interest rates and bank reserves (and through bank reserves, "the quantity of money").

Prior to the last quarter of the twentieth century, banks "set" interest rates: there was a "prime rate" for the best customers in the United States, a "bank rate" in England, and their equivalents elsewhere. The central bank by altering its "discount rate"—the rate it would charge banks for, in effect, borrowings secured by the banks' best collateral—would influence the banks to change their prime rate, which would affect business decisions. Rising interest rates would reduce the market price of fixed-income securities, which discouraged banks from lending because they felt the decline in the value of existing investments. If banks have bought 90-day government paper at 5 percent and the Fed by selling its holdings of that paper raises that rate to 6 percent, the prices on the 90-day paper the banks own will drop until they sell to yield 6 percent. To create new assets (make loans), banks either have to borrow money (at the new higher rates) or sell old assets (at the new lower price); the central bank has given banks reason to think hard before making new loans. Vice versa with declining rates: existing assets in the banks' portfolio became more valuable, which encouraged new lending as a way to use the profits.

Others could argue, equally plausibly, that the quantity of bank reserves, which the Fed could create and extinguish at will, determined the availability of money to borrowers from the banks. Putting money into the system by purchasing paper in the market, the Fed increased the banks' lending capacity and thus their borrowers' spending power. Taking money out of the system by selling paper in the market, the Fed forced the banks and thus the economy to cut back. The Fed's actions were always and necessarily pretty small by comparison with the effects desired, and their effectiveness was explained by the operation of a "multiplier" inherent in a system where banks had to keep "reserves" against some fraction of their liabilities. The bank that received the Fed's "high-powered money" might lend 90 percent of it, and the bank that received the proceeds of that loan would lend 90 percent of that, producing deposits in another bank that would lend 90 percent of *that*, etc.–Big fleas have little fleas/That come in swarms to bite 'em/And little fleas have littler fleas/And so ad infinitum.

It is by no means clear that this ever worked, past the extraordinary decade of the 1950s when American banks funded their lending activities by selling the government bonds the Fed had helped them acquire to finance the war. That was then, and this is now. Today, Fed decisions that change banks' capacity to fund loans mean very little, partly because the most significant lending occurs directly in the markets and partly because the banks don't want to fund loans, anyway: they want to package their loans into salable "asset-backed securities" or in more sophisticated form. In the modern world, a bank loan is a bundle of risks–risk that the borrower won't repay, that interest rates will change, that the lender will need the cash he has put out before he thought he would need it. These risks can be separated out, traded, sold, hedged by the creation or purchase of derivative instruments. This process, writes Henry Kaufman, the premier Fed watcher of the 1980s, "has had the significant side effect of dispelling the illusion that nonmarketable assets by nature have stable prices."

But while the intrusion of market values everywhere in the banks reduces the confidence of those enterprises, they and the Fed and the markets all take heart from the often ingenious calculus of probabilities expressed in the new instruments. The new interplay of borrowers and lenders in the market, Kaufman writes, "allows the private sector to withstand monetary restraint for a longer time. As a result, the central bank will need to engineer considerably higher interest rates–with correspondingly lower asset values–to achieve noninflationary growth."[16]

These lower asset values will not be restricted to the segments of the bond market where the Fed sells. Especially at a time when obscure companies can fund themselves by selling equity–when funding for investment is provided not through the intermediation of institutions that have continuing relations with their borrowers but through the presentations of stock salespeople who are gone the moment the deal is concluded–the Fed must pay attention to the stock market. 'Twas not always so. In the 1920s, Benjamin Strong–who ran the Federal Reserve Bank of New York and thus, at a time when the Board of Governors in Washington was weak, the Federal Reserve System–had occasion to write to the head of the Federal Reserve Bank of Philadelphia that "if the Federal Reserve System is to be run solely with a view to regulating stock speculation instead of being devoted to the interests of the industry and commerce of the country, then its policy will degenerate simply to regulating the affairs of gamblers."[17]

In the mid-1930s, when a stock market boom heralded a false dawn of recovery from the depression, the president of the New York Stock Exchange (then an unpaid part-time post) made a speech saying that if the market went pop, the blame should lie with the Federal Reserve, which had loosened money too far; and Fed chairman Marriner Eccles responded with a statement endorsed by all the governors to the effect that the rising stock prices had not been financed with Fed credit and the Fed couldn't do much about it anyway. Roosevelt sent Eccles a letter warning him against "any statement relating, even remotely, to actual stock market operations. This is where Coolidge, Mellon and Hoover got into such trouble. A word to the wise!"[18]

Erik Hoffmeyer, longtime head of the Danish National Bank, observes that players in markets are motivated by "what they expect the market to do," and that these expectations "are heavily influenced by the behavior of the monetary authorities concerned."[19] Still, new economy or no new economy, the values asserted by the stock market represent the price of an anticipated stream of future earnings ("even if," as Alan Greenspan rather grumpily told a conference in summer 1999, "no market participant consciously makes that calculation").[20] Higher interest rates mean a greater discount in those values looking forward, and thus lower stock prices today. Once an economy reaches a certain level of development, with a body of existing debt that must be rolled over periodically, everybody hates high interest rates, debtors because they have to pay them, creditors because the market value of their assets falls. Central banks have been given independent authority over interest rates because high interest rates are the necessary prophylactic when inflation threatens, and politically there is no constituency for increasing interest rates even after inflation has taken hold. The willingness of political leadership to abdicate responsibility for interest rates has been one of the most remarkable aspects of the postmodern political economy. As a German cabinet minister said many years ago, explaining this phenomenon in Germany, "every politician knows that some day he may need a central banker to hide behind."

To say that central banks must now seek their objectives through the market rather than through the banks masks the essential change. Securitization, derivatives, worldwide markets, and the vastly increased liquidity of once non-marketable assets (represented in the household world by home equity loans and easy access to margin values of stock market investments) have made the idea of the "quantity" of money a historical curiosity, like belief in a flat Earth. Credit may be amorphous, but credit risk is specific, and leverage–the fraction of the money at risk that the lender or investor or speculator must repay to his creditors–continues to rise. Henry Kaufman worries that securitization and derivatives will act as rubber bands allowing the system to keep stretching as the central bank pulls at it; an equal worry is that the chaos theoreticians may be right, and that a system where receipts and payments are tightly bound together may shatter beyond easy repair if a minor event far away—the Indonesian butterfly's wings feared by the chaos maven—leads with awesome inevitability to systemic disaster.

As the Asian crisis of 1997 demonstrated, much of this risk remains with the banks. The finance ministries and the central banks can probably protect them and their creditors, though there is a lot of work to be done to assure that government and central bank protections cannot be abused self-destructively by the participants in the system. But in a market-dominated age, most of the burden inevitably lies on investors who no longer use banks as their intermediaries, and who need unprecedented access to information and even more unprecedented capacity to analyze and use it.

The burden lies on you.

Chapter 2

The Magician at Home

"Get away from that wheelbarrow. What the hell do you know about machinery?"

–attributed to Elbert Hubbard by Eugene Manlove Rhodes (1934)

A YEAR AFTER HIS FEAT OF PRESTIDIGITATION on the world markets, Alan Greenspan performed what may have been an even more remarkable magic trick in the world of U.S. governance, enlarging the role and probably, over time, changing the nature of the Federal Reserve System. At a time when other countries were revising the charters of their central banks to give them only one function–"Price stability," said the Roll Panel that prepared *A New Mandate for the Bank of England* at the request of Chancellor Gordon Brown, "should be the sole statutory objective of the Bank"[1]–Greenspan got the Congress and the White House to make the Fed a financial tsar in America. Under the terms of the Gramm-Leach-Bliley Act of 1999, the Fed will be the "umbrella supervisor" of "financial holding companies" that will own the nation's largest banks, its securities houses, its insurance companies, and much else. Each activity will be "functionally" regulated–securities subsidiaries by the Securities and

Exchange Commission (SEC), banks by the Office of the Comptroller of the Currency or the state banking departments, insurance companies by the state insurance commissioners–but the Fed will have responsibility for the entity that owns these subsidiaries. To understand Greenspan's accomplishment and its significance will require a little American history, and a little international background; but the story is interesting on its own terms. And important, too, though the press has missed it.

The year 1999 was a peculiar one for central banks. In continental Europe their role in monetary policy was ceded to a new European Central Bank (ECB), a supranational institution charged with introducing and maintaining the value of a new currency which would replace the old marks and francs, pesos and lire, gulden, escudos, and kroner, punts and schillings. Short-term interest rates for the Euro–for all the nations of "Euroland"–would be set by this new institution in Frankfurt, housed in a rather nondescript office building just outside the city's best office-and-shopping district, nowhere near as glamorous as the twin towers of Deutsche Bank half a mile away, nowhere near as menacing as the elongated squat structure of the Bundesbank in its own park out in the suburbs. The European Central Bank would be run by a governing board of technocrats and would have the authority to set an inflation rate for Europe without consulting any of the European governments (though it does report to a toothless European Parliament); and it would have no function other than the achievement of that rate.

The regulation and supervision of the different national banking systems remains with national institutions–in a few countries, central banks, and in others some agency of the Ministry of Finance–and they will supervise the transition from national currencies to the Euro, which is to occur in 2002. With the end of the national currencies, the national central bank of each country lost its role as manager of the national debt, which would no longer be denominated in the national currency. Because each nation's debt in Euros would be functionally similar to the debt of private corporations (the nation servicing its debt could not escape by printing its own currency but would have to arrange the availability of Euros, just as a private corporation had always had to arrange the availability of its own country's currency), the governments turned to private-sector investment banks to manage domestic debt. With monetary policy housed in the ECB, the national banks no longer had a role in creating a yield curve that measured interest rates against the expiration dates of fixed-interest government liabilities.

The Bank of England, in a country that had at least temporarily rejected the Euro, retained its pound, and for the first time since its nationalization after World War II received legal status as an independent agency not subject to orders from the chancellor of the exchequer. Nevertheless, the new banking act written by Tony Blair's government imposed upon the Bank of England a significant loss of status and function. All regulation and supervision of British banks (and the local affiliates and branches of foreign banks authorized to operate in the United Kingdom) was transferred from the Bank of England to a Financial Services Authority, which also inspected securities houses, mortgage lenders and insurance companies, futures and options markets, as well as securities exchanges. Its headquarters are on Canary Wharf along the Thames to the east, far from the Bank of England's late-eighteenth-century building on Threadneedle Street in the heart of the City, and on the wall of its reception area are carved not the minatory warnings to bankers of Hugh McCulloch, the first U.S. Comptroller of the Currency (which are posted in the waiting room of the Cashier's Office at the Bank of England) but the text of a rock ballad: "You've got a lot of nerve to say you are my friend. When I was down you just stood there . . ."

It was while the European central banks were in retreat that the Federal Reserve in fall 1999 sought and gained new powers and new responsibilities, winning a war with the Office of the Comptroller of the Currency (OCC) that had been fought in the battlefields of Congress for more than sixty years. That Office predated the Fed—it had been created in 1864 by a Congress eager to use the proceeds of new bank charters to help pay for the Civil War. Nationally chartered banks would be permitted to issue bank notes up to 90 percent of their total holdings of U.S. Treasury bonds. States would not be permitted to tax nationally chartered banks (a provision that remained in the law until 1969, when Congress authorized states to collect from national banks whatever taxes they assessed against state-chartered banks). Meanwhile, the federal government would tax the issuance of notes by state-chartered banks, which presumably would drive them out of existence. But after the 1880s, demand deposits accessible by check and cleared by private-sector clearinghouses were clearly preferable to national banknotes. Many of the nation's biggest banks were built on state charter (in New York, Bank of New York and Chase have state charters, and the only reason HSBC does not is that Muriel Siebert as state commissioner of banking in the late 1970s was damned if she would let a Hong Kong bank buy the Marine Midland Trust Co., and the deal could be consummated only after John Heimann as Comptroller of the Currency approved the switch of Marine from state to national charter). Ninety percent of the two hundred–odd U.S. branches of foreign banks are still chartered and empowered and supervised by a state rather than an agency of the federal government.

The Office of the Comptroller of the Currency is lodged on the organization charts of the Treasury Department, though no longer housed in the same building. Its powers include the authority to charter new banks and to declare banks insolvent, neither of which the Fed can do. The Federal Reserve Board, like other central banks, reports to the legislative rather than the executive branch of government. All banks chartered by the OCC are automatically members of the Federal Reserve System and must invest 3 percent of their capital in the stock of their district Federal Reserve Bank. (Another 3 percent of their capital must be regarded as "on call" for the benefit of that district Fed, in case it needs the money, which is a quaint conceit.) As Fed members, the national banks had to keep reserves in an interest-free account at their district Federal Reserve Bank, but in return they received access to the discount window, where they could borrow funds at a lower rate than market rates, plus free services, including check clearing and settlement, custody and transfer of their government bond holdings, and management consulting in the form of Federal Reserve examination reports. The Fed could prohibit the merger of national banks under the Clayton Act of 1914 and approve or disapprove the launching of foreign branches by national banks, and after 1933 it could set ceilings on the interest rates banks could pay depositors. But except for those specific provisions and some flexibility in mandating reserve requirements, the Fed had no authority to give orders to nationally chartered banks until the Securities Exchange Act of 1934 authorized the board to set margin requirements for all lenders on loans for the purpose of buying stocks.

State-chartered banks could decide whether or not they wished to be members of the Fed, and most smaller state-chartered banks decided that the Fed's services were not worth what they cost. In practice, what happened was that bigger state banks were members, and retailed the Fed's check-clearing, wire transfer, and trust services to smaller banks, which paid for them by keeping *their* reserves in "correspondent accounts," where some of the money earned interest and some did not, depending on how much the larger bank wanted the use of the money and how many services the smaller bank got for nothing.

The Fed did not until fairly recently consider itself a regulator or even a supervisor of its member banks. Fed bank examinations, Benjamin Haggott Beckhart wrote in 1972 in a book sponsored by the American Institute of Banking and approved by a panoply of Fed officers, "are designed to be helpful to the bank's management."[2] It was not until 1933 that Congress required the Federal Reserve Board to keep itself informed of the "general character and amount of the loans and investments of its member banks." At one point in the 1930s, Marriner Eccles as chairman of the Fed got some senators ginned up to move for the elimination of the OCC and the transfer of its powers as charterer, regulator, and examiner to the Fed. He thought the OCC was delaying recovery from the depression by unnecessarily forcing banks to "classify" loans and take reserves against them. "If the [Federal Reserve] is committed to a policy of monetary ease in times of depression," he argued in a memo to Franklin Roosevelt, "then bank examination policies should follow a similar commitment."[3]

A congressional report in 1931 noted that the typical Federal Reserve examination of a bank "is less formal and usually much less complete, than in the case of the examinations prescribed by statute for the legally-constituted [state and federal chartering] authorities. . . . This is a natural consequence of the fact that the Federal Reserve examination is designed in the main to determine the soundness of rediscounts or advances secured by United States Government bonds made by the reserve bank to its members, as well as the soundness of the member institutions in relation to the activities of the Federal Reserve Bank as collecting agent for out-of-town checks."[4]

Testifying before the committee that wrote that report, the Federal Reserve Bank of Chicago noted that "Supervision of national banks rests with the Comptroller of the Currency, and of State banks with the State banking departments. Copies of the reports of examination of all national banks are filed with us by the Comptroller's representative, and copies of reports of examinations of all member State banks by the respective State banking departments. . . . Our field work in actual examinations is confined to a limited number of State banks, principally the smaller institutions."[5]

There was no tradition of central bank examination of banks. The Bank of England, which until the 1970s did not even attempt to define what was meant by the word "bank," never employed bank examiners, relying instead on a rule that the auditors hired by the banks themselves to prepare their own reports were presumed to report to the Bank any problems they found . . . and meanwhile the governor or his deputies would meet periodically with Sir Toby or whomever to discuss the grouse season and how the Bank seemed to be doing. Indeed, the Bank of England *avoided* learning about the condition of individual banks, executing its monetary policy by making money easier or tighter for a community of note brokers largely created by the Bank, and in the absence of crisis relying on those note brokers of the City to measure the creditworthiness of individual banks. When a London bank threatened to sink, the Bank of England organized a "lifeboat" of other financial institutions that kept it afloat until its affairs could be settled. Before World War II, while it was still a privately owned undertaking, the Bank in deference to its stockholders avoided helping failed banks in situations where it was likely to lose money; after World War II and the nationalization of the Bank, its reluctance to put up any of its own money in any rescue was heightened by fear of political reaction in the House of Commons.

Until 1956, the Fed's supervisory functions were concentrated in the discount window, where officers of the district banks could examine the quality of the collateral banks offered when they had a need to borrow. That year, however, the Congress got mad at bankers who were violating state laws against branching–and (worse) the McFadden Act that prohibited interstate banking–by forming "bank holding companies" that might own a number of banks in a number of places, and might also violate the Glass-Steagall Act that restricted banks to banking by including a lot of non-banking activities under the holding company umbrella. Holding companies owned both state-chartered and nationally chartered banks, and the only agency that had continuing relations with both those categories was the Fed, so the job of approving bank holding companies, their acquisitions, operations, and activities, was turned over to the Board of Governors. This was done at a time of great good feeling between the Fed and the OCC: the Comptroller was a former president of the Federal Reserve Bank of Cleveland, and the Fed's official position before Congress was that it would be happy to see the regulation of bank holding companies added to the Comptroller's responsibilities but would take the job if Congress insisted. In any event, the Comptroller's authority over banks themselves was not diminished. The board could decide that some activity was not "so closely related to banking or managing or controlling banks as to be a proper incident thereto," but the Comptroller could okay that activity as permissible under a national banking charter. Thus a national bank I visited in Toledo, Ohio, owned and operated a travel agency with the consent of the Comptroller, though it was a Fed member and the Fed had forbidden the holding company that owned the bank to own a travel agency.

Then, in 1961, John F. Kennedy appointed as Comptroller James Saxon, a Washington lawyer and former First National Bank of Chicago executive who had first come to Washington in 1956 to be staff director for a committee of bankers asked by Senator A. Willis Robertson of Virginia, chairman of the Senate Banking Committee, to write a bill that would replace Glass-Steagall. It passed the Senate unanimously, but fell afoul of Chairman Wright Patman in the House Banking Committee, and died. Saxon had a taste for adventure, and his experience in 1956–57 had given him a distaste for Congress. And Kennedy gave him a job that he thought embodied powers inherent in the executive branch. Saxon began throwing stuff at the fan. He changed definitions and regulations, permitting banks to lease personal property, declaring that loans from one bank to another could be construed as purchases or sales of Fed Funds (reserves at the Federal Reserve Bank), and thus not subject to limits on loans to one borrower; that municipal revenue bonds were really the same as municipal general obligation bonds and could therefore be bought and sold by banks even though the statute said otherwise; that a national bank could buy stock in a foreign bank; that a nationally chartered bank could own and operate travel agencies, insurance agencies, finance companies, and computer service centers. In each case, the Fed screamed bloody murder–in public statements contradicting Saxon's definitions and rules–but Saxon went ahead, with the result that a number of banks previously state-chartered, including Wells Fargo, Mercantile Bank in St. Louis, and Chase Manhattan (which later switched back to a state charter as one result of its merger with Chemical Bank), changed their status to federally chartered and with Saxon's blessing began doing the profitable things the Fed said they couldn't do. When Congress mandated that banks like other corporations disclose their financial condition to shareholders, Saxon authorized a reporting form for national banks that provided much less information than the forms established by the Fed.

The result–in addition to a number of lawsuits, many of which the Comptroller lost–was a fair amount of bad blood between the agencies. The Comptroller's budget has to be voted by Congress; the Fed spends its own money (in every sense) and does not need congressional approval–under law, indeed, the district banks are privately owned by their members (and can thus pay much higher salaries than anybody else in government receives, including the governors of the system, which *is* a federal agency). The Board of Governors has only one limousine, for the chairman; the district banks have three to five each. National bank examiners who worked for the Comptroller were typically paid less than Federal Reserve Bank examiners, who carried authority from the board but worked for the district banks. The Fed could not close a bank, but it could keep any bank alive, even after its depositors fled, by lending it money at the discount window. A deputy comptroller said sarcastically that no Fed examiner ever spoke to anybody in a bank with a rank below executive vice president; a slightly less senior officer spoke of the Federal Reserve System as "the evil empire."

Meanwhile, some of the big banks found a loophole in the Bank Holding Company Act, and turned themselves into "one-bank holding companies," which had not been touched in the law because Congress had not wished to choke off the activities of small banks in small towns, organized as holding companies to provide other financial services to customers who otherwise would not have had access to them. So the Bank Holding Company Act of 1956 had exempted "one-bank holding companies" from its strictures. Conservative John Medlin at Wachovia Bank in North Carolina and then adventurer George Moore at First National City Bank of New York spotted the loophole, and found it large enough to permit the passage of their own huge vehicles. "From 1955 to 1968," Thibaut de Saint-Phalle reports, "the number of one-bank holding companies had grown from 117 to 783, and their deposits increased from $11.6 billion to $108 billion (approximately one-third of all commercial bank deposits).

Furthermore, these banking entities were engaging in a wide variety of commercial activities ranging from agriculture, mining and oil and gas to various types of manufacturing, real estate, and wholesale and retail distribution."[6]

Amendments to the Bank Holding Company Act were clearly required, and were passed in 1970, with considerable difficulty, on the last day of the year, which was also the last day of a lame-duck session of Congress. There was no grandfathering here. The new law told the Fed to make the one-bank holding companies divest themselves of everything that was not "so closely related to banking or managing or controlling banks as to be a proper incident thereto." Over the next dozen years, the governors of the Federal Reserve spent more time debating the application of that language to specific activities than they devoted to any other purpose, including monetary policy. Some insurance activities were permitted (until the Garn–St. Germain Act of 1982 explicitly forbade anything to do with writing, selling, or brokering insurance). Courier services were out, but data processing services were okay, and so were brokerage services on both securities and commodities markets.

Until the passage of Gramm-Leach-Bliley in 1999, this legislation was the bedrock of the Fed's claims to authority in supervising banks. "The Bank Holding Company Amendments of 1970 are not getting the attention they deserve," Fed governor Andrew Brimmer said in 1973. "Congress told the Federal Reserve Board, 'We've done the best we can—now you make the decisions.' And we are, frequently by split votes, remaking the banking system of this country." Donald Rogers, president of the Association of Bank Holding Companies, noted sourly the same year that "There's been talk over the years about the need for a single Federal Banking Commission. Well, under the Holding Company Acts, we're getting one—by chance."[7]

Between the 1970s and the 1990s, the Fed came into conflict more often with the third leg of the federal regulatory stool, the Federal

Deposit Insurance Corporation (FDIC), which had been formed in 1933 by a Congress that raided the Fed's accumulated surplus for the purpose to assure depositors (of $2,500 or less at the start) that they would get their money back if their bank failed. The FDIC was a separate agency supported by premium payments from the insured banks, with a line of credit at the Treasury to convey added confidence. Because these premiums and the interest on its accumulated reserves were greater than its payoffs year after year, Lyndon Johnson put the FDIC on the federal budget to help pay the combined costs of the Vietnam War and the Great Society. The FDIC had its own force of examiners, but without invitations from the Comptroller or the Fed they were restricted to state-chartered banks that were not members of the Federal Reserve System, which could be as many as eight thousand banks, nearly all of them quite small. But when a large institution was endangered, the insurance funds were put in peril to repay its depositors—in their bosoms, indeed, both the Fed and the Comptroller looked upon the FDIC fund as the easy way to pay off lenders to a bank other than the depositors on whose deposits insurance had been paid.

When the Fed lent money to a failing bank, it was against the best collateral that bank had to offer, which meant that if the bank subsequently collapsed the FDIC as receiver was left with a carcass from which the value had been stripped, and didn't like it. Twice in the mid-1970s, large banks died. In 1973, U.S. National of San Diego collapsed under the weight of hundreds of millions of dollars of stand-by letters of credit written to permit the sale of commercial real estate by other ventures of its owner H. Arnholdt Smith (a buddy of Richard Nixon's, who had been among the select group with the president on election night 1968). U.S. National had to be infused with cash by the FDIC before it could be sold to Crocker Bank. In 1974, Franklin National of New York, which had expanded recklessly from its suburban roots into the big city, sought rescue first from Larry Tisch of Loew's and then from the supposed foreign exchange trading skills of the Italian wheeler-dealer Michele Sindona. The Fed wound up with more than $2.2 billion of face-value collateral, including foreign exchange positions, as security for the $1.7 billion it had advanced to keep Franklin alive until it could be sold (to a mostly European consortium; Joan Spero reports that the Fed asked the FDIC to accept a lower bid from a U.S. bank.[8] The FDIC claimed that its charter forbade it to pay off on foreign exchange losses. This was hairy for a while, but eventually the foreign exchange market turned and the positions rose above the waterline.

Through this period, think tanks and presidential and congressional commissions kept proposing new systems to get away from the divided supervision of the banking industry, most commonly a Federal Bank Commission that would take over the regulatory and supervisory powers of the OCC, the Fed, and the FDIC, and perhaps the state agencies as well. There was not much support for giving the job to the Fed. J. L. Robertson wrote to Senator William Proxmire of Wisconsin in late 1974, "[I]n my opinion, based on forty years experience in the field of federal bank supervision, including twenty-one years as a Governor and seven years as Vice Chairman of the Federal Reserve Board, the merged supervisory function should not be vested in the Federal Reserve System. The function of formulating and implementing monetary policy and the equally important and coordinate function of supervising banks and bank holding companies cannot be performed by one agency without seriously compromising the effectiveness of each function."[9] Fed governor Jeffrey N. Bucher chimed in: "[W]here the same agency has both the responsibility for monetary policy and a major role in bank regulation and supervision, conflicts of objectives may arise. . . . Examiners should be insulated from any possible temptation of the monetary authority to use supervisory powers to implement monetary policy and they should be at all times free from evaluating certain loans differently from others."[10]

Over the years, the highly redundant and confusing American system of bank regulation has drawn much critical comment. Howard Davies, chief executive of the new British Financial Services Authority, visiting Washington in 1998, noted that he had been told that his opposite number in America would be an amalgam of the heads of seventy-eight agencies. But after 1961, no Treasury report on banking or ballyhooed independent scholarly study called for consolidation of regulation in the Federal Reserve. The Fed itself, however, became increasingly aggressive in proclaiming its rights and powers. In 1983, responding to a working paper of the Bush Task Group on Regulation of Financial Services which called for the establishment of a new Federal Banking Agency that would absorb the Fed's supervisory authority, the Fed claimed quite falsely that "the 'monetary' functions [of the Federal Reserve System] were largely grafted onto the 'supervisory' functions, not the reverse."[11]

In 1998, as the Fed began its full-court press toward its coronation as "umbrella supervisor" for all financial service institutions, Governor Laurence H. Meyer in a talk to the Institute of International Bankers insisted that quite apart from the central bank's need to know whether an individual institution is suffering because of a systemic problem or because this bank is just no good, a central bank has to be examining its charges all the time to find out how monetary policy is working. William Ryback, associate director of the Fed's division of supervision operations, added that "without such assessments, micro-adjustments in monetary policy would be impossible." When a member of his audience pointed out that the new European Central Bank has no role whatever in supervising banks, though it has complete, exclusive, and independent authority over the new Euro currency, Ryback said he wished them luck.

The larger fight in Washington through these years was on the question of repealing the Glass-Steagall rules against the blending of banking and other financial activities, and the Bank Holding Company Act restrictions on non-banking activities of any kind. The inflation of 1978–82 had made it impossible for the Fed to maintain controls on the interest rates banks could pay, and the Deregulation and Monetary Control Act of 1980 ordered a phaseout of such controls over the next half dozen years. The Reagan administration took a particularly strong deregulatory line, and accelerated the end of interest-rate controls in the Garn–St. Germain Act of 1982. There was much else, mostly foolish, in the law; Gerald T. Dunne, editor of the

Banking and Law Journal, described it as a "ham-handed, overblown, and trivialized effort to legislate sound banking."[12] Ronald Reagan and his first Treasury Secretary Don Regan (who came to government from the Wall Street house of Merrill Lynch) had a fondness for the German style of universal bank, which engaged itself heavily in non-financial activities like manufacturing automobiles. Paul Volcker was then chairman of the Fed, and shot that down relatively easily, but he did launch a process by which bank holding companies were permitted to buy or start securities affiliates provided the capital of these subsidiaries was kept separate from the bank's capital and the total revenues derived from the activity were less than 10 percent of the earnings of the holding company. The slogan/rule was that any non-banking activities must be a "source of strength" to the bank, while the bank could never serve as the "source of strength" for the other activities.

Alan Greenspan has a religious faith in the values of diversification for financial institutions; as a private consultant in 1986, he even supported the application for exemption from the rules by the S&L monster Charles Keating (he was paid $40,000 for doing so), supporting Keating's practice of investing insured deposits in junk bonds and resort hotels. But after the foolishness in the Garn–St. Germain Act played itself out in the S&L fiasco, where the cost to taxpayers of diversified bad investment of insured S&L deposits ran into the hundreds of billions of dollars, Congress had less enthusiasm for the blending of banking and commerce. (Walter Bagehot had warned in the 1870s that "There is a cardinal difference between banking and other kinds of commerce; you can afford to run much less risk in banking than in commerce, and you must take much greater precautions.")[13] When the Treasury Department in the Bush administration put forth recommendations for the restructuring of the banking system, the strongest argument it could find for permitting the marriage of banking and commerce was that "substantial losses to the government from a failed bank might be avoided only by allowing a commercial firm to purchase the failed bank."[14]

By 1991, when this document was published, nobody doubted

the need to do something about the restrictions the 1930s legislation had put on the banks; indeed, the regulators were stretching the laws pretty far to try to adjust them to conditions at the end of the century. The arrival of computers had meant that above a certain size all financial institutions–banks, S&Ls, brokerage houses, insurance companies–offered similar products to the same public. The idiocies were most visible in demand deposits, the banks' very own sacred turf, where S&Ls and brokerage houses and credit unions were all issuing checkbooks to people who could not be called depositors. Even more serious from the Fed's point of view was the great reduction in the banks' role as a lender. More than half the nation's mortgage loans were instantly securitized (packaged into "bonds" or other fixed-income instruments that could be sold in the markets) through privately owned but federally sponsored corporations that did nothing else. Auto loans were securitized through the financing wings of the automobile companies. And larger loans to business were being "participated out" to insurance companies and pension funds as well as to other banks. I visited Mike Milken's junk bond shop in Beverly Hills, sat beside the toupeed master at the center of the X-shaped desk where his traders worked, and watched as they bought and sold loan participations and junk bonds interchangeably to the same customers. Milken's firm was an investment house (Drexel Burnham), but all the large banks had similar installations.

Meanwhile, the options masters and their computers were designing "derivative" instruments that could convert fixed-rate 30-year mortgages to floating-rate 1-year notes, domestic currency to foreign currency, risky to safe, and vice versa–instruments that could be and were traded by financial and non-financial institutions of all stripes. Designers from these derivatives markets were creating "Catastrophe Bonds" to permit insurance companies (and indeed banks, through "credit swaps") to price their risks by selling paper in the market. And none of the definitions in the laws fit that reality.

As the Treasury Department's minions got to work to modernize the financial system for George Bush, there was only one inviolable boundary: one could not touch the distinction between state-chartered and federally chartered banks, and the rule that the former were subject to supervision by the Federal Reserve and the latter by the Office of the Comptroller of the Currency. The Bush Treasury reached desperately for a solution, leaving the state-chartered banks with the Fed and putting the national banks and their holding companies under the wing of a new Federal Bank Agency "under Treasury." If the biggest bank in the holding company was state-chartered, it would fall under one jurisdiction; if the biggest bank in the holding company was federally chartered, it would fall in the other. In its final recommendations, the Treasury team proposed a dual structure: "The Federal Reserve would be responsible for all *state-chartered* banks and their B[ank] H[olding] C[ompanies]. . . . In addition, a new federal regulator, the Federal Banking Agency (FBA) would be created under Treasury, and would be responsible for all *national* banks and their BHCs. . . . When a BHC contains both state-chartered and national banks, jurisdiction over the entire organization would go to the charterer of the largest subsidiary bank." Among the advantages of this proposal, the Treasury suggested, was that it would "ensure that there was regulatory accountability in the Administration." Proof that this was the right way to go was found in the fact that it was like the procedure followed in Japan.[15]

Bills to "modernize" the regulation of banking were introduced into every Congress—how else could the members of the Banking Committee raise their reelection funds? Problems were tackled piecemeal: there was a Financial Institutions Reform, Recovery and Enforcement Act (FIRREA) that reorganized the bankrupt thrift industry; there was a Federal Deposit Insurance Corporation Improvement Act (FDICIA), which sought to limit the discretion of all the regulators in determining which failing bank institutions had to be supported in their time of troubles and which (the majority) should be put out of their misery quickly. In 1994, Democratic senator Don Riegle of Michigan, long the chair of the Banking Committee, worked through the Congress a bill permitting branch banking interstate, unless a state opted out (only Texas did).

But none of this dealt with the growing homogenization of financial services, the fact that banking, securities underwriting, securities brokerage, consumer finance, real estate mortgaging, and commercial lending were no longer separate enterprises. And into this maelstrom of dysfunctional definitions and agencies President Bill Clinton flung an old friend, the Wall Street lawyer Eugene Ludwig, to be Saxon's spiritual successor as Comptroller of the Currency. Ludwig was a Wall Street lawyer whose clients had been national banks, and whose instincts were for the aggrandizement of national banks in the overall picture of financial intermediation. State banking authorities became nervous, and many states passed laws to permit the banks they chartered any powers authorized by the Comptroller for national banks. These were known, charmingly, as "wild card" laws.

Now the Fed became nervous and asserted that the holding company acts gave the board the right to investigate and limit the flow of funds between banks and their operating subsidiaries, just as it controlled the flow of funds between the parts of a holding company. Ludwig's most striking changes in the old rules permitted banks to own and operate mutual funds and to sell insurance products. Specifically, Ludwig authorized NationsBank of North Carolina in effect to offer the public any money management products that it was offering to its trust customers. Then he okayed a request from Barnett Banks to sell insurance in Miami and Jacksonville and Orlando, because one of the bank's branches, which would be the ostensible source of the service, was in a community of less than five thousand inhabitants.

Saxon in the 1960s had tried to authorize insurance sales by banks in places with more than five thousand population, and had been smacked down by the Fifth Circuit Court of Appeals.[16] Now, in Ludwig's two cases, the Supreme Court heard challenges to what the Comptroller had permitted his nationally chartered banks to do, and in both the Court ruled unanimously that the Comptroller as interpreter of the banking laws was entitled to great deference.[17] The Investment Company Institute, representing the mutual funds, found it could live with the eruption of banks into that business (Matt Fink, its president, said rather apologetically that his organization's strong objection to banks in the mutual funds business had diminished a lot once the majority of its members were banks). But the insurance agents were not amused. And the investment banks remained threatened by Ludwig's decision in November 1994 that he had the authority to permit nationally chartered banks to do a securities underwriting business through an operating subsidiary (which would not, incidentally, be regulated by the SEC–a GAO study in June 1994 found 287 banks that offered securities brokerage services that were not subject to SEC regulation).[18] Ludwig found himself one of those people Congress dislikes because they are the source of irritated mail and phone calls from constituents.

The Clinton administration's first crack at "reform" of banking legislation stressed a "Federal Bank Administrator" who would coordinate the supervision of all state-chartered banks, leave the Comptroller as boss of the nationally chartered banks, open the door a little ways to permit banks to operate non-financial businesses and non-financial businesses to own banks, and reduce both the examination and the rule-making roles of the Federal Reserve. Greenspan was able to derail that one by mobilizing the state banking commissioners who would be subject to second-guessing by superior federal authorities. Sometimes he testified that the Fed had to keep its supervisory functions with relation to the fifty biggest banks so that it would have sufficient information to manage crises and "the clout that comes with supervision and regulation." Sometimes he testified that it was important to leave the final word on what banks did to the Fed because an institution with no function other than the maintenance of safety and soundness (the Comptroller) would "inevitably have a long-term bias against risk-taking and innovation," which under the circumstances was a splendid illustration of chutzpah.[19]

Having beaten off the Treasury's challenge in 1994, Greenspan turned his attention to legislation that would establish once and for all the primacy of the Federal Reserve in the regulation of American financial enterprise. This became possible in 1995 when the Republicans won the House and Jim Leach, the soft-spoken, gray-haired intellectual from Iowa, became chairman of the House Banking Committee. Leach admired the Fed and Greenspan and was prepared to take the guidance of the Fed staff in writing the new bill. The political impetus for a bill was less from banks wanting additional powers—because the Comptroller was getting them the new powers—than from the reregulation hopes of the Wall Street investment houses, which were concerned that banks might get power to poach their customers when they did not have authority to start their own banking business, and the insurance companies, which wanted to block (and if possible roll back) the Comptroller's plans to let banks into the insurance business. And the SEC wanted to be sure that if banks were going to plunge into the securities business, they would be properly registered and supervised by the Commission, which was guaranteed by law if securities activities were conducted in an affiliate of a holding company under Fed supervision, but not if they were conducted by an operating subsidiary of a bank. Previous legislation had exempted banks from SEC oversight, and some nationally chartered banks—plus branches of foreign banks operating in the United States—were already engaged, even without Ludwig's final assent, in a range of securities activities without SEC licensure.

Many of the issues were trickier than they looked. The question of separating banking from commerce, for example, cannot be answered by drawing a bright line somewhere. A company that prints checks is clearly engaged in an activity "incident to banking"—but suppose it also prints coupons to be mailed or distributed in-store? Runs the catalogue company that distributes the prizes for coupons? Makes the trinkets for which the coupons can be traded? Many insurance companies and brokerage houses had non-financial interests, and certainly could not be forced to divest them.

Lobbyists, congressional staffs, Treasury, and Fed congressional liaison people negotiated through 1997 and the relevant House committees produced a monster that all the actors eventually would oppose. "Have the various industries resolved their differences and gotten behind this bill?" the newsletter of the Conference of State Bank Supervisors asked rhetorically. "Well, no," the newsletter answered. "Like exhausted parents giving in to whiny children, the members of the House Commerce Committee just wanted all the different industry advocates to *go away*. The fastest way to make that happen was to move this bill out of committee, and make it someone else's problem."[20]

Republican senator Alphonse D'Amato of New York, chairman of the Senate Banking Committee, aggressively ignored the House bill. His ambition was to craft a law that would end the separation of banking and commerce, allowing banks to own non-financial companies and such companies to own banks. Its preamble opened with "findings" that "restrictions on ownership of depository institutions and affiliations with other business organizations interfere with their ability to attract and retain capital."[21] He also had a reelection campaign coming up for 1998 (he lost), and wished to milk his status for as many contributions as he could. I wrote cynically in August 1998 that "Sen. D'Amato in kindness wishes to send something to the floor so all senators, not just members of the Banking Committee, can dip into the mother lode of contributions from financial-services lobbyists this election year."[22] But what blocked the banking reform bill in 1998 was not the rivalry of the different financial services trade associations but a war—revealed rather starkly in testimony by Greenspan and Treasury Secretary Robert Rubin before D'Amato's committee in June 1998—between the Fed and the Treasury. The blood spilled in that one got over the hubcaps and brought the traffic to a stop.

Driven in part by the knowledge that he was going to be term-limited out of the chair of the House Banking Committee even if the Republicans retained control of the House in the 2000 elections, Leach returned passionately in 1999 to the subject of banking reform. In the Senate the chair had passed to Republican Phil Gramm of Texas, who also believed in erasing the line between banking and commerce. House and Senate passed different bills, and went to conference, the House bill reflecting the wishes of the Fed, the Senate bill closer to the taste of the Treasury. The bill was going nowhere. Gramm and Leach, seeing the conclusion of forty years of legislative effort so near and yet so far, asked Greenspan and Rubin to find a compromise.

And then Rubin resigned as secretary of the treasury. Ludwig's term as Comptroller had ended in April, and he had returned to the practice of law. President Clinton's choice of a successor was another banking lawyer, John B. (always "Jerry") Hawke, Jr., himself at one time general counsel of the Federal Reserve Board, who would move laterally from his post as undersecretary of the treasury for domestic affairs to the Comptroller's Office. Hawke is the best kind of lawyer, a counselor with broad interests and a desire to keep the parties in a dispute from each other's throats, but he had angered some senators by his insistence that the new legislation give banks a free hand to sell or underwrite insurance and establish uniform national rules of what state insurance regulators could and could not do. It would be a while before he could be confirmed, and once you get onto the chairman-secretary level, the Comptroller has at best the thin edge of a wedge. The secretary of the treasury was now Lawrence H. Summers, a Harvard economist with Nobel Prize winners on both sides of his gene pool, himself winner of his profession's brilliancy prize for the best of the under-forties, an analyst whose instinct (he knew better on Monday and Tuesday, but not necessarily on Wednesday) was that economics provides answers for political and social problems, too. He and Greenspan were members of the economists' guild (as was Gramm); the Comptroller's Office was dominated by lawyers.

I argued for the Federal Reserve's position in the Great Turf War of 1999, not because I thought the Fed a good or effective supervisor of banks or even bank holding companies, but because I thought the structuring of financial enterprise in holding companies was an intelligent way-station on the road to market discipline. And I did not wish to risk a situation where the Comptroller of the Currency, whose only interest is the promotion of the banks he has chartered and regulates, would be responsible for securities firms and insurance companies.

When the Financial Accounting Standards Board ruled that banks should report their P&L and balance sheets according to the market value of their assets and liabilities, which is the way their internal information systems work, Greenspan uttered dire warnings that honest accounting would mean the end of Western civilization as we know it, but he knew he was conducting a holding operation and could not in the end prevent the SEC from imposing better accounting rules on bank holding companies. But under the old law, banks chartered by the Comptroller and not in holding companies were not subject to SEC accounting rules, or SEC reporting rules, or SEC regulations in their conduct of a securities business. In the late 1980s, Comptroller Robert Clarke changed the valuation formulae for banks' real estate loans to enable them to claim profits in years when they actually were sustaining losses, and nobody could say boo.

Moreover, the OCC has not historically been willing to share responsibilities. In 1997, the FDIC wanted to examine the First National Bank of Keystone, West Virginia, about which rumors were rife. Ludwig's OCC insisted at the time, in what turned out to be the key examination, on its exclusive right to handle that problem, and reached a deal with the bank that both would accept the results of an independent audit by Pricewaterhouse Coopers. The officers of the bank lied to the accounting firm, which was not obliged to and did not investigate to see if the information it had been given was valid, with the result that crookedness festered for two years after the first signs of trouble emerged. William Isaac, former FDIC chairman, says this delay created a loss to the deposit insurance funds almost as great as the loss suffered from the collapse of the major international bank Continental Illinois fifteen years before.[23]

The Fed is a creature of the Congress, and the Comptroller is an agency of the executive branch. Greenspan had enjoyed an amicable relationship with Rubin—their weekly lunches were reported as jovial, both being highly successful in their separate spheres, sharing a sense of humor and an instinct to avoid contention if possible. But this dispute was an area where Rubin felt both an institutional responsibility and personal loyalties. Moreover, from a national economic policy point of view, there could be no question that a large bank with operating subsidiaries would be more efficient than a holding company with separable affiliates. Answering a question at a conference at the Federal Reserve Bank of Chicago in May 1998, Greenspan said, "If you have a new power and you can stick it in the bank, you will do so, because the cost of capital is lower for the bank."[24] But the reason for the reduced costs, Greenspan insisted, was the implicit subsidy given banks by the world's knowledge that the Fed and the FDIC stood behind the banks' borrowings from their depositors and even from the market.

Summers, one suspects, accepted Greenspan's arguments as one economist to another. In the agreement they passed back to Congress, which became the law, the Comptroller was given a fig leaf of powers he could define that could be executed in an operating subsidiary (mostly, one imagines, data processing activities), but on the large things—his power to authorize insurance activities within a bank, affirmed by the Supreme Court, his exemption from SEC regulation—the legislation was simply devastating. "You call it functional," said a very senior person at the OCC, referring to the new scheme by which agencies other than banking supervisors will control what banks and their affiliates can do outside banking itself. "We call it 'fragmented.'"

A memorandum from the Washington offices of the law firm of Gibson, Dunn & Crutcher notes that the limited specified powers of the Fed as regulator will inevitably be enhanced by its "umbrella authority" over the Financial Holding Company (FHC): "As the direct regulator of the parent FHC, the Fed will have a lever to cause the FHC to affect the activities and operations of its operating subsidiaries. The G[ramm]L[each]B[liley] Act structure suggests that the Fed in practice is likely to be a 'first among equals' regulator with an ability to invite itself to the table with other federal or state financial regulators whenever serious issues arise regarding the financial conditions, management activities, etc., of a FHC, its subsidiary banks or of any affiliate that has significant interaction with a bank affiliate."[25] Four days after the legislation was signed by the president, Greenspan made a speech to the American Council of Life Insurers, saying in effect that he was now their umbrella regulator, and, in the immortal words of Washington mayor Marion Barry to the white middle class that had voted overwhelmingly against him, they had better get over it.[26]

Carter Golembe, witness to developments in banking and banking law for almost sixty years, chairman of the group the national banks had formed to make the operating subsidiary the means of the expansion of banking powers, wrote a report at the end of 1999 asking: "Did the Fed chairman and his staff pull off a great victory, or will it all unravel as its significance becomes clear? 'Perception,' we are often told, 'is reality in Washington.' At least in that sense, and perhaps even more fundamentally, the Federal Reserve appears to hold the high ground at the moment."[27]

It is in some ways a more miraculous accomplishment than Greenspan's *Perils of Pauline* rescue of fall 1998. For the irresistible force in world finance is the triumph of the markets over the banks, and everywhere else the adjustment of the government apparatus has been toward reducing the regulatory and supervisory authority of the central bank. Howard Davies of Britain's Financial Services Authority notes that "it is fair to say that the U.S. system is not now typical of international practice." The Fed will be in the process of adjusting to the new system for some years, and the structure of American governance may make mud of all the arrangements.

Golembe points out with astonishment the reconciliation features of the new law as they affect the relations of the Fed and the SEC. The Fed will have the power to request the SEC to set aside any securities regulation (like definitions of when a loan sold off in its pieces to other banks and insurance companies and mutual funds should be considered a security–and, perhaps, like market value accounting) that the Fed does not wish to see enforced on an FHC or any part of an FHC. If the disagreement between the agencies persists, Gramm-Leach-Bliley provides that the Fed may challenge the SEC rule in a proceeding before the U.S. Court of Appeals for the District of Columbia. The court is enjoined in the legislation *not* to give deference to either party to the dispute; the conference report sending the legislation to the floor, remarkably, describes the situation as a "jump ball."

The Truth-in-Lending Act of 1969 gave the Fed the authority to write regulations, and left enforcement of those regulations divided among nine agencies—the three banking regulators, the Home Loan Bank Board, the Bureau of Federal Credit Unions, the Interstate Commerce Commission, the Civil Aeronautics Board, the Agriculture Department, and the Federal Trade Commission.[28] But at least it didn't encourage agencies of the U.S. government to sue each other. Legislating what should be done by the two agencies that have the most effect on the financial markets, Congress abdicated not only its authority to write the rules but its power to delegate that authority. As the wars of the future will be over disclosure, which the SEC promotes, as against regulatory discretion, which is the natural trope of any central bank, the failure of the new legislation to grant SEC exclusive authority over bank reporting may make financial crises more likely in the future.

PART TWO

Central Banks

Chapter 3

What Is a Central Bank?

The fluctuations in the value of money are therefore greater than those in the value of most other commodities. At times there is an excessive pressure to borrow it, and at times an excessive pressure to lend it, and so the price is forced up and down.

These considerations enable us to estimate the responsibility which is thrown on the Bank of England by our system and by every system on the bank or banks who by it keep the reserve of bullion or of legal tender exchangeable for bullion. These banks can in no degree control the permanent value of money, but they can completely control its momentary value. They cannot change the average value, but they can determine the deviations from the average. If the dominant banks manage ill, the rate of interest will at one time be excessively high, and at another time excessively low; there will be first a pernicious excitement, and next a fatal collapse. But if they manage well, the rate of interest will not deviate so much from the average rate; it will neither ascend so high nor descend so low. As far as anything can be steady, the value of money will then be steady, and probably in consequence trade will be steady too.

–Walter Bagehot (1873)[1]

THE FED

THE IDEA OF A CENTRAL BANK as a major instrument of governance first arose in the middle of the twentieth century. In an age of expansion, when political theory gave government an ever-increasing role in planning and guiding economic activity, democratic societies found that they could not rely upon—and thus did not wish to use—the traditional, supposedly automatic mechanisms that had previously connected the money world with the real world. Socially, it was a time of immense improvement in human tools, performance, and prospects—a time when public health procedures, antibiotics, and vaccines had ended great scourges, when farm yields were multiplying, vast increases in energy were at the service of society—all made possible by the expertise of the specialized professional. The central bank—the Federal Reserve System, the Bank of England, the German Bundesbank, the Bank of Japan—was the professional service that made economic policy work.

A central bank is, first of all, a "bank of issue"—that is, it stands responsible for the currency. This is profitable work, known in the history books as "seignorage." The coin was worth more than its gold content (if it was worth less than the gold content, somebody would melt it down). The difference between the price of the "bullion" in the coin and its purchasing power accrued to the mint that stamped the emperor's face in the metal. When the world moved to paper currency, the seignorage became very large. Governments farmed out the creation of the currency to the central bank, originally a privately owned institution, partly because its owners paid for the privilege (by purchasing government securities to fund the government's deficits) and partly because societies learned early that money supplied by the government itself usually loses value. A government with the power to pay its bills by printing money will eventually do so. No less a radical than Tom Paine, the philosopher of the American Revolution, felt that paper money should be issued *only* by private banks, which could be compelled to redeem their paper for gold, and that any legislator who voted for a law permitting the government to issue paper money should be killed.[2]

Still, the central bank, even if privately owned, was the government's bank. It handled the government's receipts and expenditures, and when necessary, it arranged to have money lent to the government. Central banks resisted lending the government money themselves, but that was the price of their charter, and one way or another they usually did: from 1917 to 1951, the Federal Reserve backed up every sale of paper by the U.S. Treasury and made sure no bonds went unpurchased at the government's offering price.

For people to trust the money supplied by the central bank, it had to keep a reserve, usually in gold, and as additional banks were created, convenience suggested that they pool their reserves and clear their accounts with each other at the central bank. The central bank's power to credit a bank's reserve account meant that its loans could *create* reserves. Thus the central bank became the "lender of last resort": if a rumor drew crowds to a bank to withdraw their deposits, and the bank didn't have enough cash on hand, the central bank could extend short-term credit until the panic passed. The central bank was charged with maintaining the integrity of the payments system, seeing to it that when people arranged to pay their debts through their banks—most commonly, with the passage of time, by writing checks on their accounts—their debts were paid.

And, as Bagehot suggested, the central bank could smooth what might otherwise be abrupt and dangerous transitions between boom psychologies and anxiety attacks, dictating higher interest rates to restrain what John Maynard Keynes called "the animal high spirits of businessmen" in good times and increasing the profit opportunities and thus the activities of the ambitious by lowering rates in clumps. Or so it said in all the textbooks.

When Europe's colonies were sent off as independent nations, one of the institutions they felt they needed was a central bank. Benjamin Haggott Beckhart of Columbia University wrote in 1972 that "A central bank, housed in an imposing chrome-and-glass structure, is as much a status symbol for a developing nation as a steel mill."[3] In 1994, Marjorie Deane of *The Economist* and Robin Pringle, former editor of *The Banker,* raised the level of claim to its highest pitch, arguing that central banks by themselves could do the heavy lifting of capitalism: "Developing country governments now want central banks to mobilize savings and allocate credit efficiently."[4] Nor has emphasis on the importance of central banking been restricted to the less developed world. Writing in 1987, William Greider used the subtitle "How the Federal Reserve Runs the Country" under the title of his book *Secrets of the Temple*. In May 1999, a *New York Times* reporter asked rhetorically, "How long can the good times last?" and answered with the statement, "An economist who has spent the last 15 years studying American business cycles says the short answer is: pretty much as long as the Federal Reserve, committed to preventing an outbreak of inflation, remains convinced that the danger is minimal."[5] When he was chairman of the Federal Reserve System, from 1979 to 1987, Paul Volcker was frequently described as "the second most important man in the country," and when Bill Clinton delivered his first State of the Union Address in 1993, he invited Fed chairman Alan Greenspan to sit beside his wife in the gallery, to demonstrate that all was right with the world.

The fact that the same pair of words is used everywhere conceals the extent to which different societies created different central banks. The earliest of them all, the Swedish Riksbank, was chartered as a private bank in 1656 and collapsed from bad loans eight years later. The British economist and historian Charles Goodhart suggests that some of the bad loans were to members of the government, which decided to prop up the bank quietly until someone could be found to buy it and keep its secrets. When nobody would, the bank was reorganized in 1668 under the authority of Parliament (*not* the king), and carried the name Rickets Standers Bank, the Bank of the Estates of the Realm. It was the only bank in Sweden (and its only office was in Stockholm), and its notes were the country's only paper money.

The original Riksbank was not shielded by its government status from the requirement that paper money be redeemed in gold coin, but the price of its charter was an agreement to lend money to the government. When the Riksbank got into serious trouble again in 1720, because the Swedish government failed to repay a loan, there wasn't enough gold in the vaults to redeem the paper an unnerved citizenry presented. In this emergency, the Parliament did what pamphleteer Tom Paine would have killed them for: it made the Riksbank's notes legal tender–that is, it ordered everyone in Sweden to accept this paper in satisfaction of any claim to payment. The Swedish economy ran on this basis for 153 years, though the bank in good years redeemed its notes with silver on demand, until Sweden adhered to the gold standard in 1873. By then there were other banks in Sweden, and they issued their own notes–which were *not* legal tender. They were able to compete effectively with the Riksbank, anyway: by the end of the century, the total note issue by the private banks was roughly equal to that by the central bank.

The important point about the Riksbank from an American perspective is that like our Federal Reserve Board, it was neither a private institution nor a dependency of the executive: it was an instrument of the legislature. Even in 1897, when the bank got a more defined status with reference to the Ministry of Finance and a crown agent received the right to attend the meetings of its board, the law made clear that the king had no power to give the bank orders. The crown agent could participate in the discussions–but he could not vote, and he could not be in the room when the members of the board did vote. Interestingly, in 1991, the Swedish Parliament gave the Riksbank exclusive control of the Swedish presence in the foreign exchange market and the nation's gold and foreign currency reserves, an area where other central banks are subordinate to finance ministries. When the kroner came under attack the next year, the Riksbank panicked, and raised interest rates for short-term borrowing to an annualized 300 percent in what turned out to be a vain–and, indeed, misguided–effort to defend the exchange value of the currency. When the markets forced a devaluation of the kroner, in effect lowering the price of all Swedish exports, the Swedish economy became (for a while) one of the best performers in Europe.

In Britain, the Bank of England was chartered in 1694, to private owners, as a limited liability company (the owners could not be held liable for its debts) and was given the power to issue banknotes as money. The quid pro quo was a loan of 1.2 million pounds to William & Mary to prosecute their wars with France. (This was not far off a quarter of a billion dollars in today's American money, but even that understates the contribution, because £1.2 million was probably 4 percent of England's gross domestic product in 1694.) A high fraction of the original subscribers were Huguenot refugees, who had a stake in those wars. Though it was the exclusive banker to the government, the Bank of England remained a private institution for 252 years. George Washington, among many other American colonists, owned stock in it (his dividends were sequestered during the Revolutionary War, and paid out at the end of it). The directors of the Bank were elected by the stockholders, not appointed by the government.

The Bank opened eleven branches around the country in the nineteenth century, but it was essentially a London institution, serving the private economy as a "bankers' bank." Other banks wishing to issue currency, or to have the "draughts" (checks) on their depositors' accounts honored in London, had to keep at the Bank the reserves they would transfer among themselves to their notes or checks when they were presented at other banks. In the Napoleonic Wars, the Bank suspended its noteholders' rights to redeem their paper in gold, which in the end (because all other banks had done the same) solidified its position. "The larger London payments," Henry Thornton MP wrote in 1802, "are effected exclusively through the paper of the Bank of England, for the superiority of its credit is such that, by common agreement among the bankers, whose practice, in this respect, almost invariably guides that of other persons, no note of a private house will pass in payment as a paper circulation in London."[6] At about that time, the Bank's role as a nanny to the City of London was enshrined by the cartoonist James Gillray, who drew an elderly figure sitting atop the windowless fortress walls of the massive Georgian headquarters, and described it as "The Old Lady of Threadneedle Street in Danger."

When it restored convertibility to gold for its own notes, the

Bank briefly attempted to squeeze the other English banks out of business by refusing to accept their notes from depositors or as repayments of loans. Because provincial banks were so dependent on the Bank of England for the use of their notes in London—and because the Bank was fiscal agent for the government, collecting taxes and tariffs—its power to restrict the use of other banks' notes was very considerable. But the custom of deposit banking and payment by check had already taken root, and the Bank's rivals survived. Indeed, it became common belief that the directors (the "court") of the Bank had to be prepared to extend loans to their rivals to help them meet their payment obligations—prepared but not obliged.

In 1844, an Act of Parliament officially broke the functions of the Bank of England in two. As the government's fiscal agent, managing the national debt and given exclusive power to issue paper currency in England, it would have clear public responsibilities. (An oddity of British governance still gives banks chartered to operate in Scotland and Northern Ireland independent power to issue currency, but only if they back it pound for pound with Bank of England notes.) Because the paper currency was supposed to be convertible to gold at a preestablished price per ounce, the Bank was given a public obligation to keep sufficient reserves of gold to maintain its value in terms of gold. At the same time, the new law left the Bank a private institution. Its "Banking Office," as distinct from its "Issuing Office," had no *legal* responsibility to anyone but the stockholders, and competed for business against the nation's other commercial banks.

The Bank's powers were very great. In the 1920s, Montagu Norman as governor of the Bank actually changed bank rate, the basic interest rate for all British loans, without even informing Winston Churchill, then chancellor of the exchequer for a government Norman detested. (Churchill was in France; in response to a question, he said, in French, "When I am face-to-face with the Old Lady of Threadneedle Street, I am completely impotent." Churchill never became a fan of Norman's. In 1931, as the world financial system fell apart, he wrote to a friend: "I hope we shall hang Montagu Norman. . . . I will certainly turn King's Evidence against him."[7] Later

Norman, through his continuing friendship with German central banker Hjalmar Schacht, became a buddy of Adolf Hitler's, and had his picture taken with Hitler as late as early 1939, silver goatee and mustache beside the Führer's patented brush mustache, giving Churchill further reason to dislike him.) Even after nationalization in 1946, the Bank communicated changes in its interest rates not through some governmental announcement but by a statement on the floor of the Stock Exchange by a representative from Mullens, one of the bond brokers with whom the bank worked.

R. S. Sayers in his great history of the Bank described its governor's situation when he came to work one morning in the late nineteenth century:

> If there had been an articulate Governor (they do not seem to have been born that way) he might have said that fundamentally he had three duties. He had a statutory duty to maintain the convertibility of the note into gold coin; he had a political duty to look after the financial needs of government; and he had a commercial duty to maintain an income for the stockholders. Whenever possible, he was running all three horses at once, but if there was a conflict, he knew which he had to put first. He would think of his primary duty as the maintenance of the gold standard: though rarely spoken between them, both Governor and Chancellor knew that the Treasury's needs ought not to get in the way of measures to protect the gold reserve. Similarly, the Governor might spend many hours dealing with the Bank's private customers and in arguing about remuneration for government business, but if extra expenditure was needed to prevent a fall in the gold reserve, he knew where his duty lay. It had also become accepted by this time that a far-sighted gold standard policy–as well as proper care for government finance–implied occasional action as lender of last resort, which in turn implied continuing acquaintance with the channels through which help might some day flow.[8]

The central bank maintains the integrity of the payments system, usually by finding ways that banks can settle their accounts with each other in full and on time. Deposit insurance, formal or implied, is there less to protect the depositor than to protect the payments system. A central bank serves as a lender of last resort to banks that cannot raise the cash to make the payments they or their depositors through them are committed to make. Banks are funded with short-term liabilities, deposits, or borrowings, and invest those funds in longer-term assets. This "maturity transformation" is a necessary source of profits for the banking industry. Banks keep a "liquidity ratio" of cash reserves, very short term and easily salable assets to pay back the depositors. If or when depositors and lenders to the bank want more of their money back than the liquidity reserve permits, a bank must sell longer-term assets to get the money—and at such moments those longer-term assets are likely to be salable only at greatly reduced prices. The argument to justify supplying a busted bank with the funds it needs is that the failure of any one bank to repay its depositors can reduce the confidence in *all* banks, creating a run, which endangers the payments system, the grease of any developed economy.

When the Bank of England was nationalized in 1946, decisions on interest rates became the responsibility of the chancellor of the exchequer, who told the governor what to tell Mullen as the Bank's agent at the stock exchange. Still, as Sir Leslie O'Brien argued when he was governor of the Bank, nationalization here was not like, say, the nationalization of the coal mines. "Of course we are not a nationalized *industry*," Sir Leslie said, "we are a nationalized *institution*." Indeed, the nationalization of the Bank of England had not involved any change in the formal structure of the Bank: the Labor government had simply compelled the private shareholders to sell all their stock to the government, and the queen as exclusive shareholder voted all the stock. The Bank was not a statutory corporation created by a law (like Lloyd's of London); it was legally a chartered corporation like any other limited liability company. Governors of the Bank were appointed by the queen as exclusive shareholder for a five-year term, but then could not be removed by either the queen or the prime minister. Until 1971, the nationalized Bank did not publish its accounts; until 1979, it did not *have* to reveal its accounts to anyone, including the Treasury.

The Banque de France was chartered in 1800 by Napoleon, then first consul, and planted in rather stony soil, for the French had twice been victimized by paper money. In the early eighteenth century, the Scotsman John Law had persuaded the Regent Orleans that the quickest way to boost the revenues of the state was to issue money backed by prospective tax collections, producing a great boom and a great bust. Less than a hundred years later, in the heat of the Revolution, the National Assembly had proclaimed a currency of *assignats,* with value based on what had been seized from the aristocracy and the Catholic Church. So the new Banque de France was to be a note-issuing bank with more than enough gold in its vaults to convert the currency, and while it was to lend to Napoleon (at 4 percent interest; indeed, he once said he had founded the bank to have a source of money at 4 percent), it would be owned by its stockholders. Six years later, because he was having difficulty negotiating these loans, Napoleon had the Corps Legislatif enact a law that put his own people in command of the Banque. But private ownership if not private control remained. For almost 150 years the Banque de France was a state institution with private shareholders, who received 6 percent dividend on the face value of their shares plus two-thirds of the profits.

The Banque got most of its money free, in the form of government deposits, and paid no interest on deposits by the public or businesses. It was therefore especially profitable when rates went up. This was finally noticed by the government, and after 1897 the state took for itself all profits deemed to result from a discount rate of more than 5 percent. After the Franco-Prussian War, one French observer found a unique reason for private ownership of a central bank—the Germans, he wrote, had seized Paris and the offices of the Banque, but they could not take its wealth as spoils of war because that belonged to private citizens, not to the government. It was, Charles Goodhart observes, "a more civilized century."[9] But war and the French defeat disrupted the Banque's international operations, especially its services to Switzerland, where twenty-five cantons and demi-cantons issued their own currencies and French francs served as the necessary reserves for their interchange.

This experience stimulated the first Swiss attempts to form a single national bank and a single national currency. It was not an easy venture in a trilingual country. Students of the arguments in the 1990s over the establishment of a common currency for Europe might consider that the Swiss people in referendum twice rejected the idea of a national central bank and a national currency before yielding to the inevitable in 1905. And the Swiss fondness for gold itself may be related to the fact that it was not until the twentieth century that the Swiss had a national currency that was backed by gold. At the very end of the century–in April 1999–the people of Switzerland by referendum broke the link between the Swiss franc and gold.

By contrast, the German Reichsbank had an easy birth in 1875 as a necessary expression of the newfound unity of the German Empire. Seven currencies from seven different kingdoms, grand duchies, and principalities were then circulating in Germany. Because the military victories of Prussia had unified the country, the Reichsbank was essentially an extension of the Prussian State Bank, which essentially duplicated the French structure–it was owned by the state, which appointed its directors, but funded by private investors who elected a committee that met monthly with the directors. The shareholders were entitled to a 3½ percent annual dividend on the face value of their shares, and beyond that they received one-quarter of the profits from seignorage. The Reichsbank did not really compete with the commercial banks: like the Banque de France it did not pay interest on deposits, and it restricted its investments to the highest quality short-term commercial paper.

Moreover, it was understood that German commercial banks did not have to keep any significant liquidity reserve to pay off depositors, because the Reichsbank would pour money into the market by purchasing bills when there was any danger of a run on the system. A representative of Dresdner Bank told American investigators sent to look at how the Europeans did things after the American panic of 1907, "The Reichsbank feels it has a patriotic duty to preserve the credit of the Empire. It is a state institution."

The political agitation that preceded the Federal Reserve Act went under the name of "the currency question." Three times in a generation—in 1873, 1893, and 1907—bank panics had disabled the real economy as people sought to withdraw their money from banks and there wasn't enough money to repay them. The nation's currency consisted of gold coin, paper "greenbacks" left over from the Civil War, and banknotes issued by nationally chartered banks to a total of 90 percent of their holdings of U.S. Treasury bonds. The silver dollar authorized by Alexander Hamilton and produced to an extraordinary quality in the early nineteenth century had never circulated because its silver content was so high people hoarded it or sold it to foreigners, and in 1806 Jefferson ordered the mint to stop producing the coins. Even the authorization for such coins was knocked out of the statute books in the Grant administration in what Populists (and William Jennings Bryan) came to call "the crime of 1873." Trade grew and flourished with the use of checks drawn on deposits created by banks when they made loans; but if any number of people lost faith in the banking system and decided they wanted cash, there just wasn't enough of it.

No small part of the problem was the settlement system on the New York Stock Exchange, which required brokers to post deposits daily in connection with their customers' purchases. The "call money" market in New York was thus demanding and inflexible, and in emergencies—because people who need overnight money don't feel much bite from very high interest rates—it was a whirlpool that could pull down banks far away.[10] Ten times between the Civil War and 1908, the New York Clearing House had to issue scrip—"clearing house certificates"—for insiders to use among each other in lieu of cash.

Gerald Dunne, law professor, editor of the *Banking and Law Journal,* and former vice president of the Federal Reserve Bank of St.

Louis, lists the commissions formed to create monetary reforms: "the Jones Commission of 1876, the Indianapolis Currency Convention of 1897, the National Monetary Commission of 1908, the Columbia University Conference of 1910, and the Pujo Committee of 1912. There had been the Muhleman Plan, the Baltimore Plan, the Morawetz Plan, the Warburg Plan, the Walker bill, several Fowler bills, the Williams bill, the Aldrich bill, the Vreeland bill, and the Aldrich-Vreeland bill."[11] Of these, the Aldrich bill, named for Senator Nelson Aldrich of Rhode Island, had created the greatest stir. It called for the establishment of a central bankers' co-op, a "National Reserve Association" that could issue currency against its members' borrowers' paper. The association would have forty-six directors, of which forty-two would be chosen by the member bankers and only four by the government. It was against this proposal that the Democrats, newly elected in 1910 to control the House of Representatives, launched Carter Glass's bill for a Federal Reserve that would in the end be controlled not by the bankers but by the government.

Three years later, when this bill was in the final boarding process in the House, a delegation of bankers came to call on Woodrow Wilson to get at least his pledge that the board he would choose to run the new Federal Reserve would be composed mostly of bankers. "Which of you gentlemen," Wilson inquired icily, "thinks the railroads should elect the members of the Interstate Commerce Commission?"[12] It is noteworthy that neither the bankers nor Wilson knew that at the Bank of England—"the rule," Bagehot wrote, "is rigid and absolute"—there was a total prohibition on bankers as directors, because the decisions taken by the court of the Bank were matters that might directly benefit or penalize the banks. The American compromise, which survives, rarely publicized, was a Federal Advisory Council (FAC) of twelve bankers, one chosen by the board of each district bank to serve a one-year term. (Allan Sproul, president of the Federal Reserve bank of New York, described it as "a sop to the bankers who had been ruled off the board on the theory that you don't make game wardens out of poachers.")[13] By statute, the FAC meets four times a year, the first day alone to discuss problems submitted to it a few weeks before the meeting by the secretary of the Federal Reserve Board (that day ends with a splendid dinner at the Hotel Madison in Washington); the second day with the members of the board, who listen.

Nothing would have more greatly surprised the authors of the Federal Reserve Act of 1913 than a later time's opinion that the Fed represented the ideal of the central bank. They wanted it understood that the Federal Reserve *System* was not and never would be a "central bank." "We intended," Carter Glass said nineteen years later, "to preclude all idea of central banking."[14] The Democratic Party's platform for the 1912 election had proclaimed, "We oppose the so-called Aldrich bill or the establishment of a central bank. . . . Banks exist for the accommodation of the public. . . . All legislation on the subject of banking and currency should have for its purpose the securing of these accommodations on terms of absolute security to the public and of complete protection from the misuse of the power that wealth gives those who possess it."[15]

H. Parker Willis, dean of the school of political science at George Washington University, and chief of staff to Glass—later, the first secretary of the board—wrote in 1915 that "The new act . . . generally diffuses control instead of centralizing it."[16] There would be not one central bank for all America, but twelve "district Federal Reserve Banks." Each would fulfill many of the functions historically performed by big-city "correspondent banks" for lesser banks in small cities and towns—it would clear checks, provide cash for the teller windows, rediscount commercial paper for members if they needed money, help purchase bonds for investment purposes, and handle custodial work. Nationally chartered banks would have to become "members" of their district banks; state-chartered banks could join or not, as they wished. The CEOs of the district banks were called "Governors," to make it clear that their role was comparable to that of the governor of the Bank of England.

Until 1935, the secretary of the treasury was a member of the board ex officio, which troubled Senator Elihu Root, who feared that his presence at board meetings would mean that board decisions "put in pawn the credit of the United States."[17] The question of the ranking of board members in the Washington pecking order was very important in the early days. They thought they should rank just under cabinet secretaries, but Wilson thought them no more important than members of the Interstate Commerce and Civil Service Commissions and offered a simulated ranking of assistant secretary. Treasury Secretary William G. McAdoo (who in addition to the perks of his office had extraordinary access to the White House as Wilson's son-in-law) related in his memoirs that at their insistence he took this matter of precedence to the president, who said, "Well they might come right after the fire department!"[18]

The board has never had a bank to run. The twelve "district" banks were scattered around the country–and are still today where the original "organizing committee" (President Wilson's secretaries of treasury and agriculture, plus the Comptroller) put them in 1913, only one each in the Southwest (Dallas) and in the West (San Francisco). The General Accounting Office points out that "the San Francisco Reserve Bank in 1914 served 6 percent of the nation's population; the St. Louis Reserve Bank served almost 10 percent. As of 1990, the San Francisco Bank served almost 20 percent of the population, while the St. Louis Bank served just 5 percent."[19] The Federal Reserve Board can move the district lines–the New Jersey shore of the Hudson River, originally assigned to Philadelphia, was shifted to New York in the 1920s–but twelve banks is the most (and, more significantly today, the least) the law allows.

These banks were and are "owned" by the commercial banks in their districts. Only member banks could directly use the services the Federal Reserve Banks would supply, but non-member banks could access them through their established correspondent arrangements with banks that did become members. Each district bank was and is governed by a board with nine members. The member banks elect six of them and the Board of Governors in Washington appoints the other three, one of whom it designates as chairman. These are part-time advisory jobs, like the board of a private-sector corporation. Final approval of each bank's budget is now in Washington, as is authority to raise or lower the bank's discount rate. This board selects what is now called a president to run the bank—when the Federal Reserve Act was amended in 1935, the new centralization was sealed by moving the title "Governor" to Washington. These selections, too, once made by the local board on its own, are now made very much in partnership with Washington, which can and sometimes does veto the local choice.

Each member bank of the Fed must buy stock in its district bank to a par value of 3 percent of its own capital and surplus, and as that equity rises, it must continue to allocate 3 percent of it to new shares. These shares must be sold back to the bank at par if the member shrinks or goes out of business; anything the member owes the Fed at that awful moment gets deducted off the top. Every year, the district bank must pay its members a 6 percent dividend on the par value of those shares; if there is a year when the bank doesn't earn that dividend, it cumulates and must be paid off later. When the Federal Reserve Act was written in 1913, it was not entirely clear whether this would work. The law provided that the organizing committee could decide that the sale of stock to the commercial banks of the district did not sufficiently capitalize a Federal Reserve Bank, and could offer shares in that bank to the public (up to a maximum of $25,000 for any individual or corporation). If public offer didn't do the trick, the new reserve banks could sell stock to the Treasury, which would market it at a later time.

Shareholders in a reserve bank would also be "individually responsible, equally and ratably, and not one for another, for all contracts, debts and engagements of such bank to the amount of their subscriptions to such stock at the par value thereof"—that is, the district bank could call from its members at any time a sum of money equal to the par value of the stock they had bought. When you invest in other corporations, you can lose the price of the stock, but that's all; that's the meaning of "limited liability." The bank that invests in a Federal Reserve Bank, however, is on the hook for double what the stock cost. Such arrangements were common in the capitalization of banks in the nineteenth century, and were among the reasons why bank stocks didn't trade much. They are now history for other banks, but they survive in the charters of the Federal Reserve Banks.

The district banks sold their stock easily enough, of course, and each of the twelve banks passed the $4 million capital threshold written into the act in time to open in November 1914. In addition to their capitalization, the new banks had a guaranteed source of deposits. Both state and national bank charters had required banks to keep "reserves," liquid assets that could be drawn upon if depositors wanted their money back. In 1913, these reserves totaled about 15 percent of bank deposits. Most of the reserves were in gold or "gold certificates" issued by the Treasury, but some were in earning assets like government bonds, which paid interest. The real cost to the member banks of joining the Fed was the requirement in the law that reserves deposited with the district bank would not yield interest. (In the spring of 2000, the House Banking Committee approved a new law that would for the first time permit the district banks to pay interest on reserves.) On the other hand, the district banks gave their members correspondent services without charge, and offered rediscounting services to members at the best rates in town.

It was a matter of considerable concern originally that these banks prosper as private enterprises. The 1914 *Annual Report* of the Board of Governors noted that "The Reserve Banks have expenses to meet, and while it would be a mistake to regard them merely as profit-making concerns and to apply to them the ordinary test of business success, there is no reason why they should not earn their expenses, and a fair profit besides. . . . Moreover, the Reserve Banks never can become the leading and important factor in the money market which they were designed to be unless a considerable portion of their resources is regularly and constantly employed."[20]

All the district banks opened for business on the command of Treasury Secretary William McAdoo on the same day–November 16, 1914, less than a year after the passage of the Federal Reserve Act, and more importantly, less than four months after the outbreak of World War I, which had seriously disrupted much of the American economy. (The stock market had closed the day war was declared and did not reopen even for restricted trading until a month after the Federal Reserve Banks had been launched.) It cannot be too strongly stressed that when these banks were first opened for business, the fact that local bankers elected two-thirds of their boards was very important. "The Act," economic historian Charles Kindleberger wrote, "was based on the theory that regional money and capital markets would develop around the locations of the twelve district banks. The Act implicitly contemplated separate monetary policies for the twelve districts."[21] Benjamin Strong of the New York Fed explained to a correspondent in the late 1920s that the best way to control unwise extension of credit at the stock exchange was to push the discount rates at the other eleven district Feds a percentage point higher than the rate in New York. This differential would suck money out of New York to the countryside, forcing the New York banks to call their loans to stock speculators, those being the shortest loans and the easiest to cancel.[22] At the second meeting of the heads of the twelve district banks, in January 1915, Governor Géorge J. Seay of the Federal Reserve Bank of Richmond, Virginia, grumbled that his "judgment as a banker" told him that "something unsound [was] being attempted in the effort to equalize [interest] rates where conditions vary."[23] Contemplating the creation of the Euro and the European Central Bank, the head of the German Bundesbank could have said no more—and no less—in 1999.

All the revenues of the system were in the district banks, and the Board of Governors had no independent source of income. The board could not issue banknotes (paper money), but it could authorize the district banks, one at a time, to do so. If one of the definitions of a central bank is that it issues money, the district banks are still the institutions that qualify. Though signed by the secretary of the treasury, the bills in your wallet today are all Federal Reserve Notes, and until recently there was a letter in a rosette on the obverse to indicate the bank which put in the order for this note. In the early days of the Federal Reserve System, each bank had to have its own reserves of gold, short-term commercial paper, and U.S. Treasury bonds to back its banknotes.

These were not legal tender. Until 1933, people entering into contracts with each other in the United States could require that debts incurred under those contracts must be paid in gold, not paper currency. Though the government always accepted Federal Reserve Notes for tax and tariff payments, the banknotes issued by a Federal Reserve district bank, after all, were a claim on that bank, not on the government. The Board of Governors through an appointed "Federal Reserve agent" on the board of the bank held the collateral that was required by law as backing for the notes. FedWire, which now moves more than a trillion dollars a day of interbank payments, mostly to transfer private ownership of Treasury securities from one account on the computer to another account on the computer, was begun in the 1910s (in Morse code) as a way to move book entries expressing shares in the Gold Settlement Fund from one Federal Reserve Bank to another.

Among the aborted projects of the New Deal was one that would have made Federal Reserve Notes legal tender. Even after Franklin Roosevelt had suppressed the circulation of gold coins, forcing the country to use the Fed's paper money (plus the Treasury's one-dollar "Silver Certificates"), the national prejudice against government-issued paper money prevented congressional approval of legal tender legislation. The history books told stories from the 1830s and 1840s of "wildcat banks" that issued banknotes presumably redeemable in gold, but the holder had to go search among the wildcats in remote wooded areas to present the notes and cash them in. In the 1930s, there were still people in Congress who remembered that Abraham Lincoln's "greenbacks" had circulated at less than par value for two decades after the end of the Civil War (a steel-bladed shovel for sale in the store for a $5 gold coin might cost $6 in government-issued paper money). Lincoln's National Bank Act had chartered banks authorized to issue currency against their deposit with the government of an equal (or larger) face value of government bonds, and some of those notes were still in circulation in 1933.

In that year a Public Resolution of Congress, which is not a law, described "circulating notes of Federal Reserve Banks and national banking associations" as "coin or currency of the United States" to be used instead of gold in contracts that called for payment in gold. In 1935, another Public Resolution declared that securities which stated that they were to be redeemed in gold were also to be paid in such "coin or currency." But it was not until the Coinage Act of 1965 that Federal Reserve Notes were explicitly labeled legal tender—and not until 1968, when the national stock of gold was being rapidly drained by foreign central banks which had decided they wanted to hold their reserves in gold rather than in dollars—that the individual banks were relieved of the necessity to hold "gold certificates" representing real gold in Fort Knox (still $35 an ounce) to cover at least 25 percent of the face value of their note issue. After Lyndon Johnson twisted arms, the law that permitted the banks to continue issuing their notes despite the loss of gold passed the Senate by a two-vote margin.

Until the Great Depression turned control of everything over to Washington, the decision making of the twelve district banks was inevitably infected with the self-interest of a private enterprise. The first efforts to coordinate the discounting and rediscounting activities of the separate banks, starting in 1922, were dominated by New York as the biggest and strongest of the twelve—and were successfully resisted by some of the others, often enough because they needed the revenues from their own lending to pay their bills and their dividends.

Because the law required a high fraction of gold backing for the notes printed, the district Feds' license to print money was not as profitable as had been predicted. The original Federal Reserve Act had charged the district Feds a "franchise tax" equal to one-half of the bank's earnings after expenses and dividends. The other half could be taken onto the books as "surplus" until the surplus account equaled 40 percent of the paid-in capital stock, after which all earnings would go to the Treasury. In 1919, the law was changed to let the district Feds keep all their profits until the surplus equaled the "subscribed capital," which was twice the paid-in capital–and then 10 percent of any profits thereafter. Payments to the Treasury peaked in 1920–21 at $60 million a year, then dropped like a stone; in 1930, the Fed gave the government only $20,000 as Treasury's share for its year's work. In 1933, Congress abolished the franchise tax, expropriated $139 million from the surplus accounts of the district banks to finance the launch of the Federal Deposit Insurance Corporation, and authorized the banks to keep *all* their future profits for themselves to rebuild the surplus.

In 1947, as part of the negotiations between a government that wanted to keep interest rates low and a central bank worried about inflation, the Fed instituted a "voluntary" program under which a "tax" would be applied to the issuance of that portion of the Federal Reserve Notes not covered by a gold reserve, to transfer 90 percent of the system's profits to the Treasury. By then, thanks to the war and its associated deficits, the banks had built up huge inventories of Treasury securities that generated huge earnings, and the surplus was considerably greater than "subscribed" capital. As early as 1957, the Bureau of the Budget in the Treasury, the 1950s version of what is now the Office of Management and Budget in the Executive Office, began laying claim to a much higher piece of the profits of the banks; and in 1959, once again "voluntarily" though the hounds of Congress were baying at the door, the Fed transferred all the excess surplus to the Treasury.

Once you have paid him the Danegeld, Rudyard Kipling said, you never get rid of the Dane. In 1964, the Fed reinstated its original rules, reduced the maximum size of its surplus to the total *paid-in* capital, and gave Lyndon Johnson $524 million to help pay for the Vietnam War. The inflation following that war, and the high interest rates it generated, made the Federal Reserve Banks the most profitable enterprise in the country, and by 1981 the Fed's profits contributed to the Treasury were over $14 billion a year, more than 2 percent of the federal government's total revenues. Still, when the General Accounting Office (GAO) of the Congress snooped around the system in 1994, the accumulated surplus–the Fed's mad money fund, essentially its first line of defense against any insistence by Congress that the board subject itself to budgetary discipline–totaled almost $4 billion. The reason for maintaining such a high retained surplus, the Fed said with an apparent straight face in its annual report, was to guarantee the solvency of a system with $20 billion of profits a year from its routine operations, just in case a big bank should come crashing down with giant losses to the Fed itself. On the other hand, as GAO noted, the surplus was kept in government bonds, reducing the Treasury's need to borrow from the public, which made the transaction a wash.

As part of the solution to the wretched budget battle of 1996, when a chunk of the government was shut down, Congress without hearings and without explanation required the Fed to make contributions to the Treasury of $106 million in fiscal 1997 and $107 million in 1998. And in 1999, desperate for revenues that did not involve taxation to maintain the facade of "preserving the Social Security surplus," Congress reached into the Fed's pocket for no less than $3.5 billion, which was paid out in May 2000. The reader should note that the sale of these bonds to the public adds to the national debt in public hands just as much as a $3.5 billion appropriation to pay doctors or teachers or soldiers.

The Banking Act of 1933, which brought the nation the great but eventually mixed blessing of deposit insurance, also took a first step toward reorganizing the Fed. The Banking Act of 1935 completed the structure. The secretary of the treasury and the Comptroller were taken off the board, which was reconstituted with seven members appointed by the president and confirmed by the Senate, each to serve fourteen years with no possibility of reappointment, though a governor who fills out the term of a departed governor can get a full term of his or her own when that term expires. No two governors are supposed to be from the same district, though people are sometimes accredited from their birth state rather than their residence. The chairman and the vice chairman, separately appointed and confirmed from the ranks of governors, serve four-year terms, which can be renewed in that office. Having been appointed to an unexpired term and reappointed, William McChesney Martin, Jr. (whose father, incidentally, had been the first governor of the Federal Reserve Bank of St. Louis in 1914), served as chairman for eighteen years, from 1951 to 1969.

Despite general dissatisfaction with the Fed's performance in the last years of the 1920s boom and the first years of the depression (it was, Herbert Hoover wrote with considerable understatement, "a weak reed for a nation to lean on in time of trouble"), the restive Democratic Congress could not imagine another device to do the money job. A very eminent group of University of Chicago economists (headed by Frank Knight, Henry Simons, Aaron Director, Sen. Paul Douglas, and Albert Hart) had submitted a detailed scheme to nationalize the Federal Reserve Banks and convert all commercial banks to institutions that could accept demand deposits only subject to a 100 percent reserve requirement, as the only safe way to organize government deposit insurance.[24] They got a respectful hearing from Agriculture Secretary Henry Wallace, who urged the scheme on Roosevelt, but neither the president nor the Congress wanted to upset this applecart when so many people were selling apples.

The 1933 act created a statutory "Open Market Committee" to coordinate the purchases and sales of paper by the twelve district banks. Each bank had a representative on the committee, and members of the board could attend if they wished, but individual banks were not required to mesh their activities with the recommendations of the committee. Not until 1935 was the central banking activity truly centralized in Washington by law, with the establishment of a committee on which the board members held a majority. Since 1935, all the separate banks have been required to buy or sell securities for monetary control purposes through a central office housed in New York and staffed by New York, but taking its instructions from Washington.

Each bank does retain a separate discount window, at which its members can borrow if they find themselves short some of the money they need to bring their reserves up to the designated watermark. Access to borrowings from the Fed has long been a matter of grace and favor, not a right, and banks that made repeated visits to the discount window were told to find a private-sector correspondent from whom they could do their borrowing. These discount windows are all that remain of Carter Glass's vision of separate money markets in a continent-spanning nation where in fact different regions at different times have different monetary needs: twelve vice presidents of Federal Reserve Banks continue to have independent authority to decide whether or not it will be easy for the banks in their area to borrow from the central banks. But these days it's meaningless; the discount windows go months without visitors. Nobody borrows from the district banks: it's considered a mark of weakness to do so, and a bank can lose more money by reducing its access to the market than it gains by tapping the resources of the Fed.

Between them, the Glass-Steagall Act in 1933 and the Banking Act in 1935 greatly expanded the duties and the power of the Federal Reserve. The banking and securities businesses were separated: banks were forbidden to underwrite securities and investment houses were forbidden to take deposits. It is probably worth noting, though few academic historians do note it, that the idea of separation was most strongly advocated by Winthrop Aldrich, son of Nelson Aldrich and a lawyer who had been installed as head of the Chase National Bank to clean up a stinking mess.[25] (The Republican platform in 1932 promised that if Herbert Hoover were returned with a Republican majority in Congress, they would "make a thorough study of the conditions which permitted the credit and the credit machinery of the country to be made available, without adequate check, for wholesale speculation in securities, resulting in ruinous consequences to millions of our citizens and to the national economy, and to correct those conditions so that they shall not recur.")[26] George Moore, who later converted First National City Bank to Citicorp, remembered that when he was a lad working for County Trust in 1928, he would get occasional calls from underwriters who had launched successful initial public offerings, informing him that they had put him down for a couple of hundred shares at the opening and had just sold him out, doubting he wished to hold the stock, and where should they send the check for the profits? One doubts that the academics whose studies sponsored by the banking industry now find nothing wrong in the late 1920s know more than the people who lived through that period and testified wonderingly about how the banks behaved when they were lords of the universe.

The new laws forbade banks to pay interest on demand deposits (checking accounts), and the Fed was given the power to limit the rates they could pay for time deposits (savings accounts–commercial banks were not allowed to use the word "savings" until after World War II: there were, after all "savings banks" and "savings associations" which made contributions to congressional campaigns). The Fed was also ordered to police the extension of "purpose credit"–loans taken to buy securities. "Margin requirements"–the fraction of the purchase price of securities that had to be the buyer's own money–were to be set by the Fed. Most of the time (to the present day), the Fed commanded that no more than 50 percent of a purchase order for securities can be funded by a loan, but the requirement has varied. The idea was to make sure that what were considered the limited credit resources of the banking system were not disproportionately used to finance speculation in the stock market. William McChesney Martin, Jr., and his successor Arthur Burns kept margin requirements above 65 percent from 1963 to 1971, and as part of the effort to contain inflation right after World War II, Marriner Eccles in 1946 prohibited margin entirely. Because modern finance has created so many ways to use credit to control stocks–derivatives from futures to options to swaps–Alan Greenspan has taken no interest in the subject whatsoever.

Chapter 4

The Question of Independence

*In a certain sense, it can be said that a Central Bank is never wrong.
It can always maintain its own solvency and even its own earning power
by inflation or by other methods at its disposal.*

—Eleanor Lansing Dulles (1932)

Seignorage on the currency is a wonderful central banking thing which explains why many central banks, perhaps most central banks, are both grossly overstaffed and grossly inefficient. We were no exception to that. We took the seignorage income, which in a moderately high inflation environment was always more than adequate for our needs, spent what we felt like spending and handed over the rest to the Treasury by way of dividend. There was no political oversight of what we spent. We just got first crack at the seignorage.

—Donald Brash, governor of the
New Zealand Central Bank (1999)

You cannot in a democratic society have an institution which is either fully or partly dissociated from the electoral process and which has powers that central banks inherently have.

—Alan Greenspan (1994)

UNTIL RECENTLY IT WAS UNDERSTOOD that if disagreements arose, governments would have the last say, even when the central bank was privately owned. The governments, after all, had empowered the banks. Winston Churchill could declare himself powerless before the Old Lady of Threadneedle Street because Montagu Norman had his own political position in Britain and Churchill was not willing to spend political capital to challenge him. But it was true, as R. S. Sayers noted, that before World War I and again in the years between 1925 and 1931, both the chancellor of the exchequer and the governor of the Bank of England considered the maintenance of the gold backing for the currency as their first responsibility. And the man on the firing line for that purpose was the governor.

The main advocate of an independent central bank in the United States was Benjamin Strong of the New York Fed, who operated his institution not only with minimal deference to the federal government but with little concern for the views of the board of the Federal Reserve System. In 1925, as part of his campaign to help the Bank of England restore convertibility between the pound and gold, he arranged a loan of $200 million in gold from the New York Fed to the Bank of England after an informal conversation with the governors of some other district banks. "Views were expressed by all present," he wrote in a memo to the files, "that the arrangement should be made specifically with the Federal Reserve Bank of New York, and not with the Federal Reserve System"–let alone the Treasury.[1] In 1927, Strong and Montagu Norman joined Thomas W. Lamont of J. P. Morgan in visiting Mussolini to convince him that if he wanted to keep the lira strong he should make the Bank of Italy independent of the Finance Ministry, which he wouldn't do.

Then the Great Depression which the central banks were powerless to stop gave politicians the feeling that they could do better than soulless central bankers. Marriner Eccles, Roosevelt's chairman of the Fed, a Utah banker who had worked out Keynes's approach to monetary policy before he ever heard of Keynes, unquestionably considered himself an agent of national economic policy–indeed, he believed himself to be its architect, and was highly critical of the

Comptroller because his bank examiners were not team players. After the war, the Bank of England and the Banque de France were nationalized, and everywhere the central bankers were given the task of allocating credit, persuading, influencing, or ordering the banks in their countries to finance only those activities that promoted the national "plan."

The American system presumably worked differently. Americans were not rebuilding a war-torn economy, they were gleefully banging swords into plowshares. The depression and the debt deflations did not return; instead, the problem was maintaining the value of the savings that had been built up during the war. The Federal Reserve supposedly influenced the economy by controlling the creation of bank reserves, and the private sector, encouraged or squeezed according to the Fed's actions in destroying or fattening reserves, would then do the allocations. But right after the war the banks could fund their loans by selling from their huge hoard of government paper without worrying about reserves (because the Fed was committed to maintaining the price of Treasury paper and had to buy whatever they sold). Under that pressure, the Fed in 1951 tried a Voluntary Credit Restraint Program, which wrote guidelines for banks. George Moore of Citibank, who was one of the twelve members of the national governing board of the program, described the rules of thumb: "It was okay to make a loan to build a first television station in an area, but not a competitive television station . . . sound practice to lend money to build a dairy or a flour mill, but not money to *buy* a dairy or a flour mill."

This committee maintained a liaison with bond underwriters, and Moore notes a flap that arose after the state of West Virginia could not get bids from investment bankers when it tried to float a bond issue to finance a veterans' bonus the state's voters had approved the previous fall. Governor Oakley Patterson solicited a meeting with the bankers. "I asked him," Moore recalled some years later, "what he thought the veterans would do with the money. 'About a third will spend it on women,' he said, 'and a third will spend it on booze, and the rest I guess will just waste it.'"[2] Congressmen complained, and Harry Truman sent a memo to tell the committee they were to stop interfering with the sale of state and municipal paper.

By then, the Korean War was sending the federal budget back into deep deficit, requiring prodigious sales of new Treasury paper. The Truman administration sought to resume the procedures that had financed World War II, and had left a great residue of inflationary pressure. And the Federal Reserve rebelled. It is the most important moment in the history of central banking, the first stirring of the idea that a central bank should and could be an instrument of governance separate from the legislature that created it and the executive that appointed its leaders.

Because there was a rebellion and an "Accord" in the United States in 1951, there can be a European Central Bank that sets short-term interest rates for all of Europe without input from the elected governments of the European Union, and a Bank of England where a committee of "wise men" meet with the governor to decide whether the Bank should change rates, informing the chancellor of the exchequer only after they decide. The Accord is in the pedigree of recent decisions that Mexico, Chile, and New Zealand would give their central banks authority to make pesos and NZ dollars plentiful or scarce, on their own motion, without the approval of the Ministry of Finance or the Treasury or any other elected official. When South Korea fell in an abyss of short-term debt, the International Monetary Fund refused to throw down a needed rope until the government agreed to write laws that would make the country's central bank independent of its finance ministry. When the Communist government of the People's Republic of China felt its control of the economy slipping away in 1998, it called on the Federal Reserve Bank of New York to supply consultants who could restructure the People's Bank of China along the lines of the Fed.

It is the formal independence of the Federal Reserve—its power, as Chairman William McChesney Martin, Jr., famously put it, to "take away the punch bowl just as the party is getting good"—that made the Fed the envy and eventually the prototype for so much of the world. The Fed has never had the sort of guarantee that the Germans gave the Bundesbank in the treaty that rejoined West and East Germany–that "The Deutsche Bundesbank . . . independent of instructions from the governments of the Contracting Parties, shall regulate the circulation of money and credit supply in the entire currency area with the aim of safeguarding the currency."[3] But what it has is good enough. Alan Blinder, the Princeton economist who served as vice chairman of the Fed in the mid-1990s, argues that the "hallmark of independence is near irreversibility. In the American system of government, for example, neither the President nor the Supreme Court can countermand the decisions of the Federal Open Market Committee. . . . This makes FOMC decisions, for all practical purposes, immune from reversal. Without this immunity, the Fed would not really be independent, for its decisions would hold only so long as they did not displease someone more powerful."[4]

Despite its importance, historians have largely neglected the fight between the Fed and the White House that established the ground rules for central bank independence in 1951. David McCullough's excellent biography of Harry Truman, long and detailed, does not even mention the matter. But it was among the half-dozen most important events in Truman's presidency, and its reverberations still echo, all over the world.

The fight and its denouement in a formal Accord were accidents of personality, and of the statutory arrangements that let governors of the Fed who came in as replacements take a full fourteen-year term after the expiration of the partial term to which they had been appointed. Roosevelt in 1944 had given Eccles his fourteen-year term, and a third statutory four-year term as chairman. Truman in April 1948 told Eccles–out of the blue–that he would not be reappointed as chairman but that the president would appreciate his remaining on the board. Eccles later wrote in his memoirs that he thought the president had moved against him on the intervention of Senator

Thomas Downey of California, who had been put up to it by A. P. Giannini, whose Bank of America had been in a state of war with the Fed almost continuously for more than twenty years. Eccles's decision to remain on the board–a very strange decision, for the change in status is roughly that of school principal to schoolteacher–would three years later give the board the unfettered spokesman to the president, and to Congress, who could open up to the public, to an extraordinary degree, the institutional failures of American policy making in the economic arena.

Eccles in his memoirs described what he was fighting against in the return of wartime finance:

> There were three pivotal rates of interest upon which the pattern of rates for government issues was maintained. They were ⅜ per cent for Treasury ninety-day bills; ⅞ per cent for one-year certificates; and 2½ per cent for the longest term marketable government bonds. This meant, for instance, that as the ⅞ one-year certificate came closer to maturity, the interest rate it yielded went down and the price of the security went up. Likewise, as all other intermediate and longer-term securities approached maturity, the pegging of the short-term rates forced their rates down and their prices up.
>
> . . . We wanted an increase in the rate of these bills so that banks and other investors would be induced to buy and hold them. To the extent that they did not do so, it was the Federal Reserve that would have to buy, and this, of course, would create excess reserves for the banking system. . . . By increasing the amount of bills that the Federal Reserve had to buy, the Treasury was automatically able to create excess reserves. . . . The existence of these excess reserves in turn put the banks under pressure to buy Treasury certificates and bank eligible government securities at premium prices, thereby creating the basis for "free riding" by nonbank investors.

Since the banks, and particularly the large nonbank investors, understood the government's program . . . the banks took advantage of the situation by "playing the pattern of rates," and the large investors did likewise in the process of "free riding." The banks played the pattern of rates by selling the Reserve System (which was the principal buyer) some of the short-term low-yielding securities as they went to premiums (in line with the pattern of rates) and then purchased the longer-term, higher-yielding securities. This action created high-powered reserve money, out of which the banking system was able to buy six times as many securities from nonbank investors as it sold to the Federal Reserve, and thereby to create a like amount of deposits. . . . The effect was a multiple expansion of money, with a consequent increase in inflationary pressures. . . . Countless corporations as well as individuals made a great show of their patriotism in subscribing heavily to each of these war-loan drives; but the process I've been describing, whereby they sold their holdings to the banks or to the Federal Reserve on the eve of drives or between them gave them a substantial profit for their patriotism.[5]

With the outbreak of the Korean War, the Treasury had returned to this lazy man's way of financing government expenditures. And now the economy began to pay the price. Wage and price controls had stifled inflation during the big war, but could do so no longer. Between June 1950 and February 1951, wholesale prices rose 17 percent, and the cost of living was up 7 percent. As early as August, the Federal Open Market Committee, with New York Fed president Allan Sproul in the chair, had decided, as Sproul wrote the chairman of his bank, "to act in our sphere of primary responsibility, the control of credit, by refusing to provide further reserves to the banking system at existing rates. We also decided to tell the Treasury what we had done. . . . The Secretary [John Snyder] was brief and abrupt, indicating that since we had told him what we had decided to do there was nothing for him to say. . . . Tom [McCabe, Eccles's replacement as chairman of the Federal Reserve Board] and I returned to the Board building and in a few minutes a call came through from the Secretary. He told Tom that he was announcing his September–October financing immediately, and that it was 13-month 1¼s for all maturities, totalling $13 billion plus. This was contrary to all advice he had received from any source I know of; and, of course, ran directly counter to our program."[6]

Snyder was a small-town Missouri banker with a degree of small-town elegance, a poker-playing buddy of Truman's, and a total lightweight.* What he was trying to do here was to force the Fed to back off its policies or see a government securities issue fail in the market, with unfathomable possible consequences in a banking system where more than two-fifths of the assets were government paper. Eccles's analysis being clearly correct, and all the reserve banks agreeing with it, the board was unwilling to back off, and in September the market was confronted with a surrealistic dance, which Sproul explained to a puzzled governor of the Bank of England: "We

---

*I knew him. He had a house in Shelter Island, N.Y., where I have a house. His featured a steel railway car cantilevered out over West Neck Bay, because after leaving government he had built himself a conglomerate, U.S. Industries, on the foundation of a struggling company called American Pressed Steel Car. Every Friday night in the summer, a seaplane would come out with the help, return to New York, and come out again with Snyder and his guests. One fine day in winter, the house fell into the bay, which was okay with everybody. Snyder was, however, the source of one of the great political stories of the postwar era. The weekend before the Democratic Convention in 1960, after Joe Kennedy's ability to award contracts for real property insurance had bought enough Democratic district leaders to make his son's nomination a certainty, Harry Truman gave an interview excoriating John F. Kennedy as an unworthy candidate for president. Snyder, as an old buddy, was recruited to call Truman and get him to bind up the wounds. As Snyder told the story, he said to Truman, "Harry, you've hurt the boy."

And Truman said, "I know I have. I wanted to."

Snyder said, "I can't understand that. He's got the nomination, you know."

And Truman said, "Yes, I know."

"And once he's actually nominated," Snyder continued, "there'll be nobody in the country more enthusiastic for him than you. You'll campaign for him."

Truman said nothing, and Snyder added, "I can't make any sense of it, Harry. I've known you all my life. You're not a bigot. You don't care the boy's a Catholic."

And Truman said, "I'm not afraid of the Pope; I'm afraid of the Pop," and hung up.

went our separate way, and the Treasury went its way. The result was a rise in short-term rates which made the Treasury's offering of $13½ billion of 13-month 1¼ percent notes . . . largely unacceptable to the market. We then set ourselves to buy as much of the maturing issues as we could so that the Treasury might not have a complete failure in these difficult times, and to sell as much of our existing holdings as we could, so that we would not be forced to put funds into the market, contrary to our avowed objective. The result was Alice in Wonderland in some ways. . . . This sort of thing can't go on."[7] Fortunately, it was too complicated a story for the newspapers to ask questions, and the public never knew what was happening.

Snyder asked Truman to intervene, and he did, modestly. Everybody agreed on the terms for a 5-year Treasury note to be issued in December, at 1¾ percent. The issue did not sell well. On January 18, 1951, Snyder made a luncheon speech to the New York Board of Trade, and said, "In the firm belief, after long consideration, that the 2½ percent long-term rate is fair and equitable to the investor, and that market stability is essential, the Treasury Department has concluded, after joint conferences with President Truman and Chairman McCabe of the Federal Reserve Board, that the refunding of new money issues will be financed within the pattern of this rate."

On January 22, Sproul gave his annual talk to the New York State Bankers Association, and said enough of what he thought to stimulate newspaper stories that the Fed did not accept Snyder's position. Three days later, the Joint Economic Committee of the Congress, chaired by Senator Robert Taft, was holding hearings, and invited Fed chairman Thomas McCabe to testify. Because McCabe could not testify in opposition to administration policies and keep his job, Eccles was put forward instead, and said he thought the Treasury's policies would fuel inflation. The Open Market Committee was to meet on January 31, and that morning the White House called to ask McCabe to bring all the members over to meet with the president at four o'clock that afternoon—the first and last time such a maneuver was organized. Governor M. R. Evans wrote a memo of what happened at the meeting, including the president's recollections of "his wartime experience [in World War I] when he bought Liberty Bonds out of his soldier's pay. When he returned from France and had to sell his bonds to buy clothes and other civilian things, he got only $80 or a little more for his hundred-dollar bonds. . . . [H]e was principally concerned with maintaining the confidence of the public in Government securities as one way of presenting a unified front against communism. . . . He reiterated that we should do everything possible to maintain confidence in the Government securities market."[8]

The next day, the White House issued a press statement that "The Federal Reserve Board has pledged its support to President Truman to maintain the stability of Government securities," and a Treasury press release followed up: "the White House announcement means that the market for government securities will be established at present levels and that these levels will be maintained during the present emergency." And Truman followed up with a supposedly private "Dear Tom" letter to McCabe thanking him for his "assurance that the market on Government securities will be stabilized and maintained at present levels. . . . I wish you would convey to all the members of your group [a lovely word: the Board of Governors as an NGO] my warm appreciation of their cooperative attitude." The board, much agitated, voted to have McCabe seek an appointment at the White House to straighten the president out–it could be done, the members thought, because the letter was private. And then the White House released the letter to the press.

And *then*, on February 3, on his own motion, without telling anyone except his secretary that he was doing so, Eccles released to the press Governor Evans's memorandum of what in fact had been said at the White House. Eccles had never been subordinate to anybody, and was not going to start now. McCabe came to a boil. Truman sought advice from Fred Vinson, Snyder's predecessor as treasury secretary, whom he had elevated to be Chief Justice, and Vinson recommended Robert Anderson, a lean, leather-skinned Texas oilman who was deputy chairman of the Dallas Fed and would later be Dwight Eisenhower's secretary of the treasury–and white-haired boy. Eisenhower floated a trial balloon in 1956 to see if he could get his party to nominate Anderson rather than repeat Nixon for vice president; many years later, after Eisenhower's death, Anderson as an old man got in criminal trouble with the promotion of oil fields. "Tom McCabe wasn't talking to Marriner Eccles," Anderson recalled twenty-seven years later, "and neither of them was talking to John Snyder. I insisted on a letter from Truman giving me power to tell Treasury what to do."

Eccles ends his memoirs with his leak of the board's report on the meeting with Truman, and the comment that "it is difficult to predict the long-run significance of bringing the controversy between the Treasury and the Federal Reserve out in the open for public and congressional discussion."[9] He would not have had to hold the presses long to report the denouement. On February 7, the Open Market Committee sent a letter to Truman: "You as President of the United States and we as members of the Federal Open Market Committee have unintentionally been drawn into a false position before the American public—you as if you were committing us to a policy which we believe to be contrary to what we all truly desire, and we as if we were questioning you and defying your wishes as the chief executive of the country in this critical period." What would really reduce the value of the savings bonds the soldiers and sailors and production workers had bought during the war, after all, was a tearing inflation: asset values are in the end more important than asset prices. Meanwhile, McCabe and Sproul met with senators from the Banking Committee and the Joint Economic Committee, and then hand-delivered a letter to Snyder at the Treasury. "At this meeting for the first time," Sproul noted, "Mr. William McC. Martin, Assistant Secretary of the Treasury, took part in the discussion." "Assistant Secretary" was a larger title then than it is now: Bill Martin had already been president of the New York Stock Exchange, and was a major figure in his own right.

The Fed now had the upper hand. Democrats were the party of low interest rates, but Senator Paul Douglas of Illinois, a former professor of economics on the left wing of his party, was wholeheartedly on the Fed's side; he was about to make a speech on the Senate floor urging among other things that "the Federal Reserve gird its legal loins and fulfill the responsibilities which I believe the Congress intended it to have." Snyder went into the hospital for an operation, and Treasury "sought a commitment from the Open Market Committee that there would be no change in the existing situation in the Government securities market during the period of his hospitalization. This was a commitment," Sproul reported thirteen years later, "which the Committee felt unable to give in the face of mounting inflationary pressures, and a Government securities market which was demanding heavy purchases by the Federal Reserve, contrary to the policy and program which it thought the economic situation required. The Committee asked the Secretary to name someone at the Treasury with whom it could talk, in the interim, and the Secretary named Mr. Martin. Negotiations now took a turn for the better. . . ."[10]

Snyder seems to have reached out once more from the hospital, because Truman on February 26 called a grand council to meet in the White House: the director of Defense Mobilization; the undersecretary of the treasury; in addition to Martin, the chairman of the SEC, the chairman and vice chairman of the Open Market Committee, the members of the Council of Economic Advisers, and John Steelman, the president's special counsel. The president read these worthies assembled in his office a memo he was releasing to the press, calling among other things for a committee consisting of the secretary of the treasury, the chairman of the Fed, the chairman of the Council of Economic Advisers, and the director of Defense Mobilization to make a study of the overlapping responsibilities of the Fed and the Treasury. The memo included the president's hope that "while this study is under way, no attempt will be made to change the interest rate pattern, so that stability in the Government securities market will be maintained."

But it was too late. With only perfunctory consultation of the still-hospitalized Snyder, Martin and the Treasury staff, professionals all, had come to general agreement with the Federal Reserve Board staff. If Anderson is taken as credible, he got Truman's approval. On February 28, an oral presentation of the deal was made to the Open Market Committee, and two days later the formal document was ready for consideration. The preamble stated an agreement on "purpose—to reduce to a minimum the creation of bank reserves through monetization of the public debt, while assuring the financing of the Government's needs." Most of the long-term 2½ percent bonds would be retired by a non-marketable 2¾ percent issue, and the Fed would for a year support the price of the 2½s that remained on the market. "With the exception of this support, the maintenance of orderly market conditions, hereafter, to be without reference to the maintenance of par value of any Treasury issues." The final point in the document was that "The public statement of agreement to be brief, financial, and nonpolitical."

On Sunday, March 4, only six weeks after Snyder had publicly demanded the Fed's subservience, a "joint announcement" by the secretary of the treasury and the chairman of the Fed told the world that they "have reached full accord with respect to debt management and monetary policies." Ever after, the document would be referred to as the "Accord." Sproul a dozen years later wrote to Murray Rossant of *The New York Times* that it was "an accord by courtesy. Actually, it was almost entirely a statement by the Federal Open Market Committee of what it was prepared to do and not to do in the related fields of monetary policy and debt management. . . . Mr. Martin's contribution to the 'Accord,' I think, was to get the Secretary of the Treasury to accede to the terms laid down by the Federal Open Market Committee."[11]

Interestingly, so doughty a warrior as Sproul did not realize that on the foundation of this "Accord," Bill Martin—who would move over from the Treasury to become chairman of the Federal Reserve Board for eighteen years—would build the theory and practice of central bank independence. Thirteen years later, Sproul wrote that "The Federal Reserve challenge to the Treasury's assertion of dominance in the area of their overlapping responsibilities prior to the 'Accord' had its ultimate justification in the achievement of coequal

status in these matters, and not as an assertion of a false independence. The Federal Reserve does not have, never has had, and never
has claimed to have an independence in monetary affairs which di-
vorces it from the general economic policies of the Government."[12]
Five years after that, in 1969, Richard Nixon would appoint Arthur
Burns as Martin's successor at the Fed, and in the press conference
where he introduced Burns as the next chairman would turn sheep's
eyes on him and say, "*Please,* Dr. Burns, give us some money . . ."[13]

The power of the central bank is to make the national currency
scarce and expensive or plentiful and cheap, and for that purpose
there are only two tools: the purchase or sale of paper in the market,
and direct loans to banks or increases in their required reserves
(which serve functionally as loans from the banks to the central
banks). We note for further exploration the truth that this power is
greatest when the currency is inconvertible and there are few
moneylike instruments that can be substituted for the real thing. The
essence of the central bank is its exercise of discretion, and critics of
central banking, especially from the right (where it is believed that
the market will create equilibria if left alone), are forever demanding
that central banks follow rules rather than exercise discretion. Politicians retain the right to second-guess, in nasty language too, but they
don't really want to interfere.

Discretion meant that an activity was conducted sub rosa, here
through unpublicized rediscounting of loans or unadvertised actions
in the market for government or commercial paper. The "Cashier's
Office" of the Bank of England worked behind closed doors to tell
the London discount houses what they were to do. The "primary
dealers" who intermediated between the Federal Reserve and the
market were legally obliged not to tell anybody where their orders
came from, and the hemispheric little auditorium at the New York
Fed where the Fed's own traders worked was as off limits to
strangers as the gold vaults in the basement. (The little auditorium is

gone, and the Fed traders–dozens of them–now work in serried ranks at desks before screens like the traders in all the rest of the world.)

Under the revised Federal Reserve Act in 1935, the chairman of the Federal Reserve had a legal obligation to file an annual written report with the Speaker of the House of Representatives, who would have it printed for distribution to his membership, but until 1978, when the Humphrey-Hawkins Act mandated twice-yearly hearings in both the Senate and the House Banking Committees, the chairman rarely spoke in public or testified before Congress. As late as the 1980s, there was a recognized Wall Street profession called "Fed watching," which paid economists who had been researchers on the Fed staffs to predict stock and bond market prices and what would happen to business, all based on gnomic utterances by Fed governors, weekly estimates of the size of various money supplies, and weekend squiggles in market interest rates (because reserves held for the credit of a bank on Friday night counted triple what reserves counted on the other weekday nights).

Not everyone is a fan of the central bankers. They have, Milton Friedman once said, two shared objectives: "Avoiding accountability on the one hand and achieving public prestige on the other."[14] John Heimann, who is sort of an honorary central banker, having been Comptroller of the Currency and chairman of the Group of Thirty, and then director of a Financial Stability Institute that depends from the Bank for International Settlements, says that central bankers are very congenial with each other because nobody else likes them.

Friedman argued against independence for central banks on the grounds that it would bring about "an extraordinary dependence on personalities, which fosters instability arising from accidental shifts in the particular people and the character of the people who are in charge of the system"[15]–in other words, you can't restrict the mission. In 1959, Britain's Radcliffe Commission reporting to "The Lords Commissioners of Her Majesty's Treasury" rejected the case for an independent central bank "because it seems to us that it either contemplates two separate and independent agencies of government of which each is capable of initiating and pursuing its own conception of what economic policy requires or else assumes that the true objective of a central bank is one single and unvarying purpose, the stability of the currency and the exchanges. . . . [This] second [purpose] . . . ties such a bank down to a single objective which is both too limited in scope and at the same time incapable of achievement without concurrent action on the part of the central government."[16] Radcliffe still has a point, because a central bank on its own certainly cannot "control the exchanges." But it turns out you can restrict the mission and dedicate the central bank entirely to the maintenance of price stability: virtually all the countries that have moved toward an independent central bank have done so as part of a drive to stop inflation and stabilize the value of the currency. Which was, of course, what gave Eccles his strength in 1951.

When the Indonesian banking system collapsed in a tangle that mixed the depreciation of the rupiah with bad loans to influential people, the American economist Steve Hanke, a professor at Johns Hopkins in Baltimore and a columnist for *Forbes* magazine, put the blame on the central bank (which had in fact been quite intelligently run until the Suharto government fired its leaders) and recommended its replacement with a "currency board." A currency board establishes a parity between a weak nation's money and the money of a strong nation, requiring for example that every Argentine peso be backed by and interchangeable with an American dollar. The only function of a currency board is to make sure that banks do not lend the local currency beyond their stock of the foreign currency that backs it. Hanke was taken seriously by President Suharto, who saw that if he adopted the idea of a currency board, he and his family and friends could get their money out of rupiah and into dollars during the interregnum. Meanwhile, the Indonesian central bank debased the currency with immense loans to the country's commercial banks that kept them looking as though they were sailing through the storm though in fact they were so profoundly holed below the waterline that they were beyond salvage.

At this writing, four currencies are in fact controlled by a currency board: the Hong Kong dollar, the Argentine peso, the Bulgarian lev, and the Estonian kroon. Ecuador and El Salvador have adopted the dollor as their currency. The argument is that investors will be drawn to these countries because the currency board guarantees that the value of their investments in their own currencies will not fall because of host-country manipulation, and there may be something to it, though Bulgaria has not lured much investment and Argentina has done less well in this regard than neighboring Brazil, where worries about the currency are endemic.

Sometimes a currency board is recommended explicitly *because* it eliminates the central bank: Rudiger Dornbusch of the Massachusetts Institute of Technology said savagely in early 1999 that "Currency sovereignty is the right to have stagnant growth because the central banks screw up all the time."[17] But it is hard to see why tying the domestic economy to a foreign currency must promote growth. By tying the quantity of the local currency to the country's stock of a foreign currency, a government virtually compels the market to bid up interest rates whenever there is a threat that the money supply will be reduced by a flight of dollars, whatever the cause. Argentine short-term interest rates went above 20 percent per year in the early 1990s—and Argentine unemployment went to 18 percent—not because Argentina had done anything wrong but because Brazil had stepped on a rake again.

In 1974, when Fed chairman Arthur Burns tried to follow traditional paths of squeezing bank reserves to damp down a mounting inflation, Walter Wriston, chairman of Citicorp, publicly complained that Burns (a college professor, after all) simply did not understand modern banking, and the extent to which a modern bank made its loans first and only thereafter went hunting for the money that would fund them. Burns in response said that Wriston didn't understand the function of the central bank. Both men were right. As early as 1922, Benjamin Strong, then head of the Federal Reserve Bank of New York, had told a Harvard audience that "Practically all borrowing by member banks from the Reserve Banks is *ex post facto*. The condition which gives rise to the need for borrowing had already come into existence before the application to borrow from the Reserve Bank was made."[18] Burns knew perfectly well that by preventing the banks from easily gathering the reserves the law made the banking system keep against its deposits, he was forcing the banks to disrupt their relations with their borrowers. What he did not know, and Wriston did know, was the extent to which changes in information technology and communications would alter all the relationships of commercial banking, making it possible if not always easy for banks to fund their new loans whether the central bank liked it or not.

In the next decade, changes in the function of commercial banking and the tools of central banking would indeed overwhelm the Fed—but the result would be to make the central bank seem ever more powerful. Banks live in the here-and-now, and make adjustments day-by-day; markets are forever guessing the future. The statements of Fed chairmen would become more significant than the actions of the board. In October 1998, a Chairman Greenspan could come on stage with his top hat and his scrawny rabbit and add $150 billion to the paper value of paper assets by ruminating in public about the gap between the interest rates on Treasury paper with thirty years to run and the interest rates on Treasury paper with twenty-nine years to run, and what he had to do to fix it.

PART THREE

Avoiding Catastrophe

Chapter 5

The System and Its Risks

The 1980s exposed various excesses which I think, to some degree, were becoming apparent in the 1970s. I can remember very clearly sitting in my office then, as President of the Federal Reserve Bank of New York, thinking that what this country needs is a first-class bank failure to teach us all a lesson—but please God, not in my District. When I went to Washington, I had the same feeling—we need a clear lesson from market discipline, but please dear God, not in my country. Then, if I read correctly the 1990s, and what happened when the Mexican crisis came along, Bob Rubin and Alan Greenspan thought what we need is a good country failure to teach everybody a lesson, but please not in a large country in my hemisphere. . . . There isn't a developed country in the world in the 1980s and early 1990s that did not run into banking crisis. I don't know of any of those countries that didn't act to protect the banking system with assistance whatever the law said.

–Paul Volcker, former chairman of the Federal Reserve Board,
at a conference sponsored by the
Federal Deposit Insurance Corporation, 1997[1]

"THE LIFE OF THE LAW," Justice Oliver Wendell Holmes, Jr., wrote, "has not been logic but experience." The life of central banking has not been theory but practice. Part of what makes the subject difficult to comprehend is that the practice occurs in conditions of maximum stress, like airplane crashes, and the traumatized survivors have a tendency to block the memory. But what central banks do for a living is, they prevent systemic failure. The Federal Reserve of the Great Depression is despised and rejected because the system failed while the board fiddled. The truth may be that nothing the board could have done would really have made that much difference, but what history records is that the system didn't even *try* to do its job.

Among the oddities of the 1990s has been the rise of a school of thought holding that there is no systemic risk in finance—that the markets will rebalance quickly if only governments will permit the foxes of economic growth to eat the lame ducks of unwisely sunk costs. Central banks, in this theory, have fostered a culture of "pseudo-systemic risk" to puff up their own importance. Writing in 1995, when the emerging markets were booming, Anna J. Schwartz and colleagues wrote that "investors . . . will shun entities where they perceive uncompensated risk and flock to entities with more inviting returns. Emerging stock markets are an example."[2] Two years later, the collapse of these markets, coupled with the collapse of the currencies of the countries where they were situated, plunged much of Asia and some of South America into the worst depression since the 1930s.

The cause of that depression was a banking crisis made worse by the procrastination—the self-comforting belief that the problem is liquidity not solvency, that it will all turn out all right if we just keep the banks alive until they can turn a corner. But pretending that busted banks are somehow viable enlarges their losses and creates a flight of domestic depositors and international investors, a flight that cannot be quickly stanched even by the international financial institutions. All the East Asian countries deepened their crises by trying to keep bad banks in business. Andrew Sheng, then a World Bank staffer and adviser to Bank Negara Malaysia (later deputy head of the Hong Kong Monetary Authority and chairman of its securities commission), told an IMF conference in 1990 that "central bank lending to banks during capital flight only adds fuel to the fire and is self-defeating."[3] (Some years earlier, Sheng had asked his then boss at the Bank Negara, the Malaysian national bank, what lesson could be drawn from their horrendous experience with the 1980s banking crisis in their country. The answer was: "Never hire monkeys to look after bananas.")[4]

The avalanche can start with a few relatively small rocks. As intermediaries–agents for their customers–banks do business with each other in a banking "system." The failure of one bank, by interrupting the anticipated cash flows of other banks, may create a reverberating crisis well before the depositors take flight. If an anticipated payment is not received, a bank is thrown into the credit market at a time when that market may be hostile. No one who lived in proximity to the Herstatt crisis of 1974 (when an obscure German bank defaulted on foreign exchange contracts in the New York market), or watched the severe degradation of all markets as morning moved to noon on October 20, 1987, could doubt the damage done to all credit-financed activity when banks become reluctant to make the payments expected from them until they see the arrival of the payments expected by them. Alexandre Lamfalussy while president of the Bank for International Settlements in Basle propounded the definition of systemic risk as central banks perceive it and as they are prepared to deal with it: "the risk that the illiquidity or failure of one institution, and its resulting inability to meet its obligations when due, will lead to the illiquidity or failure of other institutions."[5]

Both Walter Bagehot's *Lombard Street* and Karl Marx's *Capital* were responses to the great crises of British financial life after the Peel Act of 1844 gave the Bank of England a monopoly on the issuance of paper money. By the terms of that law, the Bank was permitted to maintain its previous Napoleonic-era issuance of £14 million of paper money that was not backed by gold but otherwise would be required to have in its vaults a value of gold equal to its issue of paper banknotes.

When bank crises come, people don't want accounts in banks: they want cash. Marx gave what may still be the best description: "Since every one is dependent upon the other for the coming in of these means of payment, and no one knows whether the other will be able to meet his payments when due, a stampede takes place for the means of payment available on the market, that is, the bank notes. Every one accumulates as many of them as he can secure, and thus the notes disappear from the circulation on the very day when they are needed most."[6] (Compare the very similar modern definition of financial panics, by Jack M. Guttentag of the University of Pennsylvania: "a general loss of faith in the capacity of financial institutions to deliver on their promises, and a consequent rush by those to whom these promises have been made to convert them quickly, before others do so, and before the institutions' resources are exhausted.")[7] Withdrawing money from the banks, people impose upon whomever it is that circulates the money a need to produce a lot of cash. In the gold standard model, and in the theoretical universe occupied by Anna Schwartz and Milton Friedman, this situation theoretically controls itself: the banks raise their interest rates high enough to persuade depositors to bring in their gold, and call in loans to get the cash to pay those depositors who aren't convinced.

Marx, again, gave a modern statement when he quoted *The Economist* on the panic of 1847: "We see here how rapidly and strikingly the raising of the rate of interest exerted its effect, together with the subsequent money panic, in correcting an unfavorable rate of exchange and turning the tide of gold, so that it flowed once more into England." Marx then observed, "This effect was produced quite independently of the balance of payments. A higher rate of interest produced a lower price of securities, of English as well as foreign ones, and caused large purchases of them for foreign accounts."[8] It is worth noting that Karl Marx a century and a half ago understood (sometimes) that higher rates of interest meant lower prices for securities, and that bankers had to consider such matters.

But this shrinkage of securities prices can trigger what the Yale economist Irving Fisher (who personally lost his shirt in the crash) was the first to call "a debt deflation," as businesses and people scramble to sell assets to pay back the banks, which deny credit to those who—if they had credit—might be interested in buying the assets. As money gets to be worth more, debts become an ever greater burden, and the wheels of trade, normally lubricated by credit, grind to a halt. Banks fail, because their liabilities have to be paid out immediately on demand at their nominal value, while their assets must be sold at a reduced price. By the time the banks have admitted failure, the damage has been done.

Andrew Sheng wrote in 1990, reflecting on his experience with the Malaysian central bank: "Bankers have a tendency to sit on a problem until it becomes too big to handle."[9] Sheng cites a rule of thumb derived from Spanish experience by Aristobulo de Juan in 1985: "Loan loss provisions by external auditors tend to be double those made by bank managers. Bank examiners would double the provisions made by the auditors, and in a liquidation situation, loan losses would turn out to be double those estimated by the bank examiners." Gerard Caprio, Jr., and Lawrence H. Summers (while still a professor) add bleakly that "both political and economic forces lean towards supervisors keeping silent about problem banks until net worth is already negative."[10]

From the central banking point of view, this is the ultimate disaster. The central bank is responsible for the money supply. Most of the money supply is in bank accounts. When a bank fails, the checks written against those bank accounts become worthless. To maintain the money supply, which is its primary business, the central bank must therefore search about for ways to maintain the value of the deposits in the failing bank. The easy way is to buy some of the assets (or take them as collateral against a loan) at a price higher than the market price, but this can work only if large supplies of cash are available to the purchaser. It is not a question of "Too big to fail," a slogan that has spilled carloads of ink in the United States. In a fragile banking system, the accounts in *any* bank known outside its immediate neighborhood will have to be rescued.

The most obvious remedy is that somebody keep a lot of cash around to meet the community's demands for the stuff in a crisis. (This holds internationally as well as nationally: testifying in spring 1999 about the world financial crises of the previous two years, Alan

Greenspan told the House Banking Committee that the best way to avoid such things was for nations to keep reserves of foreign currencies sufficient to meet at least a full year's anticipated expenditures and loan-servicing obligations.) Bagehot argued that this reserve should be centralized in a single institution, which would recognize its function as a "central bank." And this in effect is what Parliament did in the Peel Act. A bank with exclusive right to issue the currency would of course have to keep the reserves for that currency. Issuance itself being a profitable activity–for the issuing bank acquires assets with the money it prints–the government could reasonably expect the central bank to keep a good share of its reserves in sterile form, held for an emergency. Bagehot thought that something between one-third and two-fifths would probably do it.

The demand that a central bank keep a large sum idle for emergency use conflicts with every instinct of the commercial banker. "A nineteenth-century quasi-central bank," R. H. Timberlake argues,

> had to restrain itself during prosperous periods from lending on all good paper, which would have maximized its earning assets, so that it would have some metallic reserves to parlay among commercial banks if they were threatened by liquidity drains. When a panic occurred, the now-central bank had to lean into the wind, and, as Bagehot prescribed, lend on what might be called subjunctive paper–paper that would be good when general business conditions were again normal. Thus the commercial-public-central bank had to be more conservative than its fellows during a boom, and radical to the point of foolhardy in a crisis! No wonder the directors of these institutions had such difficulty afterwards explaining their operations to governmental investigating committees. Central banking policies could never be rationalized by recourse to commercial banking principles.[11]

The same arguments, incidentally, work against a government central bank in a less developed country keeping the kind of cash reserve Greenspan advocated. Invested in U.S. Treasury paper, the only certainly liquid investment, the money earns much less than the nation must pay on its borrowings, which leads the central bank to seek more profitable uses for the money. In South Korea in 1997, that meant handing it over to the nation's own commercial banks, which bought high-yield Brazilian bonds and took immense risks in the derivatives markets, betting (with a company organized in Malaysia by J. P. Morgan specifically to handle the bet) that the Thai baht would hold its value by comparison with the Japanese yen. "Central banks," James Grant of *Grant's Interest Rate Observer* told a conference in fall 1999, "have sought to make their assets sweat."[12] Unbeknownst to Grant at that time, but revealed to and by him later, the Federal Reserve Bank of New York was covering up the fact that foreign central banks were buying not only U.S. Treasury paper for their reserves, but also government-sponsored collateralized mortgage obligations, which paid higher rates. By February 2000, the total holdings of the Fed of New York for foreign central banks were $700 billion, of which $83 billion was mortgage paper.[13]

This number, incidentally–"U.S. government paper held at the Federal Reserve Bank of New York for foreign official account"–is a significant indicator of foreign investment in American enterprise when the United States has a current account deficit with the world. Foreign businessmen find themselves holding dollars earned from exports. When investment opportunities in the United States are unattractive, they take that money to their central bank to get their own currency for use at home, and that central bank invests its reserve in U.S. government paper, through the Federal Reserve Bank of New York. When the foreign businessmen like American investment chances, however, they take the dollars to the United States themselves and buy companies or build factories or support the stock market. Foreign central banks may acquire U.S. government paper for their own reasons, as the Japanese did in 1999 in their effort to keep the yen from appreciating too far against the dollar. And they sell for their own reasons, as the Europeans did in the autumn of 2000, cashing in their U.S. Treasury paper for the dollars they would sell to purchase what was then a fading Euro. But week in, week out, the published number of foreign holdings at the New York Fed is a good measurement of whether our trade deficits are being financed by foreign governments (which will necessarily become increasingly reluctant to do so) or by an inflow of private foreign capital.

In the United States before World War I, when there was no central bank, the function of establishing and maintaining a reserve was thought to fall on the big banks in New York, the residual users of funds, because the securities market was always ready and willing to borrow. Banks from the agricultural states sent their money to New York for investment except in the spring planting season, when the farmers needed loans for seed, and the fall harvests, when the purchasers of the crops had to be financed. It was noted that financial panics almost always occurred in the fall, when the banks from the farm states took back their money, but the New York banks were not prepared to hold money idle to be sure they had it when it was needed. Charles Kindleberger reports that O. M. W. Sprague, the economic historian who wrote the basic background paper for the Aldrich Commission that looked at American finance in 1910, kept growling at the New York banks for their failure to understand their reserve function: "New York is not meeting the obligations of its position as our domestic money center, to say nothing of living up to future international responsibilities, so long as it is unable or unwilling to respond to any demand, however unreasonable, that can lawfully be made upon it for cash."[14] The law that established what everybody now concedes to be an American central bank was called the Federal Reserve Act, and the institution created was called the Federal Reserve System, because its prime function was to maintain the reserves that the banking system would need in times of trouble.

What Bagehot said the central bank should do with those reserves in a crisis is perhaps the most famous economic prescription ever written, and few would quarrel too loudly with it today. If depositors were taking their money out of an institution that would fail if it could not meet their demands, Bagehot wrote, the Bank of England should lend "freely" on "good collateral," at "penalty rates of interest." We consider the three rules.

(1) "freely": If a panic is to be stopped, the people who are panicked must be convinced that they have no cause for alarm. In Stephen Fay's splendid formulation, "Central banking in a crisis is like a conjuring trick that creates the illusion that nothing is happening."[15] Marx sneered at the Peel Act of 1844 because the chancellor of the exchequer had to suspend its provisions to permit the Bank of England to issue new currency that would not be backed by gold. But once government removed the limit on the Bank's issue of money to people who wanted money, panic subsided–first in 1847 and then again in 1857. In *It's a Wonderful Life,* Jimmy Stewart finally convinces his town that their little bank is safe. There are those who claim that the Asian crisis of 1997–98 could have been stopped if the package the International Monetary Fund put together for the Thais had been $50 billion instead of $28 billion, and the United States had put up some money for the Thais on a bilateral basis. But after the Mexican bailout in 1995, Congress had temporarily forbidden the use of the only discretionary funds the president had–the Exchange Stabilization Fund created by Franklin Roosevelt's revaluation of gold in 1934 and boosted by the creation of IMF Special Drawing Rights in 1967–and there was no way Congress was going to authorize, let alone appropriate funds for lending to Thailand in 1997.

It is far from clear that more money would in fact have saved the situation in Thailand. Unbeknownst to the IMF, the Thais had already wasted their apparently substantial reserves of dollars in futile efforts to defend their baht by purchasing it in the forward market. William R. White of the Bank for International Settlements mentions in a footnote to his report on the central banking implications of the Asian collapse that "One feature of the Asian crisis was that a number of governments supported their currencies extensively using forward and other forms of off-balance sheet intervention. This information was hidden from the public and, when revealed, indicated that the true level of reserves was much less than thought. This contributed to the aura of panic and the sudden desire on the part of creditors to withdraw."[16] But the argument of insufficient help remains one that respectable people make, quoting Bagehot.

(2) on "good collateral": The central bank should not lose money on its intervention to prevent systemic risk. If a bank needs cash for its depositors and cannot sell its assets because of the general sickness in the market–the incipient debt deflation–the central bank can interpose itself in front of the market and buy good paper that before (and after) this crisis would have been easily salable at a much better price. In the absence of central bank intervention, a failing bank that is solvent at this moment may become insolvent as the fire sale of its assets reduces their market price. Implied in this argument is a conclusion that this bank is *really* solvent–that its assets properly valued exceed its liabilities. "[T]he act of liquifying an illiquid asset cannot help to hide insolvency," H. Robert Heller, president of Visa U.S.A. and a former Fed governor, wrote rather hopefully.[17] From greater experience, Andrew Sheng, then on leave from Bank Negara Malaysia, suggested that "when bankers come to the central bank for liquidity help (after they are not able to obtain help from other institutions), it is no longer liquidity assistance, but a question of solvency."[18]

If in fact there are not enough sound assets to cover the bank's liabilities, advancing money on good security may preserve the books of the central bank itself but damages the future interests of the other creditors of the bank, who will now have to collect what they are owed from an institution that has irrevocably pledged the good stuff to the central bank. Art rather than science may be involved in classifying a troubled bank as "illiquid" and thus worthy of rescue rather than "insolvent" and subject to closure. And the truth of the matter is that the central bank will always have a great incentive to say a bank is not really insolvent, not only to protect the money supply but also on grounds of day-to-day practicality. Bailing out is a lot easier than closing down a bad bank and creates fewer problems for both its depositors and (especially) the businesses that borrow from it.

One should also note in passing that quite apart from the market collapse, the systemic implications of a bank failure, and the theoretical structures that have been built around central banking, a failing bank is something from which the fastidious will avert their gaze. Brian Quinn, who had been chief of supervision for the Bank of England, observed at a Group of Thirty conference on financial insolvency that "The typical failed financial institution is a mess. Nobody knows where things are or where things should be; to put it mildly, there is a degree of dislocation."[19] And there are always things you don't know about.

(3) at "penalty rates of interest": This, interestingly, happens only rarely. The rule assumes that the institution in question is still a going concern–that it is solvent–and can thus pay penalties. But the usual borrower from the central bank these days is solidly insolvent. With rare exceptions–the Federal Reserve Bank of New York hit Bank of New York with a heavy penalty rate to carry overnight a multi-billion-dollar position in U.S. Treasury paper that a computer glitch had prevented the bank from delivering to its trading partners–it makes no sense to assess a penalty rate against a bank that needs Fed money because it can't get what it needs elsewhere. The central bank will usually be delighted just to get its money back, interest be damned, from an institution that has come for a loan in extremis.

The idea has surfaced again, however, on the international front. Money from the International Monetary Fund comes to sovereign borrowers much cheaper than the rate the market will charge (if the market will provide money at all). Once the borrower has got back on a plausible economic track, it is supposed to repay the IMF before it repays its other creditors, which it will be loath to do if the IMF money is cheaper. Several of the larger IMF "programs" for struggling countries in the 1990s established a sliding scale of interest rates, rising precipitously as time passed. On the table at the IMF as these words are written is a proposal that *all* IMF lending carry this Bagehot-like provision that as the borrower regains his feet, he must pay off his IMF debt or pay a penalty rate of interest.

One of relatively few big banks actually to be closed down in the late twentieth century was BCCI, a Pakistani institution incorporated in Luxembourg and gathering funds around the world, wherever people from the Indian subcontinent had settled. Its assets were also widespread, and many of them were pretty rancid. "The Bank of England and other regulatory authorities immediately involved," Quinn told the bankruptcy practitioners, "were not sure exactly what they were dealing with, but they knew there was criminality in the organization, perhaps going right through it. It was vital that the preparations to close BCCI were kept as quiet as possible. Otherwise the people could walk, and so might the money. We kept the lid so tight that when it came time to apply for an order to close the bank at its headquarters in Luxembourg, we discovered that it was the day of the annual Luxembourg Judges' Picnic, and there was no judge on hand to sign the necessary order. The clock was ticking towards the opening of the business day in New York, and the process of closure was stalled. I had Jerry Corrigan [president of the Federal Reserve Bank of New York] on one phone, and Eddie George [chairman of the Bank of England] on the other phone asking, 'What is keeping you, Brian? Why can't we send in the inspectors and inform the markets?' You will appreciate I am giving a rough translation here and that the actual words used were a little bit more industrial. We did find a judge in the end. . . ."[20]

BCCI could be closed in 1992 because–though Bank of America had helped get the enterprise off the ground in the late 1970s–the club of bankers had decided some years before that these people were crooks, and there were few interbank loans on the books. (And most of those were in the United States, where politicos like presidential adviser Clark Clifford and Jimmy Carter's budget director Bert Lance had cheerfully tied up with the Pakistanis to start a "First American Bank" in New York and Washington.) In important ways, then, BCCI was not part of the banking system the central bankers had to defend. But in other cases, the Bank of England has taken an expansive view of a central bank's responsibilities, usually by organizing what the British call a "lifeboat" for sinking banks.

In 1974, the so-called fringe banks–deposit-taking, checkbook-issuing institutions not licensed or regulated by anybody in the permissive legal climate of 1970s England–threatened to disappear in large numbers under the joint hammer of the oil price shock and the collapse of the London property market. The Bank of England put together a consortium of the five nationwide "clearing banks" to offer credit to the fringe banks to replace the money their depositors were removing. By the end of the year, the total amount required to prevent the public failure of these banks had reached about $3 billion, the equivalent of $12 billion in end-of-the-century money. The clearing banks provided 90 percent of it–and issued their own guarantee to depositors in the fringe banks that checks drawn on accounts in those banks would be honored by the clearing banks. Even after the revelation that some of these deposit-taking but unlicensed banks were in deep trouble, no written records of conversations with their officers were kept by James Keogh, then chief cashier and senior supervisor of the banks (and a good guy, by the way, straightforward and funny, who had done what they told him to do and found himself out on the street when the Bank needed a scapegoat). "The Bank had taken its role as a supervisor for granted," Stephen Fay wrote, "but had not taken it seriously."[21]

This was in every way embarrassing–the institutions that were saved were not recognized "banks," though some of their paper had been bought by the discount houses that worked with the Bank of England and had wound up on the Bank's books. Most of them were clearly insolvent, and one of the worst of them was owned by the crown agents, who invest the money of the royal family. To get a grip on the situation, the Bank of England "invited" these unrecognized banks "to submit themselves to voluntary supervision."[22] Governor Leslie O'Brien, whose term ended just as the size of these problems became apparent, said later, "We did think that, through the discount office, we had sufficient insight to realize that banks would not go over the top. With hindsight we could see that was not the case."[23]

Four years afterward, his successor Gordon Richardson defended the Bank's actions to a House of Commons committee: "We had to support some institutions which did not themselves deserve support on their merits, and, indeed, institutions which fell outside the Bank's established range of supervisory responsibilities. But I felt, as I saw the tide coming in, that it was necessary to take the Bank beyond the banking system proper, for which it was responsible, into those deposit-taking institutions, because collapse there was capable of letting the waves come in on the institutions themselves; and the fact that very rapidly we had to extend our support to a wider circle, which included some reputable banking institutions, showed that our instinct that we were on very treacherous ground was sound."[24]

Even after the disaster of the fringe banks, it took until 1979 for Parliament to beat down the Bank's opposition to any statutory specification of its role as a "supervisor." The head of the new department that was supposed to supervise banks noted his view that "Frequent discussions between senior managers of banks and senior officials of the Bank of England are more conducive to the maintenance of good banking practices than the technique adopted in many other countries of sending in teams of inspectors to examine the bank's books."[25] The Banking Act in 1979 presumably gave the Bank of England power to authorize both classic banking institutions and "licensed" deposit takers. But the Bank had not asked for such powers and did not wish to exercise them.

One of the classic banks was Johnson-Matthey (JM), which was one of the five dealers who bid twice a day at the famous "gold-fixing" around a table in the upstairs room at Rothschilds in London, tipping over little Union Jacks to indicate that they and their clients were willing to do business at the price that had just been called. JM turned into a rogue operation in the early 1980s, and the Bank, looking at nothing but raw numbers submitted by JM itself, had seen nothing wrong. Loans had gone from £135 million in 1982 to £309 million in 1984, holdings of bullion from £804 million to £1.359 billion, while profits had declined from £16.6 million to £9.4 million. JMB's reports included a statement that reserves had been taken against all doubtful loans, but in fact the bank was involved with some highly promotional types, not to say crooks, and several of them had borrowed far more than prudence would have permitted. But the Bank of England had learned only what JM wished to tell it. The tradition of the Bank was still that the head of a "proper" bank came and visited with the chief cashier to discuss how his bank was doing—there were no examiners who went visiting the site and looking at the books of the famous London houses. This failure to monitor produced the aphorism among American bankers in London that the Bank of England didn't care what you did as long as you didn't frighten the horses.

The horror story in Johnson-Matthey was that customers had left large quantities of gold on deposit with the bank, to be sold or augmented at the twice-daily price-fixing. If JM simply failed, these customers would lose their gold—and the other London bullion dealers might well lose their customers. The Swiss and the futures market at New York's Commodity Exchange ("Comex") were already making inroads on London's position as the center of gold trading. This was 1984, when all the big banks were in trouble on their loans to Latin America, and in the United States Continental Illinois, the seventh largest American bank, had required immense infusions of funds by government agencies or under government agency guarantees. The Bank of England called in the bullion dealers and worked hard to sell JM to Canada's Bank of Nova Scotia, which was interested in getting into the gold business. Though the Bank perceived a threat to the "clearing banks," they themselves did not, and they felt no obligation to man a lifeboat. Finally the Bank of England had to take over JM itself, guaranteeing customers and depositors, to keep the operation going.

The Johnson-Matthey case decisively changed political attitudes in England. The "big bang" of deregulation in the financial markets in 1986 was accompanied by a new Securities and Investments Board that would regulate and supervise the securities exchanges and their dealers, the "unit trusts" (in American usage, the mutual funds) and the insurance companies that sold market-linked annuities to the public. Banks were permitted for the first time to purchase and operate securities houses. The *concept* of detailed supervision was now in the law, and while the Bank of England was permitted to continue its reliance on reports by the auditors the banks themselves had hired, it was also given power to commission reports on its own. Parliament clearly expected that in the future the Bank would know enough to intervene before the City discovered the crisis.

The Barings affair in 1995 disabused the politicians of that expectation. Baring Bank had been in the same hugely distinguished family for 233 years, and appeared to have used wisely and profitably the new powers banks received in the 1986 act. In particular, it had acquired and enlarged an Asian securities and derivatives business. Among the people who carried on that business was Nicholas Leeson, a twenty-seven-year-old eager beaver who had gone to work in the back office of a securities house right after secondary school and had been sent to Singapore to supervise Baring's processing for its own and customer accounts. He polished up the handle so carefully that he got himself made head of trading, too. He was supposed to be running a client-service operation and was not supposed to accumulate net positions in Baring's account (he could be long one contract and short a countervailing contract, but his net position at the end of each day was supposed to be zero). As the head of the back office, however, he could set up fictitious accounts to bury his losses while other accounts reported his winnings.

Leeson's superiors were quite enthusiastic. Ron Baker, the young Australian head of the Financial Product Group at Barings, who had been in this business for Bankers Trust in New York and London before Barings bought him away, made a phone call to London four weeks before Leeson blew up to describe what he had found on a recent visit to Singapore. "Nick had an amazing day on SIMEX [Singapore International Monetary Exchange]," he reported. "Baring Singapore was the market. I mean, he just has a corner there. So everybody wants Nick to do their business. . . . He just sees opportunities that are phenomenal, and he just takes them."[26] By February 1995, Leeson had committed the firm to more than a billion dollars of margin against trades in futures contracts on the Japanese Nikkei stock index in Singapore and the 10-year Japanese Government Bond (JGB) in Osaka.

In September 1993, Peter Baring, chairman of the bank, had tea at the Bank of England with Brian Quinn, executive director of banking supervision. The year 1992 had been a difficult one for the bank, but now that the securities operation was in gear, 1993 was turning into a corker. Baring's conclusion from the experience was that "it was not actually terribly difficult to make money in the securities business."[27] In any event, when Leeson ducked out–taking a glorious weekend with his wife at a luxury resort in Sumatra while the accounting firm of Coopers & Lybrand, which had certified the statements of Baring's Singapore branch just a few weeks before, returned to look into a hole almost twice the size of Baring's total capital–the Bank of England was left with the baby. The search for a lifeboat reached across the Atlantic, and senior executives of Merrill Lynch, Morgan Stanley, and Goldman, Sachs were summoned to a late night meeting with Eddie George, governor of the Bank of England, who had himself hustled back to London from a ski vacation in Switzerland. The next day, the Bank, the Americans, and the heads of the clearing banks tried again, and failed again. Calls were placed to the Ministry of Finance in Japan and to the Sultan of Brunei. The clearing banks were prepared to put up $900 million, but that might not be enough–indeed, the Leeson positions lost *$370 million* on Monday alone.

In this instance, the Bank of England decided that the failure of Barings did not have systemic implications. It was a medium-small bank, only $9 billion in total footings, and only a minor fraction of that was in checkable deposits or interbank loans. News of the collapse of Baring would not, the Bank of England thought, spook any of the communities that can turn a bank failure into a panic. This was a serious misjudgment: in fact, the world spent the better part of a week teetering on the edge of a major crisis. But it was not a banking crisis, and the central banks–the Bank of England, the Federal Reserve, and for a while the Singapore Monetary Authority–simply did not understand what was going on. On normal days, the clearinghouses that handled the settlement of trades in the futures and options exchanges were not *users* of bank credit whose repayments of loans were crucial to the health of the banks; they were lenders to the banks whose deposits of customer margin were among the significant sources of funds for the banks in the cities where the exchanges were located. Thus the failure of a participant in the market to meet a margin call from the exchange–to put up additional collateral because the value of his contract had dropped–would not put a *bank* in distress. E. Gerald Corrigan had warned in 1989 at a meeting run by the Federal Reserve Bank of Richmond that during the market plunge of 1987 "the greatest threat to the stability of the financial system as a whole in that period was the danger of a major default in one of these clearing and settlement systems."[28] But by 1995 Corrigan was gone, to Goldman, Sachs, and the Bank of England had never really thought about clearinghouses.

Baring had defaulted on a margin call, and had been "put into administration," the form of bankruptcy inherited from British colonial days. Very well: SIMEX sold out Leeson's positions, further driving down the market, and exhausting the Barings margin. Prices in the contracts Leeson had traded became even more volatile, and as is the custom of a clearinghouse, SIMEX sent a notice to all participants that everybody had to pony up more margin to make sure the next day's trades could clear. From the point of view of the American traders and brokers who had money frozen in accounts at Barings, SIMEX was trying to hold them up to pay off the Barings losses. Out of courtesy, because the Singapore market was joined to the Chicago Mercantile Exchange in a Mutual Offset System that permitted people to cancel a contract in one market by selling the identical contract in the other market,[29] Merrill informed Mary Schapiro, chair of the Commodity Futures Trading Commission in Washington, that it was about to renege on a call from SIMEX. Ms. Schapiro could see SIMEX and the Merc and London's International Financial Futures Exchange and God knows who else unable to open for trading as the Merrill default reverberated around the system. She roused the head of the Singapore Monetary Authority at three in the morning, and he went to his office to prepare and send off a guarantee to Merrill that its money would not be used for any purpose other than the fortification of its own positions.

This was still hairy, because the accountants administering the Baring estate still held $350 million of deposits from American traders and showed no inclination to release the money (the Merc's London lawyer told Stephen Fay that the Brits' attitude was "fuck the U.S.A.").[30] The Americans' money, indeed, was not released until the administrators found ING, the Dutch banking-cum-insurance conglomerate, to purchase the shards of Barings. ING paid one pound for the lot, and allocated a billion dollars to make the creditors whole, and another crisis was history. Significantly, perhaps, it was the first great financial crisis since the mid-nineteenth century when center stage had been occupied by someone other than a central bank.

In 1997, the new Labor government brought forth yet another Bank of England Bill, which took bank supervision away from the Bank of England. Victoria Robb of the Bank explained what had happened in a genteel piece on "The Genesis of Regulation" published in the Bank's own short-lived *Financial Stability Review:* the new legislation "provided the opportunity to transfer banking supervision to a new and strengthened S[ecurities and] I[nvestments] B[oard]. . . . The Bank will remain responsible for the overall stability of the financial system."[31]

Chapter 6

The American Lender of Last Resort

Until experience has demonstrated the contrary, I fear we must calculate that the American banker by and large will do in future emergencies just what he has done on similar occasions in the past. He will gather up every dollar of reserve money that he can lay his hands on and lock it up so tight that the Reserve Banks will never get hold of it until the crisis is past. I personally saw that happen in the early '90s, 1907 and 1914. Frankly, our bankers are more or less an unorganized mob.

—Ben Strong, Governor, Federal Reserve Bank of New York, to Adolf Miller, October 26, 1916[1]

IN HINDSIGHT, IT SEEMS CLEAR that the United States, never having had a lender of last resort and having suffered a depression where the Fed seemed powerless, set up a deposit insurance system as the way to prevent bank panics. Everyone in the United States knows that if the balance in an account is less than $100,000 (a number fixed in 1980; the original number, in 1934, had been $2,500; FDIC in 2000 proposed increasing it to $200,000), the Federal Deposit Insurance Corporation will pay, instantly, making arrangements to assure that you can continue to get cash from the ATM machine and

120

your checks will not bounce. Usually, the collapse of a bank is announced to the public with a statement that some other bank has taken over the operation, with a subsidy from the FDIC to make up for the losses in the asset portfolio.

Only federal insurance works. In the late 1980s, panicked depositors in savings associations in Ohio and Maryland and credit unions in Rhode Island forced the closing of solvent as well as busted state-insured institutions after one or two publicized fraud-induced failures drained the state insurance funds. Carter Golembe, a lawyer, historian, and banking consultant whose past includes a stretch with the FDIC, has always insisted that the New Deal Congress demanded deposit insurance less as a protection of individual depositors than as a device to protect the banking system from runs.[2] Bert Ely, an energetic banking consultant and libertarian (and an accountant, not an economist), has promoted with occasional allies in Congress a private deposit insurance scheme that would be better than the government system, he argues, because private banks would monitor each other if they were on the hook for each other's performance. The argument is plausible on its own terms–looking at the current systems of "prudential supervision" by government agencies, skepticism about the protection they provide is clearly warranted. But to the extent that the purpose of deposit insurance is to prevent bank runs, nothing but the deep pockets of government will do to give the insurance credibility.

Where there is an independent deposit insurer, there will be a conflict of interest between the central bank and the insurer. "The Fed," as FDIC chairman L. William Seidman once explained to Congress, "is a liquidity lender. They were never contemplated to lend to any institution that was insolvent. The fact is that as the information comes out that the Fed is making large loans, instead of stopping runs, it starts runs because people know that they are taking all the good assets to support their loans. Given that, it is not surprising that other people say, well, if they're in there, we'd better get ours out. Therefore, it has come to the insurance fund to be the ultimate supporter of this."[3]

The matter first came to a head in the failure of the Franklin National Bank in New York in 1974. This was a suburban bank that had overstretched by moving into New York and extending its normal construction lending into a market where commercial real estate is feast or famine. In a frantic effort to keep the thing afloat, management of the bank was turned over to Michele Sindona, an Italian banker whose dubious past was shadowed by the glory of his supposed Vatican connections, and the bank plunged heavily into foreign exchange trading. Acting in large part on the argument that declaring Franklin insolvent would roil the world's foreign exchange markets—and with some concern about the systemic impact of closing down the nation's twentieth largest bank—the Fed advanced Franklin more than a billion dollars, much of it against paper nobody in other situations would have called "good collateral." I had occasion to say to Tom Waage, a senior vice president of the New York Fed, that it would be fun to watch the bank try to dispose of this collateral when Franklin's doors were closed, and Tom said, "Martin, you're not entitled to that much fun."

The Fed tried to peddle Franklin to Manufacturers Hanover, which was interested only if the FDIC would assume responsibility for a big chunk of Franklin's assets. As the Fed already had possession of the good assets in the bank, the FDIC would have had to take all the loss, which it was not prepared to do, and it had on its side the fact that its charter did not permit it to deal in foreign exchange. This was more than a year in working its way out—and required the services of 778 FDIC employees—before the Fed and the FDIC made a deal with four foreign banks to take over what was left of Franklin, which was opened with greater dignity as the European-American Bank. The lesson from Franklin was that in the modern world the big losers from a bank failure were likely to be the borrowers. One way or another, the creditors get taken care of, but the builder who has arranged a loan from the failed bank finds that no other bank will pick it up, and he is left with a hole in the ground or a steel framework and no source of funds to continue the work. Because the stench of death is everywhere, the good loans get punished with the bad loans.

The irrelevance of deposit insurance per se in modern American banking was pointed out dramatically in the 1980s with the disasters at Continental Illinois and then throughout the state of Texas. Continental Illinois coming into 1984 was the seventh largest bank in the United States, and the largest commercial lender in the country. It had 21,000 shareholders and offices in 29 foreign countries. Illinois was a "unit banking" state, where the law prohibited banks from branching (indeed, as Continental grew, it had to build a bridge across a downtown Chicago street to link the two buildings where it had offices, so that they could be treated as a single building under the law). Most of its funding therefore had to come through borrowings from other banks (it had more correspondent banking relations than any other bank in the country) and through sales of commercial paper by its holding company, which downstreamed the money to the bank. Ninety percent of its $30 billion in deposits were uninsured foreign deposits or jumbo domestic deposits well over the $100,000 insured maximum. The General Accounting Office says that after 1982, Continental routinely bought $8 billion of Fed Funds (other banks' excess reserves) overnight, every night.[4] Confident of its ability to borrow at rates cheaper than those at which it could safely lend, Continental had opened loan production offices and had become the biggest single customer of Penn Square Bank, a bunch of cowboys with a shopping center office in Oklahoma City, who made oil and gas drilling loans to other cowboys, funded themselves to a large degree in the interbank market by paying more interest on deposits (29 commercial banks, 44 S&Ls, and 221 credit unions had some money on deposit at Penn Square when this shopping-center bank went under in 1982), and then sold the loans (with a neat markup for themselves) to banks in the big cities. Chase, Michigan National, Seattle First were also purchasers, with Continental alone holding a billion dollars face value of loans originated by Penn Square.

Publication of this story in 1982–and it was a great story, complete with officers of Penn Square drinking champagne from cowboy boots and wearing Mickey Mouse ears to conferences–put such pressure on Seattle First that it had to be acquired by Bank of America. And it knocked Continental off its perch as a preferred borrower from American institutions. By 1984, $17 billion of Continental's funding, almost five times the total of insured deposits in the bank, came from foreign sources. And there was more than a billion dollars of junk bonds issued in the Caribbean by the holding company. Every penny except the deposits had to be bought at prices higher than the bank could earn on good loans, so the books were filling up with bad loans: bad borrowers are always willing to pay more.

In his book *Bailout*, Irvine Sprague, who served two terms as a board member on the FDIC, suggests that the "wire run" on Continental began in May 1984 after some American investment bank fishing for business suggested to some Japanese banks that Continental might be available cheap. A man from the Comptroller's Office who was in a position to know told me once that the run began because several bank examiners questioned the safety of deposits at Continental by small correspondent banks they were examining. Once the rumors were on the street, the Chicago Board of Trade Clearing Corporation withdrew its $50 million account from Continental, an action that could not be kept quiet. The bank lost $6 billion in funding in ten days. "Inside the bank," Sprague reports, "all was calm, the teller lines moved as always, and bank officials recall no visible sign of trouble–except in the wire room. Here the employees knew what was happening as withdrawal order after order moved on the wire, bleeding Continental to death. Some cried."[5]

The Federal Reserve Bank of Chicago lent Continental $3.6 billion, and then the board went for a lifeboat, Bank of England style, pressing sixteen banks into service with a $4.5 billion 30-day line of credit, announced on Friday and pretty much all gone by Tuesday morning. On Wednesday, Fed chairman Paul Volcker, FDIC chairman William Isaac, Comptroller Todd Conover, the CEOs of six of the seven largest American banks, plus the vice chairman of the other one met at J. P. Morgan to decide what to do. There was nobody there from Continental: Continental was gone. So the Fed couldn't put up any more money; the Fed was not allowed to lend to insolvent banks. The commercial banks basically wanted to be paid back for what they had already advanced. Only the FDIC could keep Continental meeting the demands made upon it for cash. The FDIC committed $2 billion—and, more important, guaranteed that "all depositors and other general creditors of the bank will be fully protected and service to the bank's customers will not be interrupted." On the heroic assumption that Continental would some day "resume normal patterns of funding in the market," the Fed agreed "to meet any extraordinary liquidity requirements of the Continental Illinois Bank during this period." When the deal was reached (on Thursday), Alan Whitney, the FDIC's press director in Washington, was informed by Joe Coyne, the Fed's press director—a man who for a whole generation represented the Fed to the outside world, and could behave to those who disagreed with what he perceived to be the Fed's positions the way the People's Liberation Army behaved in Tiananmen Square—that Coyne was going to issue the press release. Bill Isaac, a tough lawyer from Kentucky, spoke with Whitney: "Tell Joe Coyne," he said, "that if the Fed wants to put up the $2 billion, they can announce it any way they want."[6]

But in the end, the Fed might have to become the source of the money, because the Fed can create money and the FDIC cannot. As an insurance company, the FDIC charges banks a premium for the insurance the banks offer their depositors. When the pledge was made to Continental, the "reserve fund"—i.e., the credit for the FDIC on the books of the U.S. Treasury; there is no FDIC reserve fund any more than there is a Social Security trust fund—was about $15 billion, and on top of that the FDIC had the right to borrow $5 billion from the Treasury. But a sequence of bank failures could conceivably eat up all of that—and might easily eat up enough of it to weaken the FDIC guarantee. Indeed, Continental itself could strain the FDIC's resources. In addition to its subordinated note, FDIC bought $5.1 billion face value of Continental's questionable assets (for $3.5 billion). There was lots more where that came from, if the FDIC was to guarantee the repayment of all the debt a bank holding company had acquired. The Garn–St. Germain Act of 1982 had given the FDIC carte blanche to rescue banks–even if the cost of rescue would be much greater than the cost of liquidating the bank–if there had been a finding of "essentiality," of great damage to a community should the bank close its doors. Continental had something like two thousand correspondent banks all over the Midwest, most of which were still operating under "unit banking" laws, which required strong correspondent relationships. It could be and was argued that some enormous number of these banks would go under if the FDIC simply paid off the insured depositors, which was the extent of its legal obligations, and walked away. The FDIC board voted a grant of "essentiality" to Continental Illinois.

Even under those circumstances, paying off the debt of the holding company that owned the bank was of doubtful legality–and paying off paper that had been sold to foreigners in the Caribbean, where no purchaser had the slightest reason to believe that the debt was guaranteed by an agency of the U.S. government, was off the wall. Secretary of the Treasury Donald Regan, who had run a large financial services enterprise (Merrill Lynch) without government guaranties, thought what the FDIC wanted to do was scandalous. So did I: I wrote an article for *Financier* saying that the guarantee to the paper issued in Aruba was demonstrably *ultra vires*.[7] But $17 billion of the funds in the bank was money owed to foreigners, who quite specifically threatened to withdraw their money if they were stiffed on the junk bonds. In his book, Sprague noted that Continental in 1983 paid only $6.5 million for insurance on what turned out to be all the $69 billion of its total on and off balance sheet liabilities, and that five of the nation's ten largest banks had more foreign deposits (on which insurance did not have to be paid, because in theory they were not covered) than they had domestic deposits. As a result, Bank of America, the nation's second largest bank, with two-thirds of its deposits domestic, paid $40 million for insurance, while the largest, Citibank, with only three-eighths of its deposits domestic, paid only $18.5 million. Sprague thought the law should be changed. The law was changed, but the truth is that the big international banks continue to get free coverage on the non-deposit liabilities of their holding companies.

Still, Sprague was serene about what the FDIC had done: "We believed the very fabric of our banking system was at stake."[8] The opinion is not unanimous: with the advantage of hindsight on the S&L disaster and later analysis showing that only a few dozen small correspondent banks would have been seriously harmed, and less than ten would have been made insolvent, by a Continental failure—and with the belief that the banking crisis of 1990–91 had been made worse because the government had rescued the investors in Continental from their folly—Bill Isaac a dozen years later said flatly that he thought Continental should have been closed.

The deal was done a few days before a meeting of the Federal Open Market Committee, and I had breakfast in Washington the morning before the meeting with one of its participants, Bill Ford, a saturnine westerner who had been chief economist for Wells Fargo when I first knew him and had moved on to be president of the Federal Reserve Bank of Atlanta. He too had no high opinion of the Continental deal, which unquestionably had been driven by Fed chairman Paul Volcker, a child of the depression who was genuinely scared about bank failures (he had wanted to save the egregious and minor-league Penn Square, but he couldn't find anybody who would touch the contingent liabilities). I said that much as I disapproved of the Continental deal, I could see how if I sat in Volcker's chair, I would think, "Well, maybe—but not in my time." Ford shook his head. "Wrong word," he said. "It's 'not in my *term*.'" The quote at the head of the previous chapter argues that Ford, as usual, got it right.

But how could the FDIC, with its limited resources in the form of a reserve fund and capped borrowing authority, absorb the Continental contingent liabilities? Answer, not offered to the world: by borrowing from the Fed. Continental at the end had a debt of $1.5 billion to the Federal Reserve Bank of Chicago (the Federal Reserve *Board* has no money to lend). Silas Keehn, president of the Federal Reserve Bank of Chicago, noted that his money was not to be repaid to him as part of the overall deal, and notified Washington that he was going to call the loan. Volcker was appalled, and persuaded Keehn to maintain the credit. When L. William Seidman became chairman of the FDIC in 1985, he was committed to building the agency's public stature and to repairing what he perceived as the damage Isaac's backwoods rudeness had done to relations between the deposit insurers and the banks. ("Banks," Seidman said in a dozen speeches in his first months, "are our clients, customers and constituents"; one of Isaac's held-over staffers said he conspired with others to remove the "c" key from Seidman's secretary's keyboard.) FDIC now owned a controlling share of Continental; the agency arranged to pay back to the Chicago Fed the $1.4 billion still owed by the bank–and substituted a loan of $2.5 billion from the Federal Reserve Bank of Chicago to the FDIC itself.

The same device, this time with the Federal Reserve Bank of Dallas on the other side, was used when the Texas banks fell out of the trees two years later, and Seidman told everybody to whom these banks owed money that the FDIC would take care of them. The House Banking Committee held hearings, and Representative Stan Parris of North Carolina asked the cutting question: "Should a printing company that makes the checks for a bank in Amarillo be insured by the insurance fund of the FDIC?"

Seidman answered, "The reason that we protect 100 percent of deposits and creditors is to stop runs on those banks so that they won't become insolvent and deny either the community or any other party services. So we take this action reluctantly, but it is the only way we have found to stop the kind of situation we had at First Republic [a Texas bank holding company]. At First Republic, the money that was going out of the banks was not only deposits, but also other creditors, overnight creditors and so forth. . . . We have become, although we certainly were not designed to be, the ultimate stability for very large institutions which, in the opinion of the people who are responsible for a safe and sound financial system, [they] feel are too large to close down."

Representative Parris, after a brief additional colloquy, put his finger once more on the sore spot: "The Federal Reserve System has become the next-to-the-last point of last resort. You're it."

And Seidman said, "That's correct. The Federal Reserve is a liquidity lender. They were never contemplated to lend to any institution that was insolvent." One notes that in the previous response the effort was to stop a run that was threatening to make a bank insolvent, and now the FDIC is there because the bank already is insolvent.

Representative John LaFalce of New York tried to put a number on it: "If I add up Continental Illinois and First Republic, in about a year or so, that comes to between $5 billion to $6 billion, closer to $6 billion. . . . How much will the FDIC owe the Fed in toto in 1989 as of this time?"

Seidman said, "If the Fed continues to require us to pay in 1 year, which I don't believe they will–"

> LaFalce interrupted: "Well, assuming they do."
>
> Seidman: "Assuming they do, we'd owe them roughly $2 point some billion for this transaction."
>
> LaFalce: "About 2.8."
>
> Seidman: "And about $1.8 billion or something for the other transaction. It might come to as much as $4 billion."
>
> LaFalce: "I thought it was $2.6."
>
> Seidman: "Well, it could be. It goes up and down."

Finally, House Banking Committee chairman Henry Gonzalez pulled the questioning back to the larger issue. "This idea of saying, don't you worry," he told Seidman. "Be happy, because we are guaranteeing deposits no matter what the amount–you don't have the authority to do that, the statutory authority to do that. We never gave it to you."[9] In 1990, the Conference of State Bank Supervisors replied to a request from the Treasury for comments on deposit insurance reform with a report that was all over the lot, but noted in passing that "The FDIC has shifted its focus from direct protection of depositors to protecting the economy from the shocks that would accompany a major bank failure. While this role protects the depositor indirectly . . . it would appear to be a duty that falls more appropriately to the Federal Reserve."[10]

But with Continental Illinois, this torch had publicly passed from the Federal Reserve to the FDIC. It made a difference that Seidman was colorful–totally bald, with pointed ears and a confident manner, a growly voice and a turn of phrase–and played the press every day the way Volcker played trout on vacation. "When Frank Wille had that job," said Fed governor Martha Seeger, a University of Michigan economics professor four or five inches taller than Seidman and just as aggressive, "nobody in this town knew who he was." Seidman was good company, and intelligent, an accountant with a Harvard law degree and experience running a big copper company (where he broke one of the longest strikes in American history) and the business school at the University of Arizona. Gerald Ford had brought him into government, as a key economic adviser; it was he who designed the "Whip Inflation Now" campaign launched at a White House do just as the economy started its slide into recession in 1974. Seidman and I sat together over drinks at a Garn Institute conference on Key Largo in 1989, and talked for more than two hours, because he honestly did not understand why I was criticizing him and he was sure he could charm me out of it. At the end, he said, "Your problem is that you think there are substantive issues here. There aren't. It's all turf. Everybody would do the same thing; it's just a question of who is going to do it. And I want to do it." In fairness, it also made a difference that the rash of bank failures in the 1980s had given the FDIC a much more prominent role than it had played at any time in the fifty previous years.

The people who worked for Seidman in the upper cadres of the FDIC liked him, which is a lot to say for any man. But his approach to the relations of government and banking was incoherent, mostly because his political beliefs did not encompass the possibility of what he saw in his office every day. Under his direction, his staff put forth a theoretical document assuming that deposit insurance was a "merit good"–something that benefited the community as a whole and did not cost anything. This is not true. The costs of deposit insurance are very high, because in a fully insured banking system bankers have good reason to reach for the highest-yielding assets and give lending officers quotas that must be filled regardless of the quality of the borrowers. Kenneth Arrow of MIT had introduced the term "moral hazard" to economic literature in 1971, borrowing it from the insurance industry, where it has a straightforward definition: if you insure a house for more than its market value, you increase the odds that somebody will burn it down.[11] "Banking failures in the 1980s," Andrew Sheng writes in his study for the World Bank, "were largely market failures, caused in large part by moral hazard induced through implicit or explicit deposit insurance."[12]

The S&L crisis, simplified, was a case history of moral hazard: by giving the operators of S&Ls a contract to sell their assets to the government for as much money as would be necessary to pay off the depositors (including in the payoffs whatever interest the management of the S&L had promised to get the deposits), the government had removed all incentive for an S&L operator to behave prudently. You took the depositor's money to the racetrack and bet it on number six. If number six came in, you kept the winnings; if number six dawdled up the track, the government paid the losses.

Another structural element had pushed the FDIC front-and-center. The Federal Reserve System as originally operated and organized relied mostly on the discount window for monetary control. Bernard Shull, professor of economics at Hunter College, points out that through the 1920s the proportion of member banks borrowing at the window was consistently around 60 percent. The Fed thus had day-to-day acquaintance with the asset portfolios of the banks, because some fraction of those portfolios was presented daily as collateral for borrowings from the district banks. By the 1970s, the Fed had shifted entirely to buying or selling Treasury paper in the open market as the means of monetary control.[13]

There is certainly a strong case for preferring open market operations to discount window operations, even in time of crisis. James Hoehn of the Cleveland Fed liked to tell a tale of riots in the streets of London because there was no money. The Lord Chancellor had a choice. He could climb up to the top of the Tower and scatter gold to the populace to still their protest, which was open market operations, or he could go to the back door and give the gold to his friends, which was the discount window. There is a democratic quality and a capitalist efficiency associated with a policy that allows emergency funding to be allocated by the market rather than by vice presidents of a quasi-governmental agency. But in a situation where a bank is seen to be struggling, the market will not sell it money however much gold the Lord Chancellor throws onto the street.

The loss of daily contact with the loan portfolio diminished the Fed's ability to predict trouble, especially when prosperity eroded prudence. Banks did not come to the discount window for funds until they had entirely lost their access to funds from the private market, by which time the problem was almost certain to be insolvency rather than illiquidity; other banks will lend in the interbank market to any bank that is even remotely plausible if it will only pay an extra eighth of a point. The FDIC does not concern itself with the question of whether the failed bank is insolvent or just illiquid, because deposit insurance makes no distinction between illiquid and insolvent banks. In real life, deposit insurance makes illiquidity all but impossible as a cause of failure, because the failed bank can bid any interest rate to lure deposits from the markets, and the depositors know the FDIC will pay the interest "earnings" if the bank collapses. Indeed, when the government began to close down the S&Ls pursuant to the FIRREA Act of 1989, brokerage houses like Merrill Lynch which had put their customers into these high-rate deposits for a commission to themselves raised holy hell that the CDs were being paid off before their term, reducing the length of time the owners would receive the high risk-free returns their broker had promised them.

In the modern world, it is the deposit insurer who serves as the lender–and guarantor–of last resort. In most countries the central bank *is* the deposit insurer, *faute de mieux,* but even if there is a specific insurance agency the central bank must stand behind the depositor insurer as the source of his money. "I guess they could foreclose on us if they want," Seidman told the congressmen in his most jovial manner.[14] Walker Todd, while associate general counsel of the Cleveland Fed, raised the question everybody else ducked: why should Texas have a claim on the Federal Reserve System for billions of dollars, to be met outside the usual political process, because its problem was bank failures rather than water supplies or AIDS or services to immigrants?

The Fed's greatest triumph was the rescue of the markets in October 1987, and the slow draining of liquidity thereafter that contained what could otherwise have been significant inflationary pressures. In terms of the numbers, the panic of October 19 was the greatest one-day disaster a market has ever suffered. The Dow Jones index was down almost 23 percent; the price of an S&P futures contract on the Chicago Mercantile Exchange was down more than 29 percent. The systems did not hold up under the pressure. At the New York Stock Exchange, the "tape" that reports sales was two hours behind by the end of the day–that is, the sales being reported at four o'clock were those that had been made at two o'clock. Thus there was a complete disconnect between the bids and offers that customers might receive if they called their brokers for quotes (and got through) and the sales being reported as current. And activity itself was similarly delayed. The "Designated Order Turnaround" (DOT) system at the stock exchange that automatically delivered orders to buy or sell up to 3,099 shares, used by individuals and by program traders matching their orders to traded stock index futures, was swamped with orders for 396 million shares (more than any previous day's total trading, including the dominant very large institutional trades); the mechanical printers that delivered the orders to the market makers' posts on the floor of the exchange fell many minutes behind. The only current price information was the price of the futures contract for the S&P

index of 500 stocks, which in theory was linked by arbitrage activities to the performance of the shares themselves, but in fact became quite independent. The index itself could not be priced for comparison with the futures contracts, because the prices of so many of the stocks were uncertain.

In Chicago, the Mercantile Exchange where the stock futures are traded had to send out an intraday call for more than a billion dollars of additional ("variation") margin from holders of contracts that paid off if the market rose and lost money if it fell. This money was due Monday afternoon from the losers, but would not be paid out to the winners until Tuesday. At the end of the trading day, calls for another $1.3 billion went out, and by the Merc's rules the banks that handled payments for the brokers (futures commission merchants or FCMs, to use the correct term) would have to certify by seven o'clock the next morning that the money was en route. When Tuesday came, the shell-shocked Merc staff neglected to credit the margin payers of the day before for the payments they had already made, and excessive calls were sent—and not all the payments to the winners were credited at the opening. "This occurred," the Commodity Futures Trading Commission observed laconically the following January, "because the CME permitted the posting of letters of credit in lieu of cash to meet the exceptionally large intra-day margin calls on October 19 and its settlement systems had not been programmed to handle non-cash payments."[15] FedWire, the money transfer system from one city to another, suffered a still inexplicable two-hour outage in Chicago—especially damaging because in Chicago (and Chicago alone) the local FCMs used FedWire as their means of paying the commodity exchange clearinghouses. Two very large New York brokers—Kidder Peabody and PaineWebber—did not receive $678 million and $916 million, respectively, until after 3:00 P.M. for one and 5:00 P.M. for the other. Rumors flew around Wall Street that the Chicago clearinghouses were insolvent. In this atmosphere, the FCMs and the brokers on the options exchange needed among them credit extensions of $3 billion from the Chicago banks.

They got it. There were not many heroes on October 19 and 20, but Harris Trust, which had recently been acquired by Bank of Montreal, will qualify. It had long been the "settlement" bank for the Merc, the bank to which the banks of the losers were to send their payments and from which the banks of the winners would collect on Merc contracts. On October 20, some of the so-called settlement banks that were supposed to feed Harris Trust were, to say the least, sluggish. A system that was based on payments being irrevocably pledged by the traders' banks by seven in the morning required that morning a large quantity of loans from Harris Trust. Bruce Osborne, a fortysomething banker in white shirtsleeves who handled the Merc and options exchange accounts at Harris, called Montreal and was told that he could increase credit lines to FCMs to the maximum permitted by law, and he did. These were the best customers in the bank, and the bank had an obligation to save them; anyway, if the Merc went under, the banking system didn't have much future either. "There was gridlock," Osborne said a few weeks later, "but we oiled the system."[16] The other Chicago banks responded to the urgings of Silas Keehn, president of the Federal Reserve Bank of Chicago—but Harris was there before the Fed woke up. Putting together the scarce numbers from that week, it would appear that Harris more than doubled its lending to help the Merc clearing corporation get the markets open. It is a story that the good man will tell his son; at least for this generation, Harris will remain the lead bank of the Merc.

In New York, the banks were a much worse problem. The "specialists" at the trading posts at the New York Stock Exchange were charged with buying the shares of the companies assigned to them when people wanted to sell them and selling the shares when people wanted to buy, to maintain an "orderly market." They were charged also with filling customer orders that had come in on the DOT system within three minutes of the time stamp on the order, which meant in the chaos of that week that they had become committed to fill it before it was delivered to the post, at a price usually above the price when they actually saw the order. They were much too lightly capitalized to absorb these waterfalls of sell orders, even if they felt obliged, as some did, to step in the way of ruin.

On October 19, the specialist community on the New York Stock Exchange had net purchases of $486 million, as against their total funds that morning of $2.3 billion. At the opening of the next day, after those purchases, the total funds in the specialist community were only $852 million.[17] These people traded on margin, which had to be replenished. They had lost almost 60 percent of their capital–and they were supposed to keep making orderly markets. The market opened October 20 much higher–too much higher, for many of the specialists were reaching, selling off the inventory they had acquired the day before at the best price they could hope to get. When that first burst of buying was exhausted and the markets turned down again, the specialists needed credit from their banks to keep functioning–and they didn't get it.

The American branches of Japanese banks had been moving into the "call money" overnight market, content with its very low margins; now they fled. The Europeans, whose markets were also in a state of collapse, were in stasis, which was better than the Japanese but not much. The Federal Reserve had started pumping out money by purchasing Treasury bills overnight. Alan Greenspan, who had been chairman of the Fed for less than ten weeks, issued a statement at 8:41 A.M. on Tuesday: "The Federal Reserve, consistent with its responsibilities as the nation's central bank, affirmed today its readiness to serve as a source of liquidity to support the economic and financial system." For the Chicago banks, which were dealing, after all, with participants in zero-sum markets, where every loser's loss was matched by a winner's gain, that assurance was ultimately enough. In New York, the banks were dealing with a meltdown in shareholder value in the many hundreds of billions of dollars. As the Fed beefed up their reserves by purchasing Treasury bills in the open market, the banks gratefully clutched the money to their bosoms, and told the specialists and the over-the-counter dealers to look elsewhere. They were not in such great shape themselves. They had got involved with providing financing for takeover schemes that were now rubble; they were beginning to face the fact that many of their loans to less developed countries would involve losses, and in the case of the investment banks, they were the underwriters of the privatization of British Telecom, one of the largest public offerings in history, where they were committed to pay the British government about 30 percent more than they could now hope to get from their customers when they sold it.

The bank that had a role closest to that of Harris in Chicago was Bankers Trust, which also had a division that ran a portfolio insurance scheme for pension funds. Under this nutty plan, the funds theoretically (it was an academic's plan) could lock in their past gains in the stocks they owned by selling futures contracts and buying put options and entering stop-loss sales orders on the exchanges. ("Dumbest idea ever accepted by any substantial part of mankind," said Howard Stein of Dreyfus Fund. "How could anybody believe everybody could sell at the same time?") In that division of Bankers Trust, the little techies were sending out their sell orders to all the markets. In the banking division of Bankers Trust, which served more specialists than any other two banks on Wall Street put together, the lending officers were going tch-tch about the decaying capital position of the specialists, who were sent to look elsewhere for money. Upon information and belief, as they say in the courts, E. Gerald Corrigan, large and muscular, walked over the three blocks from the Fed to Bankers Trust and entered the office of Charles Sanford, chairman and CEO, a smooth, slight southern gentleman, and remained with him until Sanford issued orders that all that cash the Fed had flowed into his bank should flow out to support the operations of the market makers in New York and the FCMs waiting to collect on their gains in Chicago. Corrigan was also in touch with others, vigorously.

Single-handedly, and perhaps without full consciousness of what he was doing (for while he is very intelligent, he was also very busy), Jerry Corrigan changed the definition and the function in the economy of the lender of last resort.

In the United States, the deposit insurer is now the lender of last resort to the banks, and the central bank is the lender of last resort to the markets. Or, rather, the Fed uses its power over the banks to force them to lend to the market. A colloquy between Senator Paul Sarbanes of Maryland and Alan Greenspan, following Greenspan's testimony that the Fed had to keep supervision of the banks among its powers so it could handle crises, tells a fascinating story:

> SARBANES: "I guess the question I'm asking is not whether you tried to introduce an element of rationality into the system, and as you just put it, tried to make [the banks] see that it was in their rational self-interest to behave in a certain direction but whether in addition, the dimension that you are their regulator enables you to apply a pressure upon them over and above the rational persuasion.
>
> "So they, in effect, okay, well, you know, we're not persuaded rationally. We don't really agree but these people are our regulators and they can cause us a lot of grief if we don't go along on this thing, and so we better go along on this."
>
> GREENSPAN: "We stay on this side of threatening. We think threatening them, which we do not do, is inappropriate."
>
> SARBANES: "A wink from you, Mr. Chairman, for many constitutes a threat, does it not? I mean, you don't have to threaten. You just have to say a few well-chosen comments?"
>
> GREENSPAN: "I hope it's only a few."
>
> SARBANES: "And I hope they're well-chosen, too."
>
> GREENSPAN: "I've said about as much on this as I intend to."[18]

Politically and economically, this is an enormously important phenomenon. Both the fixed-income markets and the stock markets have come to rely to an unprecedented degree on a safety net from the Federal Reserve. The head of one of the largest hedge funds in the world said to me shortly after the rescue of Long Term Capital

Management that the episode had carried a clear message for him: "If I get in big trouble, the Fed will come and save me." I told him that if Alan Greenspan could hear him he would turn white as a sheet and resign. But he was sure he was right.

PART FOUR

Making Money

Chapter 7

The Age of Invention

The primary function of monetary policy, with due allowance for the liquidity of the economy, is to regulate the total supply of money and to influence its cost and availability so as to help keep marginal demands–government and private–from spending themselves in speculation and increased prices in time of prosperity, and from being stifled in times of recession.

–Allan Sproul (1963)[1]

WRIGHT PATMAN, the shrewd, charming, lazy populist from Texarkana, was chairman of the House Banking Committee from the 1950s into the 1970s. He was no friend of the Federal Reserve, which he felt had extended the Great Depression by reducing bank credit in 1937 (choking off what is still in percentage terms the biggest six-month gain the Dow Jones has ever seen), and his dislike was reinforced by his belief that the board's reason for increasing banks' required reserves was that Congress had just passed a veterans' bonus that had been the centerpiece of Patman's run for office. In the 1970s, when I knew him, he liked to say that the Constitution gave the House of Representatives the power "to coin money and regulate the value thereof"–and that the Congress had "farmed out its power to the Federal Open Market Committee."

One notes the exactitude of Patman's placement. Not the executive branch, for there is no law requiring or even suggesting that the Fed report to the president or the secretary of the treasury, and the most either of them can do if they don't like the policies is bitch about the Fed's failure to be a team player–as Harry Truman and Lyndon Johnson and Richard Nixon did. (Nixon, typically, did it through an unprecedented campaign of personal vilification of Chairman Arthur Burns, anonymously out of the White House.) Not the Federal Reserve Board, whose seven governors are appointed by the president and must be confirmed by the Senate, retaining–although they hold fourteen-year terms and cannot be reappointed or removed except for gross misbehavior–some degree of political input. The hands on the wheel are those of the members of the Open Market Committee, who decide when and how to buy or sell paper for the Fed's portfolio, increasing (when they buy) or decreasing (when they sell) the reserves of the banking system and thus the money supply of the country–reducing (when they buy) or raising (when they sell) the interest rates the banks will pay for funds and charge for loans.

A unanimous board can control the FOMC, for seven of its twelve members are governors. (This was not true in 2000–2001, because two seats on the board were vacant.) Only five of the twelve reserve bank presidents are voting members of the committee: New York every year, Chicago and San Francisco every other year, and each of the other nine banks every third year. But all twelve of the presidents join the seven board members (when we have seven board members) for FOMC meetings around the splendid mahogany table in the conference room behind the eagle on the Constitution Avenue side of the headquarters building. The seven presidents who don't vote do have a voice. One former participant in these meetings, which fill two days every six weeks or so (there are eight meetings a year), notes that if each participant entitled to a say speaks for five minutes, more than an hour and a half is required for opening statements.[2] (But Gerald Corrigan, who sat in on those meetings for fifteen years, says that "One of the most valuable aspects of FOMC meetings was the go-round session, at which banks provided input. Often that was the only really new information you got.") Populists in Congress worry about a committee that makes the key decisions on the nation's money supply and interest rates with almost half its members chosen by local boards of directors of whom two-thirds are bankers or bankers' representatives.

The history of open market operations is the history of the Federal Reserve System, and the perfection of open market strategies and tactics is under the eye of eternity the Fed's great contribution to the theory and practice of capitalism. This perfection was not easily accomplished, and it was not in anybody's mind (let alone in the law) when the curtain went up. Section 14 of the act, authorizing the district banks to "purchase and sell in the open market . . . cable transfers and bankers' acceptances and bills of exchange," was added to the bill quite late in the legislative game by H. Parker Willis, chief of staff to Congressman Carter Glass, then chairman of the House Banking Committee.

The Federal Reserve Board in Washington had and has no resources of its own; only the district banks have money. Thus open market operations, and monetary policy generally, can be carried out only through the district banks. In the early years, these banks were, as the law intended, quite independent. There was no central coordination of open market operations; each of the banks bought and sold paper according to its own needs. The purpose of buying paper in the market was the acquisition of earning assets for the banks, which had to pay their bills and their annual dividends to their member/shareholders. Another purpose was to build a separate money market in each district, to some degree independent of the national money market. As late as 1922, after it was widely recognized that Federal Reserve Bank purchases and sales influenced interest rates and securities prices, Governor F. H. Curtiss, chairman of the Federal Reserve Bank of Boston, thought that different cities in the United States could and should have different monetary policies, and told a meeting of his fellows that "Local credit policies should be dictated . . . by the Board of Directors of each Federal Reserve Bank."[3]

The intent of the authors of the Federal Reserve Act had been that the district banks should earn their keep mostly by rediscounting the short-term trade-related loans written by the member banks (i.e., purchasing at a lower "discount" price, reflecting a higher interest rate, loans their members were willing to sell for cash they could lend elsewhere). These purchases by the district bank were accomplished by giving the bank that presented the paper a credit in the reserve account it was compelled by law to keep at the Fed. In the early years, these reserve accounts, one of the few nationally imposed rules, were set by law: 18 percent of their deposits for member banks in "money centers" (New York, Chicago, and St. Louis); 15 percent for banks in another 47 "reserve cities" where larger banks served as conduits for the almost 28,000 smaller banks to connect with the credit market; and 12 percent for those smaller banks to the extent they were members of the Fed (which most were not).

Banks make loans by creating demand deposits in the name of the borrower. Thus a bank in a money center city would need 18 cents in reserves—deposits at its local Fed plus cash in the vault, and checks in process of collection from other banks—for every dollar newly loaned. But in fact the process was trickier than that, because a bank had to expect that a borrower would spend the money, which meant that the bank had to be prepared to transfer funds to the banks receiving the borrower's checks. Meanwhile, other banks' borrowers would be writing checks that transferred funds back to this bank. Clearinghouses in the cities allowed banks to pay and receive funds on a net basis with all the other banks that belonged to the clearinghouse, paying off a single debit to or collecting a single credit from the clearinghouse itself. Meanwhile, "correspondent banks" in the reserve cities squared off the books of the smaller banks out in the towns. These smaller banks kept money at their correspondents for this purpose in the form of interbank deposits. The existence of this source of funds for the banks in the big cities was the reason the legislation establishing the Federal Reserve System imposed higher reserve requirements on the big-city banks. When the Federal Reserve bought paper from or sold paper to a bank, it might or might not impact significantly on that individual bank's reserve position; but it always increased or decreased the reserve position (and thus the lending capacity) of the banking system as a whole.

Reserve requirements historically had been a way for the authorities that licensed banks to assure that they were liquid and could pay off a number of depositors on demand. Cash in the vault was thus part of a bank's "reserves." In 1917, hoping to increase the transfer of gold from ordinary banks to the Fed district banks, Congress dropped vault cash as a recognized reserve, and its status was not restored until 1957. (Perhaps Congress can be excused: no less than Walter Bagehot argued that "we should not include in the 'reserve' of a bank 'legal tenders,' or cash, which the bank keeps to transact its daily business. That is as much a part of its daily stock-in-trade as its desks or offices . . . we must carefully distinguish between this cash in the till which is wanted every day, and the *safety*-fund, as we may call it, the special reserve held by the bank to meet extraordinary and infrequent demands."[4] Of course, one of the main reasons for a central bank is to maintain a single pool of liquidity from which banks can draw in a crisis.) In 1999, vault cash claimed as a reserve totaled more than five-sixths of the total reserves the Fed required of the banking system, reflecting the demand for cash by the "vaults" in the ATM machines. In a world where the banks had $350 billion of deposits against which reserves had to be kept—and almost ten times that much of liabilities that were not subject to reserve requirements—the seminal element of reserves in the creation of money had become quite irrelevant. In spring 2000, the Fed came hat in hand to the House Banking Committee to ask for the power to pay interest on required reserves collected from the banks, in hopes that if it could earn a little money on the reserves, the banks would keep more cash there. The Treasury opposed the request on the grounds that it might cost the government a couple of hundred million in revenues.

The district banks were and are participants in the clearing-houses in their cities, and often ran them. Because the district banks are correspondents for all their members, the most convenient way for one bank to pay another bank is by transfer of money between their respective reserve accounts at their district bank. That was and is how the clearinghouses worked: after each day's clearing (usually in mid-morning), they send the district Fed a tally sheet listing how much is to be debited or credited to the reserve account of each member bank. Each member also gets a tally sheet, together with all the checks its depositors have written to make payments to deposi-tors of the other member banks of the clearinghouse (and their cor-respondents); and these checks, of course, now have to be deducted from *their* individual accounts.

When the Fed acted to reduce reserves, some member bank somewhere would feel the squeeze and would come to its district Fed to "discount" a borrower's note–to sell it or to endorse it over to the district bank as the security for a loan. At first each district bank maintained its own pattern of very different interest rates for differ-ent kinds of commercial paper. Some needed earning assets and set rates low to encourage their member banks to use the facility as a source of funds. Others set rates above market rates to maintain pressure on the banks to limit their lending. The only paper eligible for discount in the original legislation was what economists called "real bills": "notes, drafts, and bills of exchange arising out of actual commercial transactions . . . [with] a maturity at the time of discount of not more than ninety days."[5] When loan demand rose, then, the banking system could meet its reserve requirements by discounting existing paper at the local Feds, which gave the district banks the earning assets they needed. Thus in an ideal world the activities of the individual district banks would serve the needs of trade in their districts, and the country would have the "elastic currency" com-manded by the preamble to the Federal Reserve Act.

The real bills idea of money responded to a body of economic theory reaching back to the eighteenth century. And by limiting the paper "eligible" for discount and specifically excluding stocks and bonds, real bills theory expressed the strong and continuing fear of politicians and commentators that left to their own devices, the banks would misdirect the credit resources of the nation to speculation in real estate and on the stock exchange. (Until the 1920s, nationally chartered banks were not permitted to lend on the security of real property, though state-chartered banks or their trust companies usually were.) The political force behind the Federal Reserve Act had been the recession of 1907, triggered by a frenzy of stock buying on margin, which drove up interest rates in the New York market to the point where banks all over the country began sending their money to New York rather than lending locally. And then New York couldn't pay it back.

Significant modern figures have supported the real bills doctrine: Fischer Black, co-author of the Black-Scholes model that made option pricing a science and created the modern world of derivative instruments, wrote in 1976 that "I believe that in a country like the U.S., with a smoothly working financial system, the government does not, cannot, and should not control the money stock in any significant way. The government does, can only, and should simply respond passively to shifts in the private sector's demand for money. Monetary policy is passive, can only be passive, and should be passive."[6]

Belief in and utilization of the discount windows peaked in the years immediately after World War I. Required reserves were under $3 billion, and borrowings by the banks from the discount window ran steadily over $2 billion every night through most of 1919 and again in 1921. (The period in between the two, when the Federal Reserve System was running down its loans to the banks, marked a very severe but short recession in the American economy. In the eyes of the real bills theorists, the system worked: the provision of funds to business had matched the demands of business on the way down and again on the way up.) The rate at which the local Fed lent to its members became the key variable in the bank's reaction to credit conditions in its district: if the bank wished the banking system to make more loans, it would establish a discount rate below the interest rate in the local market, encouraging its member banks to expand their lending by discounting paper at their Fed; if it wished to restrain its members, it would set a discount rate higher than the rate in the market. The system's principle was to supply all the loans for which the banks had good collateral, if they were willing to pay the rate; not surprisingly, both 1919 and 1921 saw major inflationary pressure.

A district bank did not have to wait for one of its members to come along with a note to discount. It could also buy earning assets in the market. Commercial paper was always for sale somewhere, and these, too, were real bills. Informed that money seemed tight to-day, a district bank could and sometimes did go out and buy paper before anyone came to the discount window. The most creditworthy assets banks had were bankers' acceptances–four-name paper that financed manufacturing, where the producer's bank that had signed the instrument could be held liable to pay if something bad happened to the customer's bank. This paper, especially useful for foreign trade (indeed, it was developed in the Italian Renaissance), had been much more common among the city-states of Europe than in the United States, and the leaders of the district banks were anxious in the Fed's first dozen years to promote its use. They bought it in the market at prices higher than those they were prepared to pay for other kinds of commercial paper, and they gave a better rate when discounting it. As late as 1928, most of the assets in the investment portfolios of the district banks were bankers' acceptances.

The real bills doctrine had as a corollary the proposition that there could be no such thing as a monetary policy for the purpose of stimulating or restricting the economy. Banks' needs for funds from the discount window were a function of loan demand but also of gold movements. With the supply of credit insulated from the vagaries of the markets for financial instruments and real estate, changes in interest rates would be caused by inflows and outflows of gold. A country losing gold would see a reduction in its money supply, which pushed interest rates higher, restricting the demand for new money from the banks and pushing down domestic prices. (Economics teachers liked to relate Samuel Johnson's comment on his trip to the Hebrides when he was informed that eggs were one penny per dozen; that did not, he said, tell him that chickens were plentiful, merely that pennies were scarce.) Inflows of gold would expand the money supply, reducing interest rates, increasing the demand for credit, and raising prices. The situation was self-equilibrating: higher interest rates brought the gold back (at the Bank of England in the nineteenth century, the saying was that 7 percent would draw gold from the moon), the inflow of gold raised the exchange value of the currency, which brought the interest rates back down and led to more purchases of foreign goods and fewer sales to foreigners, which in turn created a trade deficit that had to be met by a reversal of the gold flow. Lower interest rates tilted the gold flow out, which ran the cycle in the opposite direction.

In 1915, with the country awash in liquidity as the combatants in Europe deposited their gold in the United States, Ben Strong summoned a committee of representatives from district banks, not to assure a uniform monetary policy for the United States, which was still regarded as essentially undesirable, but to make sure that the twelve banks did not bid against each other in the New York market for the same limited supply of U.S. Treasury paper. Before World War I, the total national debt was less than a billion dollars, and most of that was locked away as required backing for national banknotes. Coordination through New York was also necessary to make sure all the banks in the system had access to a money market. But the coordinating committee simply filled the orders the district banks placed with it: any individual bank might or might not wish to participate in any given purchasing program being executed through New York.

Eventually, the banking industry and the Fed system would have to recognize that the changes wrought by World War I were forever. The national debt had gone from $1 billion to $25 billion. The Fed was the "fiscal agent" for the Treasury, responsible for maintaining the government's bank account, taking in the tax receipts, making the government's payments, managing the borrowing if the government needed money. During the course of the war, the Treasury had come to lean more and more on the Fed to ease its path, providing the reserves to give the banks the money to buy the paper and fund the war. Those reserves were provided through the purchase of the bonds by the district banks, which meant that some of the debt being piled up to finance the war was monetized from the beginning. At the end of the war, Liberty Bonds and Victory Bonds, and especially the very short-term Treasury "certificates of indebtedness," were held by banks, and by the Fed district banks, all over the country. Whatever the local economic conditions might be, these national bonds had to be worth pretty much the same everywhere: the government's credit had become the benchmark for all credit. And the combination of this nationwide investment instrument with a fractional reserve system had made it possible for the Fed to conduct a true monetary policy.

At the heart of that monetary policy, as students of money and banking learn to this very day, was the multiplier implied by a fractional reserve system. When the Fed bought an acceptance or a bond in the open market, the money paid to the seller was added to the reserves of the banking system. In 1917, as part of the drive to free up credit for the war, Congress reduced reserve requirements on the reserve city banks to 10 percent. With a 10 percent reserve requirement, assuming that any bank would lend out whatever new money came in, the first bank to receive these funds would create new deposits for 90 percent of the total. Its customers would write checks against that money, and when those checks arrived at the recipients' banks, they would lend 90 percent of *that* total, and so on through the chain of the banking system, which in sum would lend about nine times the amount of the Federal Reserve System's new purchases of bonds or bankers' acceptances. In other words, the addition to bank reserves was "high-powered money," a phrase usually though incorrectly attributed to Milton Friedman. Conversely, if the district banks *sold* government bonds or bankers' acceptances, they would drain reserves from the system, reducing the supply of high-powered money, and the banks would have to cut back their deposits–selling investments or calling loans–to a total nine times the amount of the drain.

But the banks did not have to do what theory said they would do. Any bank that owed money to its Fed at the discount window could take the new money put in the system by purchases in the open market and pay back the window instead of increasing its loans to the public. Similarly, when the Fed drained reserves from the system, the banks could seek to get them back by borrowing from the window. The total of borrowings from the discount window would tell the Fed system how much pressure its required reserves had placed on the banks' capacity to create the deposits that were most of the nation's money supply. The discount rate worked in large part because banks were less likely to borrow from the window and more likely to cut back on their assets when the Fed set a high rate. There were, then, two tools—the discount rate and open market operations—by which the Federal Reserve could influence the behavior of the banks, the ease or rigor of credit, and the nation's money supply.

It was one of the discoveries of the early 1920s that rediscounting and open market operations were symmetrical. Trying to restrain the boom in 1922, the Feds and the Treasury "sterilized" the incoming gold, keeping it in their own vaults to hold down the money supply, while selling off some of their stock of bankers' acceptances and bonds. These operations taken together decapitated the district banks' portfolios of earning assets, which shrank menacingly to the point where it was not clear that all of them could meet their dividend obligations. But whenever a district bank added to its bond portfolio, its members borrowed less at the discount window, so that its net income might not change. Real bills doctrine or no real bills doctrine, government bonds and bankers' acceptances were the same.

Under the leadership of Ben Strong, the district banks in 1923 pulled together a formal Open Market Investment Committee of five governors: New York, Boston, Philadelphia, Cleveland, and Chicago. The next year, the board in Washington published its *Tenth Annual Report*, defending the deflationary activities of the district banks in 1922–23. "The authors of the Tenth Annual Report," the British economist Roy Harrod wrote a generation later, state fairly and squarely that it is the duty of the Federal Reserve System, in accordance with the terms of the Act which established it, to maintain steady credit conditions in the country. While each Federal Reserve Bank may do what it can by way of qualitative supervision, to ensure that individual member banks do not use credit for speculation or other undesirable purposes, it is recognized that the main weapon of a central banking system for preventing speculative development must be by an overall policy in regard to the total quantity of central reserve credit vouchsafed to the economy. . . . In 1922–23, the Federal Reserve System applied a brake to the gathering boom, which might otherwise have led to a crisis like those of 1893 and 1907.[7]

Similarly, Greenspan's Fed in 1994 delivered a preemptive strike against an accelerating growth in economic activity and (especially) in the asset markets, raising short-term rates by almost 3 percentage points in one year. And after another six years of frenetic growth in the economy and escalation in the stock market (in part sustained by the interest-rate cuts of 1998), Greenspan's Fed returned to the attack in 2000.

There has been much louder controversy about the Fed's actions in 1927 and 1928, when American interest rates were kept low, facilitating the stock market bubble of 1928, at least in part to help the Europeans stay on their precariously regained gold standard. Russell Leffingwell of J. P. Morgan, a lawyer who had been an antagonist of Strong's when he was assistant secretary of the treasury in the early 1920s, told a colleague, "Monty [Norman of the Bank of England] and Ben sowed the wind. I expect we shall all have to reap the whirlwind."[8] But there is no controversy at all about the Fed's performance when the Great Depression struck. Ben Strong had died, leaving his successor George Harrison with a good sense of what had to be done but no standing to push the other banks (and the Federal Reserve Board in Washington) in the right direction. If anything, the fact that New York was advocating a policy made it unpopular. By early 1929, Montagu Norman or no

Montagu Norman, the New York Fed was ready to put its foot on the brake. In the first six months of 1929, the New York Fed asked eleven times for authority to raise interest rates to 6 percent, to damp speculation on the stock exchange, and was refused every time by the Federal Reserve Board in Washington, whose members saw the logic of trying to curb the use of bank credit for stock speculation, but thought the job could be done by direct regulation and jawboning. The bust came. The day after Black Thursday, Harrison on his own initiative went into the market and bought $125 million of Treasury bills, doubling the system's holding of government paper, but he wasn't thanked for it, and over the next three years, while the economy sank into the sea, with 25 percent unemployment and a one-third reduction in the gross national product, the Fed was essentially moribund.

Strong's Open Market Investments Committee, which ran out of New York, was replaced with an Open Market *Policy* Conference, which included all twelve heads of the district banks plus what were then the five members of the board—and was called to meetings from Washington, not New York. Harrison repeatedly asked for permission to buy more paper for the New York bank, and was repeatedly refused. One can see the reasoning: the banks already had excess reserves, there was no loan demand, and in 1920, not so very long ago, a similar violent shrinkage of money supply, employment, and economic activity had cured itself. And there was, of course, concern about the loss of gold if interest rates fell. Keynes had described the Bank of England's insistence on retaining the gold standard as a "policy to reduce the standard of life of as many people as are within their reach in the hope that some small portion of the reductions of standard will be at the expense of imports."[9] At the end of September 1931, Britain was forced off gold (announced that the pound would no longer be redeemed for a fixed quantity of gold on demand)—and the New York Fed promptly raised its discount rate from 1½ percent to 3½ percent to hang onto American gold, further crippling already disabled banks.

The result was Irving Fisher's "debt deflation," when money itself becomes a great destroyer of wealth and enterprise. The more valuable money becomes, the more onerous the obligation to repay loans taken at a time when money was worth less. When prices fell, what had been sound investments did not yield an income stream large enough to service the loans that had financed them. Goldsmith had written *Deserted Village* to denounce the enclosure movement of the eighteenth century and a society "where wealth accumulates and men decay." G. K. Chesterton wrote a parody: "And irony that glares like Judgement Day/Sees men accumulate and wealth decay."

Treasury Secretary Andrew Mellon and most economists argued that the problem was past inflation of values, which had supported iniquities ranging from speculation to bathtub gin to short skirts, and the country needed a bloodletting to restore business and personal standards. Herbert Hoover, whose presidency was destroyed, bitterly called Mellon and his followers "liquidationists." Former Harvard economist and Federal Reserve governor Larry Lindsey believes in Mellon's remedies to this day, though one wonders whether he counseled George W. Bush in the 2000 election campaign (he was the candidate's most important economic adviser) that if the market sours, he should let the chips fall. At the banks in the 1930s, what had seemed to be secure loans turned unsafe as the value of the collateral diminished. There were no long-term self-amortizing mortgages in the United States in 1933, and mortgage loans usually ran no more than five years, written in the expectation that a new mortgage would be taken as the old one expired. As earnings diminished, people could not service their existing mortgages, and when the old mortgage ran off, they could not borrow enough to pay back the principal. Millions of people lost their jobs; millions of people lost their homes. And the Fed stood by.

Hoover's chairman of the Fed was Eugene Meyer, Wall Streeter, a former partner in Lazard Frères, whose place in history comes from his decision shortly after departing the Fed to buy what was then a floundering *Washington Post*. In September 1930, as he joined the board, the Open Market Policy Conference voted decisively to target interest rates in the market as the Fed's correct objective. As there was no demand for loans, borrowers fearing that continued deflation would make repayments more and more burdensome, interest rates were low and declining. So long as the rates were low, Meyer and Mellon and their colleagues believed the Fed was stimulating the economy. Adolf Miller, who had been a member of the Fed's board almost from the beginning, objected to the conclusions: "Money is sleeping," he said to the conference, "and it is conceivable that a part of a constructive package is to wake it up and make it do something and that you may be misled into a false sense of the soundness of the general money situation because rates are low."[10]

The next year Ogden Mills, a former New York congressman, became secretary of the treasury, and began turning the screws on the Fed. Mills came to the April 1932 meeting and told the board members that "a great duty now rested on the Federal Reserve System. . . . For a great central banking system to stand by with a 70% gold reserve [against currency in circulation] without taking active steps . . . was almost inconceivable and almost unforgivable. The resources of the system should be put to work on a scale commensurate with the existing emergency." Bullied by Mills, the Open Market Conference authorized the purchase of $500 million, and then another $500 million, of Treasury paper, pumping in "high-powered money." But it wasn't high-powered. Jane D'Arista in her history *The Evolution of U.S. Finance* notes "a new problem. Despite the substantial additions to reserves, member banks were unwilling to either expand their loans or repay their borrowings to the system. The system's purchases created excess reserves held as cash balances by a majority of member banks who chose to protect their liquidity."[11] American banking and business was caught in what Keynes would later call a "liquidity trap."

Meanwhile, the public was pulling money out of what looked like and often were shaky banks. The reserve banks were losing the gold backing for the currency–and the banks were not generating the commercial loans that under the law the banks could use as a substitute for gold in partial backing of the currency. By August 1930, more than half the loans in the banking system were collateralized by securities, which made them ineligible at the discount window.[12] At one point in 1932, before the first Glass-Steagall Act authorized the is-

suance of currency against reserve bank holdings of Treasury securities, the Federal Reserve had to sell Treasury paper in the open market, raising interest rates and compelling the banks to rediscount at
the district banks what little commercial paper was still on their
books, which allowed the banks to resume the issuance of currency.

Marriner Eccles, a Utah banker and businessman, had seen it coming and understood the psychology. "The assumption of spontaneous
revival through new investment," he said in a speech to Utah teachers,

> has always rested on the belief that people and banks will not
> indefinitely hold money in idleness. This is a false idea, as this
> depression has proved. The question is not how bankers and
> those who have idle money and credit can bring about recov-
> ery, but why they should do so, so long as there is no incen-
> tive offered in any field for profitable investments. A bank
> cannot finance the building of more factories and more rental
> properties and more homes when half of our productive
> property is idle for the lack of consumption and a large per-
> centage of our business properties are vacant for the want of
> paying tenants. The government, however, can spend
> money. . . . The only escape from a depression must be by in-
> creased spending.[13]

Eccles was invited to Washington, where his banking partner had
been installed as the Republican director on the three-man board of
the new Federal Deposit Insurance Corporation, and met in his hotel
room with Roosevelt's brain trust: Rex Tugwell, Mordecai Ezekiel,
Harry Hopkins, Jerome Frank, Lauchlin Currie. He wrote later in his
memoirs: "I doubt whether any of the men in my room had ever
heard of John Maynard Keynes, the English economist who has frequently been referred to as the economic philosopher of the New
Deal. . . . The concepts I formulated, which have been called 'Keynesian,' were not abstracted from his books, which I had never read. My
conceptions were based on naked-eye observation and experience, in
the intermountain region."[14]

Roosevelt had run for the presidency on a platform that called for balancing the budget. Eugene Meyer, who also believed in balancing the budget, had resigned as chairman of the Fed two months after Roosevelt took office because he didn't believe Roosevelt meant it. Lewis Douglas at the Bureau of the Budget and Treasury Secretary Will Woodin were trying to keep policy in line with that promise at a time when government revenues were declining and deficits were growing. The Federal Reserve Board, after drifting through the four lame-duck months of the Hoover administration, had recommended the bank holiday with which Roosevelt started his term, but like the large metropolitan banks that were the system's clients, it declined to support the proposals for deposit insurance that country banks clamored for. (George Moore, later chairman of Citicorp, who was in and out of Washington during the deposit insurance debate as a gofer representing James Perkins, then president of National City Bank of New York, remembered communicating the argument that "the competence of bankers is not an insurable risk.")[15] Roosevelt didn't want deposit insurance either, but the Democrats in the House of Representatives refused to go along with the other financial-sector reform measures in the Glass-Steagall Act until deposit insurance was firmly in the bill.

The Emergency Banking Act of 1933, which reopened the banks after the holiday, was rushed through both houses of Congress in a single day before the bill was printed, and almost nobody who voted for it knew what was in it. It gave the Federal Reserve temporary authority to issue currency against its holdings of Treasury paper (not just gold and commercial paper) and to discount *any* good assets to help reliquify the banking system. It gave what was from now on to be called the Federal Open Market Committee legal status as an agency of the board rather than of the district banks, though only the governors of the banks served on it, and authorized the board to change reserve requirements on its own motion, without the consent of Congress—but it did not change the composition or operations of the Federal Reserve System. Eugene R. Black, president of the Federal Reserve Bank of Atlanta, was named "Governor" of the board without any change in mission. The reopened banks, still frightened of runs despite deposit insurance (which did not come into effect until 1934), used whatever money the Federal Reserve poured into the marketplace to increase the "excess reserves" that looked to them like a margin of safety.

In fact, Roosevelt greatly expanded the nation's money supply by cutting the link between the American dollar and gold. The Emergency Banking Act had given the president a free hand in matters monetary, and on April 5 by executive order Roosevelt prohibited the ownership of monetary gold by Americans. A month later, an amendment to the Agricultural Adjustment Act (the objective of the currency fiddling being to raise the price of wheat) instructed the president to devalue the dollar in terms of gold, and presently he did so, destroying an international conference in London that had been called to stop the march of competitive devaluations. In April 1933, an ounce of gold had been worth $20.67; in January 1934, it was worth $35, a price it would keep (ludicrously, in retrospect) through war and inflation, until 1971. Gold drawn by the high price poured directly into the Treasury, which sent it off to Fort Knox and issued "gold certificates" to the Fed, increasing the reserves of the banking system.

In theory, the Fed could have sold its holdings of government paper and bankers' acceptances to "sterilize" the inflow of gold and keep it from becoming money, but in fact nobody wanted to see interest rates rise—and the district banks needed the earnings on their investments to pay their bills and their dividends. It was not until 1937 that the Fed again bought paper in the open market—and then the purchases were made only because the board had raised reserve requirements, creating panic in the bond market; the purchases, the Federal Reserve Bank of New York explained, "were not undertaken primarily with a view to affecting the reserve position of member banks, but rather with a view of exercising an influence toward the maintenance of orderly conditions in the market for Government securities."[16]

Eccles, having signed on as a consultant to the Treasury to help create the various housing authorities that would guarantee home mortgages and make them more attractive to bankers, had won over the New Dealers with the clarity of his ideas for using the Federal Reserve to revive lending in the banking system. As a highly successful businessman and banker, he had indeed "met a payroll," and could give political cover to Franklin Roosevelt (when he was nominated to be governor of the Federal Reserve Board in 1934, the White House statement included "a thumbnail sketch of my business and banking connections, written as though it was a stockholder's report. It listed the capital value of each enterprise along with the volume of business it did each year").

Eccles immediately got to work drafting a new Banking Act that really would create an American central bank run from Washington. He felt the 1933 act had essentially done nothing to make the Federal Reserve a significant player in national economic policy: "In human terms," he wrote in his memoirs sixteen years later, "before a uniform decision could be reached regarding open-market operations, with their far-reaching consequences affecting the volume of reserves and the supply of money and credit in the economy, there had to be a complete meeting of minds between the governors of the twelve reserve banks and the 108 directors of all those banks, plus the Federal Reserve Board in Washington. A more effective way of diffusing responsibility and encouraging inertia and indecision could not very well have been devised. Yet it seemed to suit the New York Federal Reserve Bank, through which private interests in the New York financial district exercised such enormous influence over the national economy."[17]

Carter Glass did not like Roosevelt or Eccles, and delayed Eccles's confirmation for five months. The natives grew restless. The Federal Advisory Council, the twelve bankers chosen from the twelve districts to advise the Federal Reserve Board, issued a public statement demanding a balanced budget. A Legislative Committee formed by the district banks and chaired by New York–on which the Federal Reserve Board had a single representative–geared up to propose changes in the law quite different from those Eccles had sold to Roosevelt. Eccles told them all to get lost, badgered the FAC into changing its procedures so that it would never again make a public statement except through the board, which would edit the statement as its members pleased (which is still the arrangement), and dissolved the Legislative Committee. In August 1935, Eccles got most of what he wanted, and the "Board of Governors of the Federal Reserve System" as it was hereafter known is pretty much as he designed it some sixty-five years ago. The title of "Governor" was taken away from the heads of the district banks, who became mere "Presidents" (Eccles wanted the real authority at those banks to be given to their "Chairman," who is appointed by Washington, but lost that one). The board got the power to raise or lower reserve requirements on its own motion, and to decide what paper would be "eligible" for discount. Eccles had made the point that by 1934, real bills having disappeared under the weight of the depression, there was only about $2 billion of trade-related paper in the country, which meant that the discount window had slid shut.

The day the act was signed was also the day that the cornerstone was laid for the marble Federal Reserve Board building on Constitution Avenue, with the huge eagle over the grand (permanently closed) main doorway to the avenue. The Fed had been housed in the old Treasury Building across the street from the White House, and both the secretary and the Comptroller of the Currency had sat on its board. Now the executive branch was to be removed from the management of the institution. And to reinforce the separate status of the Fed, its offices were being removed from the Treasury Building. The grand Fed headquarters, with its three-story 1930s-style Pharaonic atrium flanked by imposing marble staircases, is now called the Eccles Building, with a bronze plaque on the C Street side. But nobody notices.

At the century's close, Eccles's prescriptions were followed in Japan, with unimpressive results. The Bank of Japan hugely expanded its assets, pumping yen into a moribund economy and reducing interest rates to zero, while the government built roads and bridges and harbors all over the islands. It was not enough to save a bloated banking system that had supported the "bubble economy" of the 1980s, driving land prices and stock prices far beyond rational valuations. Banks had little reason to seek loans when the collateral borrowers could offer seemed overvalued and interest rates were very low. Bond buyers had good reason to fear low-interest bonds that would rapidly lose value the moment the economy turned and interest rates began to rise. A national debt rising toward 150 percent of annual gross domestic product threatened the future financial stability of the Japanese government–Moody's cut its ratings on Japanese government bonds. The Japanese situation is unique–anybody not Japanese who tells you he or she understands how Japan functions is probably mistaken–but Japan does seem subject to the general rule that in times of economic decay rescue begins with the creation of demand. A pithy comment in the *70th Annual Report* of the Bank for International Settlements notes "the unprecedented gap between the record high rate of private saving in Japan and the record low rate in the United States."[18] And a central bank cannot do much about that.

Chapter 8

Monetary Policy
in the Maelstrom

*In my speeches as a governor of the Federal Reserve, one of my hardest tasks
was to convince people of the fact that we do not know as much about
money as people think.*

–Sherman Maisel (1973)[1]

WILLIAM MCCHESNEY MARTIN, JR., served as chairman of the Board of
Governors of the Federal Reserve for more than eighteen years, and
the system as it is at the turn of the millennium is very largely his creation. The pompous building on Constitution Avenue is the Eccles
Building; the businesslike building across C Street, connected by an
underground tunnel, is the Martin Building. The Fed's tennis court
stands appropriately beside the Martin Building, for tennis was Martin's passion. Ron Chernow reports that Martin would hustle meetings of the Federal Open Market Committee to make sure he got on
the tennis court by noon.[2] After retiring from the Fed, Martin became president of the National Tennis Foundation, and supervised
the construction of a tennis center for the national championships
on the grounds of the old New York World's Fair. Before he came to
Washington, he and George Woods of First Boston (later to be chair-

man of the World Bank) had a hobby of investing in Broadway shows, and they made money at it. Sherman Maisel of the University of California, who served as a governor with Martin, wrote that he had been appropriately described as a "fun-loving Puritan."[3] Indeed, the most famous line he ever uttered illustrated both his capacity for enjoyment and his rigidity about the limits. "The function of the Federal Reserve," he liked to say, "is to take away the punch bowl just as the party is getting good."

No small part of Martin's strength when he succeeded Thomas McCabe as chairman was his origin as a Missourian—and a Democrat. Truman always trusted Missouri Democrats more than other people. And Treasury Secretary John Snyder, of course, was also a Missourian. Martin's father had been the first head of the Federal Reserve Bank of St. Louis, and Martin himself had come to New York at the age of twenty-five to represent the St. Louis brokerage house of A. G. Edwards in the New York Stock Exchange. The floor of the exchange, necessarily, is a place where a person is judged by his willingness to live by his word when it costs him money; Martin from day one inspired trust. When Richard Whitney as president of the stock exchange dishonored his family and the exchange by embezzling money from employee welfare funds, and the members had to find someone whose reputation for probity would control the damage, they hired Martin—all of thirty-two years old—to be their first salaried full-time president. It was not a job Martin much enjoyed, and when the war came, he was happy to be drafted as a private in the army. Soon he was a sergeant at the Army War College, then a lieutenant, rising through the ranks to colonel in military intelligence at the end of the war.

He was, in short, a man of parts. He was also, and this should not be omitted, an unusually nice man, a good listener who actually heard what other people were saying, friends with just about everybody in all the financial communities where he lived or visited. Maisel wrote: "One can truly say, in a slight alteration of Will Rogers's statement, that nobody who really knew Bill Martin disliked him. Whenever I traveled throughout the world, people would make a point of meeting me in order to be remembered to Bill Martin. They wanted to express their great fondness for him."[4] He was perhaps the only chairman of the Fed ever who relaxed easily, deadpan mouth over the square jaw, an earnest Midwest look about him while he told stories. Milton Friedman, attending the swearing-in ceremonies at the White House when his protégé Arthur Burns became chairman of the Fed, noticed Martin in a group with Richard Nixon and a bunch of senators. "I still think," he said, "Bill Martin is the best politician in the room."[5]

Martin was a compromiser: the small band of reformers at the New York Stock Exchange who had been excited by his election as president ultimately felt that he had failed to lance many of the boils, and when he returned to the exchange after his Fed service, to chair a committee on how to reform floor procedures, he gave away entirely too much to the old-timers. His survival at the Fed, with reappointments by Eisenhower, Kennedy, and Johnson, demonstrated his ability to get along with all sorts, and to operate in different states of independence. His reign was the time when the Fed became a centralized institution, greatly diminishing the role of the New York Bank, to the disgust of its president Allan Sproul, who retired to his native California (where his brother was chancellor of the University of California). But it was the first rumblings of the communications revolution, not Martin, that created a single command center for a nationwide market. In the 1940s, it was still possible for the different reserve banks to have different discount rates; by 1969, when Martin left the Fed (to live almost thirty more years, all but the last half-dozen pleasurable), such differences would have been arbitraged away in the blink of an eye.

Martin was not an economist, or a scholar. (Indeed, there were no economists on the board of the Federal Reserve: the first to be appointed was George Mitchell, in 1964.) More than anyone else who has held the chairman's job, Martin was a market man, who wanted only enough information to stimulate his instincts. As a market man, he had great faith in prices, those one-dimensional reductions of complex data that guide decisions. And he knew that prices will change in response to such decisions, so he sought out varied views to give him a sense of what the reaction to his Fed's decisions might be, and how those reactions might play in terms of tomorrow's prices and the guidance market participants would find in them. He once said that he encouraged his people to hire researchers who would disagree, so he would have the benefit of conflicting views before forming his own opinion. What George Soros has called "reflexivity," which may or may not be a better word than "feedback," was built into Martin's processes of judgment.

Fortunately, the world Martin inherited as chairman of the Fed was especially well arranged to respond to price signals. During World War II, as Eccles pointed out, banks had been encouraged to stuff their portfolios with government bonds. In the 1950s there was strong loan demand, at interest rates considerably higher than those on the bonds, with nowhere near enough money flowing into the banks in the form of deposits to fund the loans. To take advantage of the loan demand, the banks had to sell their bonds. Accounting regulations adopted in the 1930s permitted them to carry the bonds they already owned at face value, regardless of market price; but if they sold the bonds for less than face value, they had to take the loss. By pushing interest rates up (which could be done simply by letting the bond market find its level without Fed intervention at a time when banks were trying to sell), Martin could discourage lending, because the banks would have to measure the additional income from the new loans against the losses they would have to take (and report) if they sold their government bonds. With interest rates very low as wartime policies persisted, a modest increase would generate large reductions in the market price of government bonds: an increase of a single percentage point, from 2½ percent to 3½ percent annual rate, would drive the price of a 20-year government bond down from 100 to about 90. In 1952, when I was working on my first long article about financial subjects, a banker at Chase said to me sorrowfully that he never thought he would live to see the day when the government would deliberately make the banking system technically insolvent.

In Martin's first years, a relatively small push on short-term in-terest rates would not just make loans expensive–it would make them unavailable. Banks could not issue corporate bonds to raise money for themselves, and they were still not organized as holding companies that could tap the market. Their source of funds to lend was the deposits their customers brought them. Under the rules of the Glass-Steagall Act, they were not permitted to bid for additional demand deposits by paying interest on them, and the interest they could pay for "time deposits" of thirty days or more (nationally char-tered banks still were not permitted to offer "savings accounts") was controlled by the Fed. In theory, banks could ration their loans by price, ratcheting up the interest rate when money was scarce. In fact, that was not the way banks worked, partly because they were afraid (with some reason) that borrowers willing to pay very high rates were less likely to pay back the principal of the loan, partly because they lived off established relations with good customers who would be poached by other banks willing to take a loss on this loan to ex-pand their customer lists.

Thus Martin could count on an almost reflexive reduction of to-tal lending (which meant a deceleration of the rate of increase of the money supply) simply by sitting still at meetings of the Federal Open Market Committee when the economy expanded and rates began to rise. The Bank of England had long operated on the basis of a wink and a nod; for a few blessed years, the Fed could do the same. After each meeting of the FOMC, a bland "directive" went out to the chief of the desk at the New York Fed, telling him in essence that the Fed wanted interest rates a little higher or a little lower, and to sell or buy government paper in the market accordingly. The contents of this directive were held secret for a year; people in the market had to guess what the Fed intended from watching what the New York desk seemed to be doing.

Three times in the Eisenhower administration, reductions in the supply of loans induced by minor increases in the open market inter-est rate curbed economic growth and blasted the stock market (mostly by sabotaging home construction, the industry most responsive to the availability of credit–an associate of the Trammel Crow construction company once said that "the successful builder is the man who, when the banks are handing out the money, you always find him at the front door in his Rolls-Royce; and when they aren't handing out the money, you don't see him anywhere"). In 1956 and 1959, the banks bit the bullet and sold off a noticeable piece of their Treasuries holdings, pushing up the interest rates on U.S. government paper as the economy strengthened. Those rising rates forced what Democrats called the "stop/go" environment of the economy in the Eisenhower years.

Martin, as noted, was not a theoretician. He was not interested in money supply numbers, in total reserves, in unborrowed reserves, in the size or nature of the portfolio of investments at the district banks (government bonds, agency securities, discounted loans). He was of course quite sophisticated enough to know what Wright Patman (and recent commentators like William Greider) did not, that higher interest rates meant lower securities prices and real estate prices and thus reduced the wealth of the rentier class as well as increasing the costs of producers and discouraging them from employing workers. Such results were unavoidable in the short term; they were the price paid by the society for maintaining the integrity of money as a unit of account and a store of value, permitting markets to allocate investment resources most efficiently and improve the productivity of the system. Maintaining the value of money against inflationary or deflationary pressures required what Martin called "leaning against the wind." For most of the time of Martin's chairmanship, an honest man of the market not burdened with theoretical concerns could believe that this goal was attainable simply through the manipulation of interest rates.

American banks have never thought of themselves as willing instruments of national policy, and in the early 1950s, responding to Martin's first increases in interest rates, J. P. Morgan developed the overnight repurchase agreement. The law forbade banks to pay interest on demand deposits. During the war, corporations had got in the habit of leaving large deposits at the bank for the days before they were to pay the government the withholding tax or Social Security tax on their employees' wages. (Such steady payment of taxes through payroll deductions was itself, of course, a World War II novelty.) Interest rates on short-term Treasury paper were one-half of 1 percent annually, and there were costs involved in buying and selling the paper: it wasn't worth the while of a company to take the money out of the bank, buy a Treasury bill, and then sell the Treasury bill to cover the check the company had to write to the government a few days later. The bank, dealing in Treasury paper all the time, did however invest the corporation's deposit in bills. When the Fed became stingy about supplying reserves, a bank could reduce the amount of reserves it needed by extinguishing corporate deposits overnight, selling Treasury paper to its depositor with a guarantee of repurchase the next day at a price reflecting one day's interest on the paper. The corporate depositor earned a little something on its money, and the bank reduced its footings—its assets and its liabilities—reducing pressure on its reserves. There was a sacrifice, in effect, of the day's interest on the T-bill, most of which the bank recouped by its reduced need for reserves. And from the companies' point of view, as Morgan pointed out, they profited from a cost-free safe investment of their funds for their benefit: Morgan was doing them a service . . . As interest rates rose, and companies became conscious of "cash management," repurchase agreements between banks and their clientele became a significant relationship on both sides.

Morgan also resurrected what had become a moribund market in "Fed Funds"—the excess reserves of the banks that were not fully loaned to customers. Arranging interbank loans from banks that had heavy reserves to those that needed them had been a good business in the 1920s, pioneered by a man named George Garvin, but it had atrophied in the depression, when all the banks had excess reserves. After 1951, Morgan sent salesmen around to its immense list of correspondent banks, suggesting that it could pay good money for what would otherwise be idle balances in reserve accounts–with a sweetener of an offer that if this bank ever found itself embarrassed in its reserves, Morgan would use its best efforts to take care of the problem. Soon Morgan was funding its own needs to a significant degree by borrowing Fed Funds from correspondents, and it was brokering money from one correspondent to another all over the country.

Puzzled technicians from the Fed came calling to find out what lay behind the rash of interbank transfers Morgan seemed to be masterminding on the books of the district banks. At first the official reaction was negative, because the transfer of Fed Funds looked like an end run around the rules: Fed Funds borrowed did not constitute a "deposit" and thus were not subject to reserve requirements. On reconsideration, however, the Fed decided to encourage the growth of this market. So long as there were excess reserves in the system, it was difficult for Fed policy makers to tighten the money supply without relatively drastic action. If reserves were fully employed, which would be the end result of an active Fed Funds market over time, the Fed could hope for additional leverage on the lending activities of the banks.

Because these transactions were booked as loans to be repaid, they were subject to limits on loans to one borrower–10 percent of capital, which in a bank with 10 percent capital meant 1 percent of total assets, which was not much money from an individual country bank to Morgan. In 1963, however, James Saxon, Kennedy's eccentric Comptroller of the Currency, issued a ruling that for national banks, which he controlled, a loan of Fed Funds would be considered a sale with an agreement to repurchase, which removed all limits on the size of the transaction. It should be noted that the ban on the payment of interest on demand deposits had been required by Congress because of the fear that the big metropolitan banks were denuding the country of lendable funds for the benefit of the call money market at the stock exchange. Now Saxon was structuring a short-term world where the big-city banks almost automatically would take money out of the country whenever the Fed tightened. The Fed was publicly upset, but it was Saxon, not the Fed, who controlled the rules affecting the behavior permitted to national banks. Little bankers liked Saxon's rules a lot. A banker in small-town Iowa in 1972, when rates were low because the economy was pulling out of a recession, told me that he was looking forward to the day "when Fed Funds will get back over eight percent, and banking will be a good business again." Even in 1972, the sale of Fed Funds provided 8 percent of the income of smaller American banks.[6]

Full exploitation of the Fed Funds market was the pioneering work of Ralph Leach, an elegant, athletic man who before coming to the Morgan bank had been chief of the government finance section of the Fed (at the age of thirty-three–Martin missed him when he left: he had been the chairman's favorite doubles partner). The reserves a bank had to keep at the Fed were calculated as its average on a two-week cycle, from the opening of the bank on Thursday morning to its closing on Wednesday afternoon, and a bank could be light one night if it was heavy on others. Friday was especially important, because the position counted triple. Through the period when Leach was running this operation for Morgan, required reserves were calculated on a lagged basis, so that this two-week period had to show sufficient reserves to cover the deposits reported in the previous two-week period. Leach therefore knew on Thursday morning exactly how much he would have to have at the Fed overnight on average for the next fourteen nights. If he thought money would get cheaper during the two weeks, he would keep low reserves in the early days, looking to buy more money toward the end of the period. Indeed, once other banks caught on to the usefulness of the Fed Funds market and there was lots of liquidity, Leach might *sell* Fed Funds in the early phases of an accounting period, knowing he needed lots of additional reserves before the two weeks were over, and use the profits from the sale to reduce the effective cost of what he had to buy later.

"It is the most incredible change in the commercial banking system," Bob Dall of the bond-dealing house Salomon Brothers said in 1974. "They used to react, just as I do. Sometime in the day, they would guess where they would be at the end of the day, and move to stay even. Then Ralph Leach said, 'Why not take a view?'" As the mechanism for the purchase of Fed Funds was refined to the overnight extinguishing of correspondent balances, and the "dematerialization" of Treasury paper proceeded to the point where repurchases and their reversals could be accomplished on FedWire by the push of a button, *everybody* was empowered to take a view and the market for overnight money became the most active market in the world. As it is to this day.

Down Wall Street from J. P. Morgan, meanwhile, First National City Bank of New York–ancestor of today's Citigroup–was planning a course that would leave it even more independent of Federal Reserve decisions. Its first ventures were in the fledgling Eurodollar market of the 1950s. The United States had made a considerable quantity of dollars available to the Marshall Plan countries to help them trade with each other, conversion from lira to dollars to guilder being easier than direct conversion from lira to guilder. And the United States had begun to run deficits with Europe in its balance of payments, as improved political stability in Europe and higher interest rates drew investment abroad.

Meanwhile, having money in America had begun to look less safe. In 1956, the United States had frozen the American bank accounts of all the participants in the British-French-Israeli war against Egypt. And there was a continuing dispute between the United States and the Soviet Union about the status of accounts left over from the lend-lease programs of World War II, which left the Russians very concerned about what might happen to any dollar accounts they had in American banks. The Russians had therefore expanded their own banks in Paris (Eurobank) and London (Narodny Bank) to do their dollar business safely away from American law. The Bank of England in 1957 clamped tight controls on what banks in London could do with accounts denominated in pounds sterling, but left the growing dollar market in London free from regulation. Dollar-denominated accounts in London, even in American banks, were also free from the Fed's reserve requirements. In the late 1950s, there was a growing mass of dollars in London that could be repatri-

173

ated overnight to help a big New York bank meet its reserve requirements at the Fed.

In 1960, Citibank issued a one-year "Bankers' Certificate" for $1 million to the Union Bank of Switzerland (UBS), writing the instrument in such a way that UBS could sell it. But there was nobody to buy it from UBS. Walter Wriston, then head of the First National City overseas division, saw that other banks would buy considerable quantities of certificates of deposit from his bank if in fact there was an aftermarket that made the paper truly negotiable. With John Exter, who had come over from the Federal Reserve Bank of New York, he persuaded Discount Corporation of America, one of the oldest and best established dealers in government bonds, to announce that it would make a market in City Bank's CDs. I described this in 1975 as a revolution in banking: a move from asset management (deciding on the right mix of loans and investments, selling government bonds to fund loans if deposits didn't arrive in sufficient quantity) to liability management (buying deposits whenever you needed money). It was quantitatively different from what Leach had done in the repo and Fed Funds markets, because it put banks in competition with their own borrowers for lendable funds.

This too, of course, was a way around the law which prohibited the payment of interest on demand deposits, but Harold van B. Cleveland and Thomas E. Huertas in their 1984 history of the bank argue that the negotiable CD was in fact a suggestion from Howard B. Crosse, a New York Fed vice president, who gave a talk to the National Credit Conference in January 1961: "As I see it, it is no more than wishful day-dreaming to hope that holders of temporarily idle excess funds will leave them as non-interest-bearing demand deposits in commercial banks when they can sell them in the market. If banks are to use these funds they will have to pay for them . . . if changes in the law or regulations are required, the commercial banks should aggressively make the case for such changes."[7] National City Bank announced Discount Corporation's agreement to make a market in its CDs only a month later.

What made the negotiable CD possible was that the Fed's ceilings on 30-day and 90-day time deposits were higher than market rates. The year 1960 had been a slow one (John Kennedy ran for president with the slogan that he would get the country moving again). Relations between the Kennedy administration and the Federal Reserve were unusually close: Robert V. Roosa had come from the Federal Reserve Bank of New York to be undersecretary of the treasury for monetary affairs, and Charles Coombs from the same bank, who had been Kennedy's roommate at Groton, was the administration's point man in relations with foreign central banks. Douglas Dillon, born to the manner of Dillon, Read & Co., very smart as well as very social (for nobody remembered that his father had come to the United States as a Romanian Jew) was secretary of the treasury.

Harry Truman had created a Council of Economic Advisers in the White House, to balance the National Security Council. Kennedy appointed distinguished economists to the council (among them, the future Nobel Prize winner James Tobin), and its chairman Walter Heller was someone whose company the president enjoyed. Dillon, Heller, and David Bell, director of the Bureau of the Budget (as it then was) met occasionally as "the Triad," and Kennedy had them all to the Oval Office every two months or so to discuss the framework for budget and tax policy. Martin did not attend these meetings, but he spoke occasionally with Heller, breakfasted with Dillon, and talked on the telephone with the president.

When Lyndon Johnson came to power, he wanted to be sure everyone got on board and stayed on board, and he began a tradition of a monthly meeting of the four significant players in economic policy—the secretary of the treasury, the director of the Bureau of the Budget, the chairman of the Council of Economic Advisers, and the chairman of the Fed. This "Quadriad" was summoned to meetings by the president and listened to him a lot. For Martin, his attendance did not imply any sacrifice of the Fed's independence; commenting once on a piece of blatherskite Treasury Secretary Henry Fowler had uttered to support one of Johnson's statements, Martin noted that "He was a subordinate; I wasn't." But as a matter of courtesy, and respect, Martin shared with the others of the Quadriad his thoughts about what the Fed should do.

Martin had his own contacts in the Senate, who soon after the introduction of President Johnson's 1965 budget began telling him that *authorizations* for the Vietnam War (as distinct from *appropriations*, which seemed to be under control) had escalated to the point where future government deficits of grand dimensions had become unavoidable. He brought his concerns about future deficits and their possible impact on the value of the dollar before the Quadriad as early as March 1965, and he was brushed aside. "By May," he said a dozen years later, "I was getting really worried, and I began trying to sell the idea [of a rate increase] on the board. I got two members with me, one on the fence. In July and August it became perfectly obvious that military spending was *soaring*, even though the figures didn't show it. I kept waiting–I think I waited too long.

"In October, I was hauled over to the White House by Johnson, just when I was ready to go. He said, 'You know, Bill, I'm having my gallbladder out. You wouldn't do it while I'm having my gallbladder out, would you?' All I could say was, 'I've had my gallbladder out. It isn't so bad.' But I went home to my wife and I said, 'Well, suppose the President is in the hospital and I raise the discount rate and he dies . . .'" It wasn't until early December, when Johnson was safely out of the hospital, that Martin moved.

By then, the banks had committed to lend great sums of money to the defense industries that had received Defense Department letters of obligation to provide escalating quantities of arms for Vietnam. The Fed raised its discount rate only one-half of 1 percentage point, to 4.5 percent, but market rates went to 6 percent. Rates on Fed Funds went higher than the discount rate for the first time ever as the discount window officers at the district banks discouraged the use of their facilities, driving what would once have been member-bank borrowers into the cold of the marketplace. Interest rate ceilings prevented the banks from competing for short-term money in the form of deposits. Not only was it impossible for the banks to sell new CDs, but they had to dig into their other funds to pay off old

CDs as they ran off and could not be renewed because the banks could not offer their lenders market rates.

The crunch crushed the savings and loans, most of them mutuals, which meant that their customers got "shares" rather than "deposits" when they put money through the teller's window. Shares paid dividends, not interest, and thus the S&Ls had been exempt from interest-rate controls. They had been bidding money away from the banks with widely advertised higher rates on their shares—and had then leveraged their resources by selling their mortgages to get the funds to write new ones. Suddenly the value of their portfolios skidded downhill, and the most aggressive of them were bust. "In 1966," the builder-academic Ned Eichler writes, "the noose on California associations tightened." Since they weren't earning the dividends they had promised, they had to disappoint their "shareholders," creating a run on the "bank" in several California thrifts. "Less able to compete for funds when interest rates rose, thrift executives stood helplessly by as money flew out the door."[8]

In theory, there couldn't be a run—people who put their money in an S&L agreed to accept a delay of up to a year in getting it back, at the option of the institution. The Federal Savings and Loan Insurance Corporation did not promise to redeem shares in an insolvent S&L for twelve whole months, at its discretion. But the fact of the matter was that people who put their money into an S&L expected it to be available when they wanted it. They accepted that they couldn't use it to pay bills the way they could use a bank account to pay bills (it wasn't until the 1970s that a smart ex-Citibanker transformed into CEO of the Five Cents Savings Bank in Worcester, Massachusetts, saw that he could offer his customers "Negotiable Orders of Withdrawal" that were the exact equivalent of checks). But it hadn't occurred to the purchasers of S&L "shares" that they weren't depositors and they couldn't redeem their shares on demand. The Federal Home Loan Bank of San Francisco bent its rules to advance enough cash to State Savings & Loan to keep it in business, and the panic subsided.

The rules changed. The Home Loan Bank system admitted that S&L shares were really deposits that could be withdrawn on demand, which meant that the government could control the interest rates the thrifts offered. To make sure that housing would continue to be a priority use of the nation's savings, the S&Ls were allowed to pay at each maturity one-quarter of 1 percentage point more for savings than the banks were permitted to pay. But because they had a burden of old mortgages written at lower interest rates, the squeeze on them was dramatic. The self-amortizing 30-year mortgage, one of the great creations of the New Deal, became in the 1960s, without anyone willing what happened, the major transmission belt of monetary policy. When interest rates went up, housing starts collapsed; when they went down, housing became the starter engine for the reviving economy. Given the political strength of both the home-building and the home-buying communities, this implement was likely to be taken out of the hands of the monetary authorities, one way or another, but in real life housing remained a residual user of funds for twenty years after the 1966 crunch.

In 1981–82, as a member of the finance committee of Ronald Reagan's National Commission on Housing, I became one of the authors of the plan by which housing could be financed with real estate mortgage investment conduits, permitting pension funds and mutual funds to get in and out of housing investments, and permitting Wall Street houses to slice and dice mortgage paper that carried an implicit government guarantee. The bankers created innumerable "tranches" that could be sold separately to risk-averse investors and risk-seeking speculators, hedged to reduce the dangers of changes in interest rates, or rolled over in repurchase agreements to multiply both risks and rewards. It is by no means clear that the future will regard this system of home finance as a good idea.

As the growth of repos and Fed Funds purchases had revolutionized the liability side of the banks, the asset side was transformed by the introduction of these new kinds of mortgage paper, and by the metastasizing growth of the Government Sponsored Enterprises that financed and repackaged the mortgages (mostly Fannie Mae and Freddie Mac, slang names for the Federal National Mortgage Association and the Federal Home Loan Mortgage Corporation).

These institutions, which today process more than half the nation's mortgages, would change beyond recognition the real direct effects of Federal Reserve actions on the real, non-financial economy. Henry Kaufman points out that "the large-scale shift from nonmarketable to marketable assets has had the significant side effect of dispelling the illusion that nonmarketable assets by nature have stable prices."[9] The health of the economy in the 1990s, and Chairman Alan Greenspan's ability to change Fed policies at the margin to match the incremental changes in the economy, have masked the great truth that conceptually–looking ahead as central banks are supposed to look ahead–we no longer understand what we are doing. Where Bill Martin had a two-factor problem and two tools with which to solve it–interest rates and control of the monetary aggregates–today's Fed has a multifaceted problem and only one tool, short-term interest rates.

It is not simply a matter of the decline of the banks, which once "intermediated" more than three-fifths of the public funds that went into the financing of enterprise and now provide something less than a quarter of the nation's credit. The composition of the investments traded in the market has changed, too. When the great Sidney Homer of Salomon Brothers & Hutzler wrote his hilarious book *The Bond Buyer's Primer,* he could in a serious vein claim that the bond market "provides 95% of the external long-term finance necessary to business, while the stock market provides 5%."[10] A change in the interest rate that banks charged each other (or that the Fed charged the banks) would quickly affect bond prices, so that both bank lending and market finance were pushed in the same direction. Now the "new economy" is financed by "venture capitalists" and underwriters who push initial public offerings, and the movement of a few basis points in short-term interest rates matters nothing to them unless the result is a noticeable change in the valuation of–one hesitates to say it–stocks. This reality may well be politically untenable–a Republican congressman in early 2000 called for a law that would require the chairman of the Fed to hold a representative portfolio of common stocks so he would feel the pain of the ordinary American when the Fed's actions in the market pushed stock prices down. And certainly the Fed will have to continue to deny, with steadily decreasing credibility, that it makes interest-rate decisions with reference to asset inflation or deflation. (Of course, nobody did complain when Greenspan stimulated a 7 percent rise in the stock market on October 15, 1998.) But to the extent that investment decisions, the driving force of the economy, are made on a basis of stock prices, central banks cannot avoid factoring them into their analysis.

The Fed's public image is of a supergovernment that determines the course of economic life, but in fact the Fed today walks softly and carries a small stick. Since the first modest increases in interest rates in early 1994 provoked a severe, unexpected drop in the price of 10-year Treasury notes,[11] Greenspan has tried to meet two contradictory goals: he wants to make certain that the market is not surprised by what the Fed does, but he wants a strong "announcement effect" in the markets when he does it. Not long ago, economists were confident in their predictions of what a given change in the administered short-term interest rate would do to the economy over eighteen months or two years. Today, that confidence is gone. At a conference in the Levy Institute in spring 1999, Preston Martin commented that in his time as vice chairman, in the mid-1980s, the staff economists at the Fed were preparing great macroeconomic models of the economy that would let the governors plug in whatever decision they were considering, and tell them a forecastable future. He asked Edward M. Gramlich, a sitting governor, who had just completed a speech, whether those models were still on tap. Gramlich, a dignified former business school dean, made a face. "I prefer little models, myself," he said.

Greenspan himself said as much in a talk during the annual meetings of the World Bank and the International Monetary Fund in fall 1999. "The fact that our econometric models at the Fed, the best in the world, have been wrong for fourteen straight quarters," he told his audience with a straight face, "does not mean that they will not be right in the fifteenth quarter."

Chapter 9

Disaster Time

"Solomon told me when he had been in office only a few months, 'I don't like the idea of the value of the dollar abroad being at the mercy of the central banks.' I said, 'Good. Then finance the deficit yourself.'"

> −Otmar Emminger, President, Deutsche Bundesbank,
> speaking of the Undersecretary of the Treasury
> of the United States and his problems (1979)[1]

MARTIN TOOK HIS CLASSIC BUCKET TO the well once more, in 1968, following a truly awful scare that the general public never even knew about. (Two decades later, William Greider's detailed and well-informed popular book about the Fed did not mention it.) What with the war in Vietnam and the consumption boom at home, the United States had been running a fearful deficit in its current account with the rest of the world, and in 1967–deeply resentful of the way Americans could print their own money and use it to buy French companies–President Charles de Gaulle began to buy gold from the American reserve stock with the dollars the French had accumulated through their trade surpluses. Inflation was approaching 4 percent, incidentally increasing the demand for cash. Law required the Fed-

181

eral Reserve to have 25 percent gold backing for U.S. currency, and under the terms of the Bretton Woods agreements in 1944, the United States was obliged to sell gold to foreign buyers (Americans were not permitted to own monetary gold) at a price of $35 an ounce. As gold ran off, Martin could see the day when the district banks could no longer legally issue the nation's paper currency.

There was a limit to how much of a public stink could be made about this problem, because a panicky flight from currency was a horror movie ahead of its time, and a grumpy Congress didn't want to move on any Lyndon Johnson initiative. Eventually, Congress did remove the gold-cover clauses from the law–and Martin got the world's central banks to agree that they would keep their stocks of "monetary" gold segregated from the growing gold markets in Zurich and London–but in the meantime there was no escaping the need to restrict the growth of the American money supply, pushing up interest rates to make American debt securities more attractive not only to the rest of the world but to Americans themselves. Indeed, interest rates rose to their highest level in a hundred years.

Once more, the banks reached into their bag of tricks and found something new–the Eurodollar, which had proliferated as the American trade deficit had spread American money around Europe, and could be repatriated. In 1969, arguably, there was a money multiplier in Europe independent of the fractional reserve system in the United States. European exporters took their dollars to their central bank to exchange for their own currency. This was a problem for the Bundesbank, to take the most frequent end recipient of the dollars, because the marks it had to create to buy the dollars would have an inflationary effect in Germany. It was tempting for the Bundesbank to "sterilize" this activity by using its dollars to buy marks from banks that could use dollars in their international activities. By recirculating its dollars, the Bundesbank would in effect create American dollars abroad that had no direct referent at home but probably could be repatriated. A few years later, Chairman Arthur Burns–it was one of very few of his actions that survivors of his time as chairman find praiseworthy–would persuade foreign central bankers to put their excess dollars back into American Treasury paper, giving birth to the situation of the 1990s, when Treasuries held at the Federal Reserve Bank of New York "for foreign official account" rose to 20 percent of the total U.S. national debt held outside the government's own trust funds. In 1969–70, however, the banks were able to dodge Martin's bullet by pulling money back from Europe, an activity in which they persisted even after the Fed extended reserve requirements to cover imported Eurodollars as well as domestic deposits, and the inflation roared on.

It would not have occurred to Richard Nixon that the Federal Reserve Board was really independent of the White House. Swearing in Arthur Burns in January 1970, the president said, "I respect his independence. However, I hope that independently he will conclude that my views are the ones that should be followed."[2] The evidence is very strong that Burns, who had been a longtime adviser and avuncular friend, did the president's bidding, sometimes by anticipating what Nixon might want and doing it before he could ask. (William Greider says that on one occasion when Burns didn't move as far or as fast as the White House wanted, stories were planted in the press that the chairman had gone after a 20 percent raise for himself while cautioning business and Congress not to permit wage increases.[3] Nixon was not nice to his friends, either.) In 1971, Burns sat still for the abandonment of the American commitment to sell gold at $35 an ounce, and the imposition of a 10 percent tariff on all imports. And in 1972, he joined with the rest of the world's central bankers in pushing the pedal to the metal after the world's finance ministers meeting at the Smithsonian Institute in Washington agreed to restore, with the dollar insufficiently devalued, the Bretton Woods system Nixon had fractured the summer before.

The fact that the economic expansion stimulated by this rapid growth in the money supply helped Nixon win reelection was not, I think, far from Burns's mind. Late one afternoon in his office at the Fed a few years later, removing his burred Oom Paul pipe from his mouth, he told me that one couldn't forget whom (George McGovern) the president had been running against. But it was also true that straight Keynesian analysis of the American economy in early 1972 called for a significant relaxation of interest rates, and the left wing of his board—Governors Andrew Brimmer and Sherman Maisel—were ardent advocates of the policies he adopted.

The most significant development of the Burns era was the end to Martin's system of controlling a boom in the economy by choking the growth of bank liabilities. That rested on the prohibition on the payment of interest on demand accounts, and the control of the interest rates banks could pay for longer-term certificates of deposit. In spring 1970, the Penn Central Railroad, product of one of the great mergers and the dominant rail transporter of the North Atlantic states, went to the wall, victim of government subsidies to the concrete rights of way of the trucking industry and of its management's incompetence. Nixon tried to keep it going through the agency of an obscure survivor of the World War II War Powers Act, which permitted the U.S. Navy to make loans to a company that did essential things, provided that the Federal Reserve Bank of the district where the company was domiciled could certify that the collateral was there to assure that the navy would be repaid. The Federal Reserve Bank of New York was thus instructed to verify the long-term prospects of Penn Central, and Tom Waage, a senior vice president, went over to Citibank to look at the loan files. What he found were annual reports: this was *Penn Central;* like the bank itself, it was too big to fail. A few weeks earlier, noblesse oblige, Chemical Bank had lent Penn Central $50 million, unsecured.

Penn Central had $82 million of commercial paper outstanding, no small part of it in the hands of widows and orphans, colleges and hospitals. That was the most junior of the company's credits, and would certainly be defaulted. Goldman, Sachs had sold the paper and made the market in it, and had completely emptied its own inventory. Like all commercial paper, it had been written with a backup facility committing the banks to advance the money to pay it off if the paper could not be rolled over in the market when due, but these contracts all had escape clauses if the condition of the borrower had deteriorated, and the banks were not going to throw any more money into this pot. The reason the innocents owned this paper was that it paid a higher rate of interest than other commercial paper, because sophisticates knew it was dangerous and avoided it. (The one big corporate holder of Penn Central commercial paper, American Express, was in those days pretty innocent itself.) The Federal Reserve System is not a place where people who are facing losses on overpriced risky paper can expect sympathy, but the economy was in a parlous state in June 1970, in the first year of that decade's "stagflation," and a default by one of the larger issuers of commercial paper would reverberate in the market for commercial paper from other borrowers, especially the Chrysler subsidiary that financed the sale of Chrysler automobiles.

Penn Central could not be saved; the $82 million of Penn Central commercial paper was going to be a dead loss (in the end, many of the holders were made whole by Goldman itself, after they sued). But the banks could preserve Chrysler by pledging to support its paper. The presidents of the district banks got on the telephone on a Sunday to convince their member banks that they should publicly and aggressively support Chrysler (and other) paper, making sure it got rolled over as it came due. The author "Adam Smith" (a.k.a. George J. W. Goodman) invented a hilarious telephone conversation between a Fed president and the son of the CEO of a big bank, who couldn't get his father to the phone from the lawn where he was practicing his golf swing because he'd been ordered not to leave the kitchen until he ate all his carrots. The next week banks borrowed more than $1.7 billion at the discount windows (the equivalent of about $6 billion in year 2000 money) to finance their activities in the commercial paper market, which stabilized.[4]

Everybody (including "Adam Smith") agreed that this week was a triumph for the Fed, but a high price had been paid. As the quid pro quo for the banks' help in the commercial paper market, the Fed had agreed to abandon controls on interest rates for certificates of deposit of $100,000 or more. After June 1970 it was no longer possible for the Fed to create a money crunch: the banks could simply go into the market and outbid everyone else. Relending the money for which they had paid a historically high price, they could show an improvement in their average return on assets. Previous assets would be worth a good deal less than they had been worth at the time of their acquisition, but "regulatory accounting" permitted the banks to continue to carry them at historic cost, so the traditional penalty on banks when they raised interest rates no longer applied. It was during this period when the Fed found it could make money expensive but not scarce that Arthur Burns and Walter Wriston had their dispute about who did and who did not understand banking.

Burns saw and understood the loss of authority that accompanied the elimination of controls on interest rates for high-value CDs, and when the stagflation (inflation plus recession) of the early 1970s persisted, he became an unexpected convert to the idea of an "incomes policy," the fancy phrase for wage and price controls. Nixon imposed them on the country (using a forgotten war powers procedure again) in summer 1971. Then his and the European central banks' expansionary policies, after the Smithsonian agreement at the end of the year seemed to assure renewed currency stability, left a lot of money on the table for the Arab oil producers to pick up when the Yom Kippur War in 1973 intensified the political instability of that region. By summer 1974, when the oil producers had begun insisting that they would take nothing but dollars for their oil (discarding the British pound, which left the British socialists naked to their enemies—first Bill Simon at the U.S. Treasury, then Maggie Thatcher at home), it was clear that only the American banks could enable the "less developed countries" to pay their energy bills.

The oil countries deposited their receipts in American banks, in dollars. The newly installed Ford administration (with L. William Seidman as the president's special adviser on economics and Alan Greenspan as chairman of the Council of Economic Advisers) decided to urge the banks to lend those dollars to the poor countries, to help them pay their oil bills. In the end, the big banks would have assets in the form of loans to poor countries that couldn't pay back the money, matched against liabilities in the form of demand deposits from the oil companies, who could do what they liked with the money in their accounts. Burns, sitting in on the meeting in the Oval Office, shook his head and said, "You call it recycling; I call it bad loans"[5]–but the fix was in. By seeking to accommodate the rise in oil prices, internationally as well as domestically, the U.S. government was moving the world to a new bout of inflation. Burns knew it, but felt trapped. Through the recession of 1975, inflation persisted. As the economy turned up in 1977, a new Democratic president called for a $50 a head gift to every American, to end what his advisers mistakenly thought was a continuing recession. The dollar began a precipitous descent that would be capped in 1979 by the second eruption of oil prices.

Burns finished his term in February 1978, and Jimmy Carter incomprehensibly appointed as his successor G. William Miller, CEO of the conglomerate Textron, a corporate lawyer from Providence, Rhode Island, unversed in central banking. The White House was going to run the Fed. Treasury Secretary W. Michael Blumenthal announced to an international gathering that the United States was going to defend the exchange value of the dollar (eight months earlier, brand new in the job, he had said that a declining exchange value for the dollar would have to "play its part" in eliminating the humongous U.S. trade deficit). Miller did not join in the statement. Treasury arranged a credit of $4 billion worth of marks to be used to buy dollars in the foreign exchange market, but the Fed continued to pump out the dollars its own international desk, acting for the Treasury's account, would have to buy with the marks. In the second quarter of 1978, the monetary aggregates grew at the fastest pace in American history. American short-term interest rates were below the rate of inflation, which meant that banks were paying their customers to borrow money. And Congress took a giant step toward destroying the credibility of the Fed as a force for maintaining the value of the dollar, declaring in the Humphrey-Hawkins Act that the Fed should consider the impact of its interest-rate decisions on employment as well as on inflation. In 1979, inflation in the United States would reach a rate of 15 percent a year.

R. S. Sayers, the historian of the Bank of England, had written in 1956 that "the worst episodes in recent monetary history–the great inflations–have been marked by the subjection of central bankers to overriding political pressures."[6] Jimmy Carter and G. William Miller, to the extent that they thought about the subject at all, believed this condition was proper. Generations of American schoolchildren had been taught about the separation of powers in the United States, the need for "checks and balances," and the American financial markets had lived through trauma in 1951, when Bill Martin and Tom Mc-Cabe and Marriner Eccles negotiated the "Accord" which made the Fed independent of the Treasury's desire to fund the government at low interest rates. But nobody tied it together. Carter and Miller did not see that the rapid decline of the dollar was a predictor of severe American inflation. In fall 1978, they tried to prop the dollar with a grab-bag of specific remedies, including an American borrowing (for the first and only time) from the IMF and the issuance of U.S. Treasury bonds denominated in marks, Swiss francs, and yen. As part of the package, the Fed raised its discount rate (and the Fed Funds rate) by a full percentage point–and for the first time ever, the increase was announced not by the chairman of the Fed but by the president himself. Treasury Secretary Blumenthal was in the middle of a conversion experience that would leave him "not a team player" in the president's mind and thus ripe for dismissal in summer 1979 after the disappointed president went up to the mountain of Camp David and perceived a national malaise. But Blumenthal's Treasury was institutionally ill-equipped to lead a crusade for a stronger dollar, and Blumenthal himself was not prepared to condemn the policies that had created the crisis: "You have to remember," he said not long after his return to the private sector, "that it was a *Democratic* administration."

Domestically and technically, the Fed found itself hamstrung by the contradictions Sherman Maisel had stressed as a governor. If the Fed targeted interest rates, then it would accommodate any amount of inflationary pressure, simply meeting the demand for money at its established rate, which would become unrealistically low. If it targeted "borrowed reserves," interest rates would rise, but the rise would not stop the growth in the supply of money, because the Fed would continue to supply additional non-borrowed reserves to keep the quantity of borrowed reserves from rising too high. Indeed, while the Fed calculated required reserves on the basis of "lagged" reporting, the amount of reserves required this week was known because it had to be the right fraction of the deposits reported two weeks before, and one way or another, through open market operations or loans at the discount window, the Fed obviously had to make sure the reserves were there.

Maisel and Mitchell, the two economists who served both Martin and Burns, had begun pushing in 1970 for the Fed to lift its sights from the targets it controlled–short-term interest rates and borrowed reserves–to something that spoke more directly to what the economy was doing. Maisel's preference was the "credit proxy"–the total loans in the banking system. Mitchell was more sympathetic to proponents of the "monetary aggregates" as the measuring instrument, though like everyone else at the Fed he had his doubts about the claims of Milton Friedman and his followers that if only the Fed would arrange to increase the money supply steadily at a rate of 4 percent a year, all its and the country's problems would fade away. Maisel was chairman of an in-house "Committee on the Directive" charged with finding new phrases to use when instructing the traders at the Federal Reserve Bank of New York.

By mid-1970, when Arthur Burns had taken over as chairman, Maisel had bought into the idea of asking the open market manager in New York to monitor the growth of M-1 (cash and checking accounts), M-2 (the above plus savings accounts), M-3 (plus large-denomination CDs), and the credit proxy. The desk would still buy and sell U.S. Treasury paper, but it would seek evidence of the effects of its actions in the changing stockpiles of money as well as their effects on "money market conditions."

In the late 1970s, after a decade of sometimes serious inflation, Milton Friedman's tautological insistence that inflation was always a monetary phenomenon had won him growing support among economists and others. Though he wrote music for them, the staff of the Fed was less willing to sing along with Friedman than other people were. He had spoken nasty about them, and, besides, they knew a lot better than he did what the components were in the seemingly simple numbers that came in every day and were published every week. Businesses accumulated cash to pay taxes on certain days; the Treasury put money in and took money from its "tax-and-loan" accounts. Social Security checks were mailed to reach recipients on the third day of the month, but if that was a Sunday and the preceding Friday was a holiday, the money might well pass through on the last day of the previous month, which was also a week earlier than usual in the money supply figures. Christmas came once a year, and holiday weekends when people took cash on their travels changed the demand for cash. Sometimes it snowed and checks were delivered late.

Unfortunately, economics was struggling to look like a science, with second order partial differential equations to enlighten the observer about when things changed and integral equations to measure the impact on the system of changes at the margins. None of this had much to do with the real world, but like every simplifying theorem, it met felt needs. Like the real bills theory of another time and Say's Law (that supply creates its own demand), Friedman's monetarism fit neatly into the psychological demands of his profession. And, of course, economic activity and the money supply tend to correlate pretty well on higher time horizons. David Hume had shown in the eighteenth century that an increase in the money supply had a short-term positive effect on consumption (because people who had more money in their pockets tended to spend more), which might lead to increased production (Roosevelt's hope in the 1930s) or increased prices (Bill Martin's dread in the 1960s), depending on whether or not the economy had excess capacity to meet the rise in demand. Friedman came from the Say's Law school, believing that if only the government got out of the way, the economy would continuously operate at full capacity. Part of the approved process to get the government out of the way was a requirement that the central bank increase the money supply every year by a fixed percentage, achieving price stability by setting that percentage at precisely the growth rate of the economy. Central banks, Friedman argued, hitting them where they lived, should operate on a basis of "rules, not discretion."

A very distinguished economist who had been a student of Friedman's once said something in my hearing that was so preposterous I could not believe I had heard it. I expostulated. He said, "You have to remember that that man is the greatest teacher God ever made." It is the only explanation for the reputation (including one of the earliest Nobel Prize awards in economics). Most of Friedman's policy prescriptions were simply wrong. It was not true that permitting the exchange value of currencies to float would "make us masters in our own house." It was not true that wide swings of interest rates would not matter if everyone knew that the money supply would continue on a straight path. It was not even true that the Fed or any other central bank could in fact determine the effective money supply, partly because when money is hard to come by businessmen find substitutes (and the nature of money, as Sayers put it, "is something determined by the commercial habits of businessmen"), partly because the effective money supply is determined by velocity, how fast the money moves, as well as by quantities. (Indeed, the creation of the money substitutes shows up in the conventional figures as an increase in velocity.) The fundament of Friedman's theory, that velocity was stable or moved on a predictable path, was simply false. Especially when money could leak out to Eastern Europe and Latin America, where it would be used for domestic transaction purposes that had no spillover to the United States, or might well disappear into mattresses.

But whatever his faults, Friedman did speak to the dangers of inflation, and in 1979 nothing else had worked. Prices were moving at a pace that would on the average double the cost of living every five years, and the dollar was plunging in the foreign exchange markets. The Shah of Iran, proprietor of the second largest source of oil to the Americas, was overthrown, and a second "oil shock" boosted prices again. The Europeans complained bitterly that American consumption, paid for by the export of dollars, was exporting inflation to them. Carter removed Blumenthal from Treasury, and filled the vacancy by moving Miller from the Fed. And he asked Paul Volcker, president of the Federal Reserve Bank of New York, formerly undersecretary of the treasury for monetary affairs, to succeed Miller.

Volcker was the first chairman of the Fed for whom the job was a personal sacrifice. His salary as president in New York was almost double what he would be paid in Washington, and the district bank had a much more inclusive health plan, which had taken care of his family's considerable and continuing medical expenses. His wife could not move to Washington; for his eight years as chairman, Volcker maintained an apartment in New York and lived all week in a studio on Capitol Hill. He smoked cheap cigars because he couldn't afford good ones. The son of a public servant, he was and is a man of extraordinary probity and dignity, setting high standards for himself and all around him, unimpressed by the rank, title, or income of the people with whom he does business, and not very receptive to tales of other people's troubles, or to their feelings (he would read the newspapers while the research staff presented their work at meetings of the board). As president of the New York Fed, he had been a permanent member of the Federal Open Market Committee, and he had been one of the most aggressive voices for tightening. At six foot eight, he could be imperiously the man above the battle. Within a month of his accession to the chair, he had pushed through the Board of Governors, by a 4–3 vote, a half-point raise in the discount rate.

The annual meeting of the International Monetary Fund and the World Bank was a month after that, in Belgrade, and Volcker went to Yugoslavia (with Miller) by way of Frankfurt, where they received a memorable tongue-lashing from German chancellor Helmut Schmidt and Bundesbank president Otmar Emminger, who knew that inflation was the easiest tax a weak government could impose—and that the Americans had a very weak government and a budget deficit. The finance ministers and central bank governors assembled in Belgrade were no more enthusiastic. Gold, which Nixon had been unable to raise above $38.25 an ounce in his effort to devalue the dollar in 1971, had risen eight years later to more than $400 an ounce. Volcker left the meeting before the formal sessions began–because they bored him, he says now, which is doubtless true as a detail, for these meetings are usually very boring, but unconvincing as a prime mover. Returning to Washington, he talked things over once more with Miller and Charles Schultze of the Council of Economic Advisers.

Thanks to Maisel and Mitchell, the Fed's staff had for some time been looking at the monetary aggregates. Thanks to Bill Weintraub, staff director of the House Banking Committee who was both a dedicated Democrat and a convinced disciple of Friedman's monetary theories, the law required the Fed to pay some amorphous attention to M-1. Volcker decided the only way to get out of the inflation was to limit the creation of bank reserves, which would in theory limit the growth of M-1. (It would also, though nobody talked that way, make loans more difficult to get from the banks; William C. Melton, who lived through this period as a staff economist at the Fed of New York, notes that "the credit availability view, though badly battered, was alive after all!")[7] Volcker summoned an unprecedented secret Saturday night meeting of the Federal Open Market Committee, where he pushed through–without significant opposition and no recorded dissent–a full point increase in the discount rate (to 12 percent), a new system of additional reserve requirements for any increase in "managed liabilities" (Fed Funds purchases, repurchase agreements, and imported Eurodollars) . . . and a proclamation of "a change in the method used to conduct monetary policy to support the objective of containing growth in the monetary aggregates over the remainder of this year."

The decision on how much the open market desk should supply in reserves for the banking system would be determined by the desired movement of M-1 from week to week. And market interest rates, including the rate for Fed Funds, would rise and fall as the market dictated, without the Fed trying to hold them to a steady path.

The only controls on interest rates that would be left were the "Reg Q" controls on what the banks could pay to retail depositors (which meant that the Board of Governors would continue to sit in solemn conclave every so often to determine how large a television set banks could give purchasers of CDs of different size as a reward for the fact that they didn't get anything like market rates of interest on their money). Miller and Schultze had told Volcker that they "thought" the president disapproved, but Carter himself never called, and Volcker did not solicit his opinion.

In the aftermath, bond prices dropped like a stone and interest rates soared; the Fed Funds rate went over 15 percent. Wall Street had been in the middle of marketing the first ever bond issue for IBM; dealers were left with most of the issue still in their hands, and eventually took a licking of $40–$50 million. The thirty-odd "primary dealers," who had the advantage of dealing directly with Fed traders at the inside price when the open market desk was active, had to be reminded that one of the conditions of their status as primary dealers was that they *always* offered to buy some of the new securities issued by the Treasury. It was a very indirect and expensive and painful way to convince manufacturers, grocers, and landlords (and labor unions) that prices and wages could not be raised indefinitely without losing business.

At the time, I was sure that Volcker's monetarist apparatus was merely a way to justify the much higher interest rates that would be necessary to change inflation expectations in the markets, and I said so in print, praising Volcker for the cleverness with which he had deflected criticism of the real policy to criticism of a theory. He told me I had got it wrong, that he really had converted to monetarism, if not to a pure Friedmanite view. In the book Larry Malkin made of lectures Volcker and Toyoo Gyohten of the Bank of Japan gave at Princeton in 1991, Volcker yielded an inch in this argument: "The general level of interest rates reached higher levels than I or my colleagues had really anticipated," he wrote. "That, in a perverse way was one benefit of the new technique; assuming that those levels of interest were necessary to manage the money supply, I would not have had support for deliberately raising short-term rates that much."[8] Or, as Miller said recently, the people's chairman to the end, "We were using interest rates, Volcker shifted to money supply, but it all boils down to the same thing."

The problem was, it didn't work. It didn't work technically, because the growth of M-1 (and later the other M's, as the Fed changed its targets and Friedman adjusted his theories) turned out not to be closely correlated with changes in non-borrowed bank reserves. And so far as could be seen in the fourth quarter of 1979, it didn't work practically, because the economy did not slow and inflation roared on.

Carter's White House, deluged with complaints from business-people whose plans had been sabotaged by high and wildly fluctuating interest rates, now approached Volcker to let investment grow and target consumer credit directly. It was, after all, an election year, and Carter was standing for reelection. A law from the Nixon days gave the president authority to impose controls on consumer credit without consulting Congress. The Fed would have to administer the controls. Carter wanted to wrap all economic policy—budget, money supply, interest rates, credit controls—into one big ball of wax that he could introduce with a dramatic television presentation, and Volcker perforce had to go along, though he and the other Fed governors were less than pleased with the idea of a compulsory credit control they would have to administer (Volcker had been undersecretary of the treasury when Nixon imposed his incomes policy, and never wanted to live through anything like that again). Nobody felt more strongly than Volcker about the independence of the Fed, but never since 1951 had that independence been so imperiled as it was by Carter's insistence on a unified program.

On March 14, 1980, the president told the country to stop buying, and it did. The credit controls had been targeted especially at department store installment sales and credit cards, with reinforcement through special reserves to be required from the money market funds that had become the big purchasers of finance company commercial paper. Department store sales collapsed, and the White House was snowed under with cut-up credit cards citizens sent in to show how they were supporting the president. In the second quarter of 1980, the gross domestic product dropped more rapidly than in any three-month period ever, including the worst declines of the Great Depression.

As a child of that depression, I thought the game was up. I went to Alabama to give a speech to the Alabama Bankers Association. Several of them said their correspondents in New York were telling them to stock up on cheap money now—the Fed Funds rate had dropped from 20 percent to 8 percent—because by summer rates would be heading up again. I said I thought their correspondents were crazy: the recession had arrived and rates would stay low for a long time. But when the Fed released the credit controls on July 1, the economy and the inflation (which had persisted only slightly diminished through the free fall of the real economy) snapped back to their pre-March levels, and soon the Fed had used up all the slack in the provision of non-borrowed reserves that had developed in the second quarter. Rates soared, and in 1981 the economy entered its worst recession since the 1930s. The only comfort was that the dollar was now buttressed by the very high real rates of interest, and its exchange value began to rise, which helped kill the inflation.

It is worth noting that from the European point of view what had happened was that we stopped exporting our inflation and began exporting our recession. And it is certainly significant that seventeen days after the Carter press conference, Congress passed the Depository Institutions Deregulation and Monetary Control Act of 1980, which made all banks (not just Fed member banks) subject to reserve requirements; compelled the Federal Reserve to make its services, especially check clearing, available to all banks, S&Ls, and credit unions, and to charge for them (they had previously been free to members as a quid pro quo for the reserves on which no interest was paid); and ordered a gradually phased-out elimination of Regulation Q controls on the interest rates banks could pay their depositors. No more free toasters for small deposits and television sets for large ones.

Nothing worked. M-1 was not controlled and could not be predicted; ditto, later, for M-2, which became the measurement of choice after the S&Ls began to issue checkbooks against accounts not included in M-1. Monetarists grumbled that the real problem was lagged reserve accounting, which meant that banks could make loans and create deposits with confidence that two weeks later the Fed would at worst lend them the money at the discount window to keep their reserves in line—so in 1984, the Fed went to contemporaneous reserves accounting, requiring the banks to have enough total reserves in a statement week to cover their total deposits during that week. (We have since returned to lagged accounting, which allows everybody to know what they're doing.) And it didn't help: the M's continued to fluctuate unpredictably—as they did also in other countries that adopted control procedures to target Friedman's aggregates. Obviously, inflation and an expanding money supply go together like chickens and eggs, but it was at least possible that the inflation caused the expanded monetary supply rather than vice versa—and trying to restrain it by holding down the money supply was an impossible mission.

The 1980s were rich in theories of the relationship of money and the economy. We had the Philips curve, which insisted that there was a trade-off between inflation and unemployment (making the Fed's official mission of caring for both a continuing oxymoron). From the Philips curve came NAIRU, the Non-Accelerating Inflation Rate of Unemployment, which said that once unemployment fell below a certain percentage of the workforce, there would be exponentiating inflation. But it wasn't so. To break an inflationary spiral might require the creation of unemployment, because workers cheated of their wages by the inflation tax demanded "cost of living" adjustments that never caught up with the price increases. But it was price increases that compelled (and later paid for) wage increases, not the other way around.

For Volcker, doggedly, the problem was the creation of credibility at the Fed. Interest rates had to remain at historically high levels until people believed that the Fed would put the purchasing power of the dollar ahead of all other considerations. And, of course, he had the Reagan administration ravening in the caves behind him. It never was clear, and it is not clear now, why Reagan's people thought that the combination of a very loose revenue-reducing "supply-side" federal budget with a very tight rein on the money supply would control inflation and stimulate growth enough to cut future deficits. (David Stockman, Reagan's first director of the Office of Management and Budget, former congressman, described the reasoning as "rosy scenario.") The first effect was to strengthen the dollar precipitously, as money poured into America to take advantage of the high interest rates Volcker's Fed was enforcing even as the demand for credit fell. Foreign travel and the purchase of luxury foreign automobiles became great pleasures for the American well-to-do.

The stronger dollar did help stop inflation as imports became cheap, and because our exports became expensive the rust belt rusted faster, industrial America went into shock, the labor unions based on the industrial plant decayed (this was an unintended but from the Reaganite point of view cheerful consequence of the policies), and unemployment reached its highest levels since the Great Depression. Meanwhile, the Latin American countries that had borrowed to pay for more expensive oil in the 1970s (Burns's "bad loans") were tortured as the interest rates they had to pay to roll over their debt skyrocketed to the moon. In July 1982, the Dow Jones Industrial Average was where it had been in 1968, hovering around 1,000, which meant that in constant dollars the value of the most widely held stocks had dropped by almost three-fifths.

All this Volcker accepted as part of the cost of achieving credibility for the Fed, and the Reagan administration accepted it because Volcker was following monetarist orthodoxy. The undersecretary of the treasury for monetary affairs was Beryl Sprinkel, a rotund economist of the Chicago School, who came to public service from the First National Bank of Chicago. Shortly after he moved into that post, his predecessors gave a dinner for him in New York–Robert Roosa (who had become head of Brown Brothers Harriman), Fred

Deming of the Minneapolis Fed, Jack Bennett (who had become treasurer of Exxon with a $5 billion-dollar book of foreign exchange to manage), Volcker himself, Ed Yeo (who had negotiated with Jacques de Larosière the deal that amended the IMF's articles of agreements to permit floating exchange rates), and Tony Solomon (who had become president of the Federal Reserve Bank of New York). These were men who agreed on nothing, Republicans and Democrats, Keynesians and monetarists, but after Sprinkel had left the dinner to go home to Washington, they did reach agreement on one proposition: Beryl was in over his head.

Volcker's new system for enforcing monetary policy put Sprinkel in a box. As a Friedmanite, he held a religious belief that the economy was controlled by the numbers in some monetary aggregate. Volcker's Fed by vote of the Federal Open Market Committee in its last meeting of each year set its goals for the next year in terms of percentages of growth in the monetary aggregates. Lines were drawn on graphs to show the minimum and maximum quantities of money that should be out there as time went by. If the actual numbers came in to either side of the line on the graph for several weeks running, there might be a mid-course correction in the goals (perhaps something as simple as re-basing the lines, keeping the percentages but moving the point of origin from the money supply on the date the percentages were declared to the money supply at the date of the revision), to make sure that the Fed was not forced to do terrible violence to the real economy to make the numbers work. As a matter of faith and morals, Sprinkel in his criticisms (which were the White House criticisms, Treasury's Regan being innocent of economics) had to concentrate on the failure to meet the monetary growth targets, not on the 20 percent plus interest rates that were doing the damage–or were the agents of restraint, depending on your view.

In early 1982, Fred Schultz, a Florida banker, resigned as vice chairman of the Fed and returned to his bank, and Reagan appointed to the post Preston Martin, a tall, bony, cool drink of water from California, the former builder and college professor who had been chairman of the Federal Home Loan Bank Board in the first Nixon administration. On leaving the bank board, Pres had founded a mortgage-insurance company that he sold to Sears, and in 1981, footloose and fancy free, he became a commissioner on the President's Commission on Housing. I was a commissioner too, and saw a fair amount of Pres, who was a good ally to have when you agreed with him, a man of dry wit and irreverent attitude if conventional views. He persuaded me, much against my better judgment, to vote with him in approving direct investments in real estate by insured S&Ls, because I felt I didn't know enough to refute his argument that without a sizable equity share in the enterprises to which it lent money, an S&L could not survive in a world where interest rates were on a roller-coaster. Pres left the Housing Commission in 1982, when Reagan appointed him vice chairman of the Fed, and he assumed that he would succeed Volcker when Volcker's term expired the next year. As a housing man, he made no bones of his belief that monetary policy was too tight, which endeared him to the yahoos in the White House (and to William Greider, who made him a hero in his book *Secrets of the Temple*), but added to the insiders' perception that he lacked the gravitas for the chair.

Pres Martin's inability to get a boom started for himself, even in Congress, where he had many more friends than Volcker had, eventually led him to resign from the Fed. If credibility was the target, Volcker was necessarily the Guillaume Tell. By then, Volcker had begun to loosen the reins, and the stock market was up. If anyone else were chairman of the Fed and loosening, the market might well disapprove. Not very happily, Sprinkel and Regan and Reagan accepted the need to reappoint him in 1983.

By 1985, the lawyer James Baker III having replaced Don Regan at Treasury and Sprinkel having achieved cabinet rank as chairman of the Council of Economic Advisers, the executive branch was tired of Volcker's hair shirt and conspired to loosen monetary restraints much further. Baker's co-conspirators were the finance ministers of the other large industrial nations, none of whom shared much of their thinking with their own central bankers. By early September, they were ready to go with the program of announcements and interventions that became known as the Plaza Agreement, after the hotel in New York where they met and proclaimed that the dollar was greatly overvalued and should depreciate in the market.

The Treasury and not the Fed has the responsibility for managing the *foreign* value of the currency, but in a market-driven world the quantity of dollars on offer would strongly affect the success of Baker's plan. (At the ceremony in 2000 unveiling the portrait of Robert Rubin as treasury secretary, President Bill Clinton noted that Rubin had ruled when he took the job that nobody but himself could speak about the exchange value of the dollar, and nobody but Greenspan could speak about interest rates, leaving the president tongue-tied in economic matters.) Volcker did not disagree that the dollar was overvalued in 1985, though having lived through the chaos of 1971–72 as undersecretary for monetary affairs he had a visceral objection to official statements denigrating the currency. And he would not permit the Fed's *domestic* actions to be controlled by Baker's international objections. If other countries sold their dollars for marks and yen, there would be a tendency for American interest rates to rise, which would tend to brake the Plaza process, keep interest rates high, and presumably keep the dollar strong. Automatic rebalancings in markets did not end with the demise of the gold standard. The Fed was happy enough to help with concerted intervention in the marketplace to punish traders who didn't believe what Baker had told them, but it would not follow through by acting to reduce rates domestically.

Relations with Baker were inescapably tricky. Baker was a Texan through and through, which meant that he cared deeply that oil prices stay high enough to support the marginal Texas producer. (Later, when he was George Bush's secretary of state, he would plead with the Arabs to enforce their cartel to help Texas oil producers.) His family had a long-standing connection with Texas Commerce Bank, and its sale to Chemical (now Chase) while he was treasury secretary brought profits in the high eight figures to the blind trust that handled his affairs while he served in government.

And he had his own "Baker Plan" solution to the heavy indebtedness of the poor countries, a solution that involved maintaining the pretense that there were no losses from the "bad loans." In Baker's proposal, which was more or less adopted, banks could in essence pay themselves the interest they claimed on their loans to foreign countries and banks by increasing the total size of the debt, meanwhile claiming profits from "renegotiation fees" taken down to the bottom line the day the deal closed. Volcker like other central bankers had considerable sympathy for any plan that postponed the recognition of losses and improved the reported profitability of American banks. (After I testified before Senator John Heinz and the Senate Banking Committee about the multiple iniquities of having banks report instant profits from the renegotiation of doubtful loans to poor countries that couldn't service their existing debt, Volcker told the senators that I had a tendency to see big problems where there were only minor questions of how to interpret accounting rules.) Volcker had propped up the banks by joining de Larosière of the IMF in insisting in 1983 that they had to roll over their Third World loans, and permitting them to continue to carry the paper at "historic cost" in reporting their results.

But the liaison between Treasury and the Fed in international matters had become so bad that the Fed often learned what Baker was doing from American banks or fellow central bankers abroad. Baker reorganized the Treasury, eliminating the post of undersecretary for monetary affairs which had been the liaison point with the Fed when Volcker and his mentor Robert Roosa had held the job. Baker's assistant secretary for international affairs was David Mulford, a veteran of Citibank and White Weld, very smart, impeccably dressed, the man on the wedding cake complete to little mustache, with a haughty manner and accent that told you instantly that he did not expect you ever to operate on his social or intellectual level. One of the pleasures of Washington during Mulford's tenure was to go to a hearing of the House Banking Committee where Chairman Henry Gonzalez, the hefty, ruminative, hardworking Hispanic from San Antonio, deceptively slow-spoken, tortured Mulford not only with his questions but with his power to keep Mulford sitting at the witness table and listening to his comments. In the little book Volcker and Gyohten published together, Mulford's name occurs twice in Gyohten's memories, but never in Volcker's.

But Mulford was not a joke: he as the lead American negotiator must take a share of the blame for the collapse of the Russian transition to a more civilized economy. He was belligerently insistent during the key years that no help could be given to the new Russia unless it accepted responsibility for servicing *in full* the debts of the former Soviet Union.

By 1986, deaths and resignations had created enough slots for Reagan appointees to hold a majority of the board. Manuel Johnson, a college professor from George Mason University, then known for right-wing views, came on the board with Wayne Angell, a pioneer in financial technology who believed that expanding the use of derivatives instruments to smooth the impact of monetary policy would cure what ailed the Friedmanite argument. By February 1986, the new governors had the votes to override Volcker and reduce the discount rate over his objections–though he still had the clout to get the vote reversed in the afternoon. At the start of a congressional election year (in which, in fact, the Republicans were to lose control of the Senate, though they were scarcely imagining that in February), the White House wanted lower rates, but did not dare risk the disruption that Volcker's resignation would have created.[9]

For the next year, a strange quadrille played out between the White House and the Fed. Volcker wanted to go; indeed, he had promised his wife when reappointed in 1983 that he would not serve a four-year term, and when asked by Senator Proxmire (D-Wis, chairman of the Senate Banking Committee) at his confirmation hearings whether he would serve the full term, he had said no. James Baker, now treasury secretary, always devious, thought he was maneuvering to get Volcker out, knowing that if Volcker had told Reagan he wanted to stay, the old man would have welcomed his continuance. So Volcker took the initiative and told Baker to tell Reagan that he wanted out. (At his subsequent meeting with Reagan he suggested two possible replacements: John Whitehead from Goldman, Sachs and Alan Greenspan.) It was a difficult year on the job. The dollar overshot on the way down, and in February 1987 the finance ministers of the big countries decided that having pushed it down they could now push it some distance back up. As the bond market quickly realized, that would require increases in U.S. interest rates, which the Fed's staff economists considered unwise; they (wrongly) saw a recession coming.

Volcker left with the Dow at 2700, which would be its high for the next three years. I was then writing a column for *American Banker,* and I compared Reagan's willingness to see Volcker go to the decision by Kaiser Wilhelm II to dismiss Bismarck, which prompted the great Tenniel cartoon *Dropping the Pilot.* By sheer force of personality, Volcker had in fact reestablished the credibility of the Fed. But there was no escaping the fact that he had left behind a theoretical shambles. Stopping inflation had required the imposition of interest rates high enough to throttle enterprise: only brute force had worked. It was still unclear whether a central bank could successfully stimulate a troubled economy. Targeting interest rates, non-borrowed reserves, borrowed reserves, monetary aggregates–all had failed to achieve with anything resembling acceptable efficiency the results the Fed had intended. Alan Greenspan, Volcker's successor, would have to start from scratch.

Chapter 10

Greenspan and the Markets

Assessing the role of asset prices in the conduct of monetary policy raises a range of issues. In many countries, central banks are charged with promoting financial stability. Since asset price cycles can trigger systemic banking failures and, along with credit cycles, often precede sharp economic downturns, some contend that it might be provident to target financial variables directly. However, unlike a target for inflation, it is difficult to quantify financial stability, and therefore it is not easy to know when asset prices threaten that stability. Moreover, there is the obvious difficulty of determining exactly what asset price should be targeted among the many potential candidates and, once chosen, what its target level should be. . . .

— *70th Annual Report,* Bank for International Settlements[1]

ALAN GREENSPAN, IMMEDIATELY ANNOUNCED as Volcker's replacement, was hailed as a savior by the supply-side cadre around Reagan and his vice president George Bush, who had been afraid Volcker might raise rates again and choke the economy in the election year 1988. But connoisseurs of central banking were of two minds. He was a queer duck, Greenspan, an owlish fellow a full foot shorter than Volcker, something of Woody Allen about him, a onetime music student and professional saxophone player. He had run an economic forecasting and consulting business since 1954, with time off to be chairman of the Council of Economic Advisers for Gerald Ford from 1974 to 1977. In his youth he had been a devotee of Ayn Rand, the right-wing philosopher/novelist, and had contributed to her magazine *The Objectivist* (for July 1966, when he was already forty years old) a truly nutty screed in praise of gold: "This is the shabby secret of the welfare statists' tirades against gold. Deficit spending is simply a scheme for the 'hidden' confiscation of wealth. Gold stands in the way of this insidious process. It stands as a protector of property rights. If one grasps this, one has no difficulty in understanding the statists' antagonism toward the gold standard."

Greenspan was an active Republican (he noted in his *Who's Who* entry that he had been a member of the Nixon for President Committee in 1968–69). He sat on the boards of Morgan, Mobil, General Foods, and Alcoa, among others, and he was a trustee of the Hoover Institution that was on the Stanford campus but had been kept separate from Stanford for fear that the university would have trouble recruiting faculty troubled by its right-wing orientation. In general, Greenspan's political philosophy was that whatever is, is right.

Still, the fact of the matter was that Greenspan had been an outstanding chairman of the council for Ford, and with help from Senator Patrick Moynihan of New York (who would later refer to him as a "national treasure") had maneuvered an intelligent set of proposals through the National Commission on Social Security Reform, which he chaired. Without for a moment abandoning his former beliefs (questioned at a congressional hearing in 1998 about the prospective uses of gold in international monetary affairs by Representative Ron Paul of Texas, a medical doctor infected with the gold bug, Greenspan said that he shared many of Paul's views, "but as you know we are the only two people in the world who do share them"), Greenspan as Fed chairman turned out to be entirely pragmatic.

Indeed, he turned out to be a great chairman, his accomplishments capped by the longest economic expansion in American history, by the good judgment that Drexel Burnham could be deep-sixed without harm to the financial or economic system, by his conversion of a deeply secretive institution into a more open institution, and by his triumph in the Gramm-Leach-Bliley Act of 1999, which enthroned the Federal Reserve System as the umbrella regulator of financial services enterprise in the United States. This new empire will require a lot more staff, and the Fed has already slopped over from its own two buildings to rented space on New York Avenue, two blocks away. The existing buildings are named for Marriner Eccles and William McChesney Martin, Jr. The new one, without doubt, whoever becomes Greenspan's successor and actually approves the building, will be named for Alan Greenspan.

Like Bill Martin, Greenspan is a good guy, which makes a difference. It is a remarkable experience to sit behind him while he testifies before the House Banking Committee, an unwieldy group with forty plus members all of whom consider themselves competent to question the chairman of the Fed. They ask the most ignorant and irrelevant questions, and Greenspan responds courteously to each, translating it into something that might have some meaning, and then answers with care, qualifying his responses to unimportant questions with the same detail that he qualifies his responses to good questions. For hours on end: like the Eveready Bunny, Greenspan just keeps going and going.

He did not have particularly warm relations with James Baker or Nicholas Brady, Reagan's and Bush's treasury secretaries, who ate their ritual weekly breakfasts with the chairman but maintained the long-standing institutional hostility of Treasury and Fed. (At one point, Brady cancelled his meals with Greenspan, who didn't much care.) Playing the international arena, Treasury insisted that economic relations were its fiefdom, whatever the Fed or the State Department might think. The argument about how to settle the Third World debt crisis of the 1980s persisted until 1990, when Nicholas Brady's adventurous deputies, especially Wall Street banker George Gould and Harvard Business School professor Robert Glauber, designed the "Brady bond" that would permit borrowers to write down some of the face value of their debt. Greenspan, like Volcker, was dead set against debt relief because it would force American banks to recognize what might be crippling losses, and encourage fecklessness in Third World borrowers. Brady chose a Washington meeting of business leaders, politicians, and academics as the venue to announce the new plan. Among those in attendance was Edwin Truman, director of the Fed's international relations staff, who scrambled with the press to get the text of Brady's speech as it was delivered to the ballroom where the meeting was held. Brady had not given the Fed the courtesy of an advance look.

The move to a Democratic presidency oddly helped relations between Greenspan and the Treasury. Clinton, who brought the art of co-opting to new heights, cultivated Greenspan (he sat next to Hillary in the balcony for the new president's first State of the Union Address). Lloyd Bentsen as treasury secretary was more *simpatico* than Baker or Brady, and from many years on the Senate Finance Committee knew where all the sore spots were. His successor Robert Rubin and Greenspan definitively buried the old hatchet of antagonism between the Fed and Treasury. They had various shared experiences from civilian life (Rubin as managing partner of Goldman, Sachs had known the CEOs of the companies where Greenspan was on the board) and a similar sense of humor: they liked each other, and considered each other allies in the never-ending war against economic ignorance in government. When Rubin needed cover from congressional incomprehension–especially in the Mexican loan situation in early 1995, when the newly elected Republican majorities were feeling their oats and whinnying like crazy, when Newt Gingrich and Robert Dole, having appeared at the White House with the president and Rubin to assure the world that the Congress would help the government cope with crisis in Mexico, couldn't deliver their own people–Greenspan testified that the Treasury was doing the right thing. According to Bob Woodward, he did even more. The radio talker Rush Limbaugh, Woodward writes, "was giving Gingrich a hard time, having great fun denouncing him and ridiculing the Speaker's support to give away $40 billion of U.S. taxpayer money south of the border."[2] At Gingrich's request,

Greenspan called Limbaugh and took ten minutes of his time trying (unsuccessfully, of course) to convince him that the Mexican loan would be okay (as it was). Imagination refuses to write a scenario in which Eccles or Martin or Volcker would call Rush Limbaugh on the telephone to seek his approval of public policy.

Greenspan was bloodied almost immediately after taking office in August 1987. The market peaked (the Dow reached 2700) at about the time he became chairman, and began drifting down, responding belatedly, as stock markets will, to the sell-off in the bonds that had occurred the previous spring. As a private-sector forecaster, Greenspan had thought the market was a bubble likely to burst, and on taking office he asked the Fed's research staff to accelerate its work on the likely dangers to the economy and the banking system of a recession led by a decline in stock prices, like those of 1974–75 and 1981–82. The almost 300-point drop on October 14–16, 1987, had left him like the traders very insecure about what would come next. Still, he had a date to speak to an American Bankers Association convention in Dallas on October 19, and he went off to Dallas midday with the market down about 200 points. Met at the airplane by the president of the Federal Reserve Bank of Dallas, his first question was about how the market closed, and he was relieved by the answer: "Five oh eight," reading it as 5.08 points. He expressed himself greatly relieved by the recovery that must have occurred in the last hours, and then learned the full extent of the disaster. Thirteen years later, it is breathtaking to think that there was no system by which the chairman of the Fed, on a commercial airliner, could be kept abreast of the greatest one-day market collapse in history. Greenspan left a surrogate to deliver his written speech, and returned to Washington.

For this was nothing like the simulations: it was much, much worse. Tuesday morning at 8:41 Eastern Standard Time, with trading in the S&P 500 index futures about to open at the Chicago Mercantile Exchange, Greenspan put out a statement: "The Federal Reserve, consistent with its responsibilities as the nation's central bank, affirmed today its readiness to serve as a source of liquidity to support the economic and financial system."[3] In New York, the open market desk was boosting bank reserves by purchasing Treasury securities from all the primary dealers, especially the banks. Greenspan has noted that it was not very difficult to know what to do on October 20—one had to give prospective buyers of securities the resources and (if possible) the will to buy. There were many hands to be held, especially in Chicago, where four "collecting" banks handled all the movement of cash into and out of the participants in the commodities exchanges, using FedWire to effect transfers—and FedWire had crashed.

For Greenspan, the real challenge was in the months that followed. Clearly, the liquidity that had been poured into the stock and commodities markets in October had to be withdrawn: the gains against inflation won at such cost by Volcker could not be thrown away. At the same time, everyone of Greenspan's generation was terrified by the likely consequences of a market crash in the real economy. In early December, I was on a platform with Maurice Mann, formerly president of the Federal Home Loan Bank of San Francisco and then president of the Pacific Stock Exchange, an amiable, rotund, very funny Bostonian economist who had worked at the Fed and at the Council of Economic Advisers as a young man. We were listening to a youthful expert in mortgage securities discourse about the likely trend of the economy after the crash, and we both shook our heads at his optimism. "He just doesn't know what we know," Maury said. "He hasn't lived through it."

Greenspan's triumph was his ability to forget what he "knew." By December, he thought there was an outside chance that the stock market and the real economy had become sufficiently disjoined that the worst crash in history would have only minor impact on the real world of getting and spending. As the demand for credit rose, he permitted interest rates to rise with it. The word that went out to the desk in New York from the meetings of the Federal Open Market

Committee was "Steady as she goes," and Peter Sternlight, the manager of the desk, worked wonders of delicacy in selling from the Fed's recently increased hoard of Treasuries, withdrawing the liquidity that had been added at the crash.

Few events have been so thoroughly studied as the 1987 market crash, most notably by the Brady Commission, chaired by Nicholas Brady (then of Dillon, Read & Co.), who would become treasury secretary for George Bush, with staffs directed by Robert Glauber, later undersecretary of the treasury, and David Mullins, soon to be vice chairman of the Fed, both Harvard Business School young grandees. The report was ready in January 1988. Its most publicized conclusion was that in the modern age of cheap and instantaneous communications, there was only "one market . . . what have been traditionally seen as separate markets—the markets for stocks, stock index futures, and stock options—are in fact one market. Under ordinary circumstances, these market-places move sympathetically, linked by financial instruments, trading strategies, market participants and clearing and credit mechanisms."[4] And the growth of large pools of international capital meant that all the world's markets for financial instruments were becoming linked. The crash had been so violent, the authors argued, because the separate markets for the connected instruments had failed to function together; when liquidity dried up in one market, participants were forced to go to the others to execute their strategies.

A point noted in passing was the fact that positions and the hedges against the positions were acquired in different markets. This meant that in stressful conditions the gains on the hedge could not quickly be used as offsets to the losses on the position. Even in the futures market, a zero-sum game where every price movement created winnings for some to equal the losings of others, the greater volatility meant that the exchanges had to require higher deposits ("margins") against the value of the contracts. These higher deposits in turn meant that the payouts from the winning bets were less than the losses that had to be met on the losing bets—and cash demands from the losers were then increased by the rise in the required margins. The task force called for the creation of a system that would permit "cross-margining. . . . Market participants with an investment in futures should be allowed to receive credit for an offsetting, or hedged, investment in stocks or options."[5] This was trickier than the authors of the task force realized (and it is by no means clear what they thought they meant with the "or hedged" in the preceding sentence). It is the essence of a clearinghouse that every member is responsible if necessary for the payments due from every other member; in the language of the trade, everybody's ass is on the table. Leo Melamed of the Chicago Mercantile Exchange likes to say that each member of the Merc clearing is "good to the last drop." One notes that the large Wall Street houses do business at the Chicago Mercantile Exchange through separately incorporated subsidiaries to limit those risks.

Asking a clearinghouse to give full faith and credit to another clearinghouse, which is what the task force was recommending, demands more than commercial caution will give. Unless, of course, there is a government backup—so the task force did, tentatively, with no encouragement from the Fed, suggest that the Federal Reserve might be the appropriate "agency [to] coordinate the few, but critical regulatory issues which have an impact across the related market segments and through the financial system."

In Basle, Alexandre Lamfalussy, the schoolmasterly, brilliant manager of the Bank for International Settlements—a Belgian who spoke all the European languages—decided that the clearinghouses had to be beefed up. Under his guidance, a BIS Committee on Interbank Netting Schemes wrote a set of six "standards" to guide their operations. The fourth standard was that "Multilateral netting systems should, at a minimum, be capable of ensuring the timely completion of daily settlements in the event of an inability to settle by the participant with the largest single net debit position."[6] The Lamfalussy standards were adopted by the New York Clearing House for its computerized international CHIPS system, and Jill Considine, a no-nonsense blonde who had been New York State commissioner of banking, was recruited to be president and install them. At the heart of the new procedures at CHIPS was a required decision by each member bank about how large a net payment promised for the clearing at the close of the day it would accept from each other member bank. The limit on the amount a bank could enter into the system in excess of the payments others had entered for its account was then calculated at 5 percent of the total of the bilateral limits imposed by the other CHIPS member banks. The New York Clearing House required that 1.5 percent of this total then be collateralized by U.S. Treasury bills and notes held in escrow but available to settle accounts if a bank could not transfer in the money it had promised to pay at the clearing.

The Fed itself ran a "gross settlements" wire transfer payments system–FedWire–in which Bank A paid Bank B by immediate transfer of some of its reserves at its district Fed. As the head of a rival, private-sector wire transfer system said shortly before his enterprise went out of business, payment through FedWire is like pushing gold under the door. It's totally irrevocable: having received the money, you own it. If the paying bank does not have the reserves at his district bank to make the payments, the district bank will give him a "daylight overdraft." Until 1985, these daylight overdrafts–which might run over $100 billion in the middle of the day, after yesterday's repurchase agreements have been unwound and today's have not yet been consummated–were essentially uncontrolled. Then the board introduced a plan of voluntary restraint, in which each bank set a cap on how much credit it would demand from its Fed on an intraday basis and pledged to live within the cap, though in fact the district banks allowed their members to exceed their caps. On October 20, 1987, the total of these overdrafts was quite substantial, and everybody was unhappy at the extent of the risk of loss these unsecured loans represented. It would be difficult to explain to Congress why and how the Federal Reserve System had lost $17 billion. "The government," Vice Chairman George Mitchell growled at the Fed's Williamsburg conference on payments, "had no business giving free credit to banks. What banks want to do with their customers is their own business."

In 1988, the voluntary caps were reduced by 25 percent, and the district banks were tolled off to pay attention. In 1994, after the disturbances we shall note later in this chapter, the board reluctantly imposed an interest charge for intraday loans. The calculation was remarkably obscure. The rate was advertised as 0.24 percent. This is an annual rate, so the actual fee to the borrower is 0.24 percent of the day's maximum overdraft divided by 365. This was further reduced because FedWire was then open only ten hours a day, which took the rate down to 0.1 percent/365–about $2.70 interest for every $1 million borrowed. In addition, a bank was entitled to a credit of 10 percent of its capital before interest was charged, an interesting privilege when one considers that overdrafts meant a bank had exhausted its reserves. The rate on daylight overdrafts was to rise in steps to 0.6 percent in 1996, but in fact the increase was never imposed.

The truth of the matter is that FedWire was in competition with CHIPS, and the Fed staff feared that if the Fed charged interest on daylight overdrafts, the banks would switch their business to the New York Clearing House, where cash payments did not have to be made until 5:00 P.M. (And CHIPS was more efficient to use: Donald P. Monley of what was then Irving Trust complained in 1988 that he needed only seven people to work his CHIPS payments as against seventy people for an equivalent amount of FedWire payments because CHIPS fed his payments directly into his computer while FedWire had to be taken off by hand.) It was not until CHIPS completed its compliance with the Lamfalussy standards, limiting the payments banks could enter for later settlement and requiring collateralization, that the Fed moved at all. Two months later, a report by Furash & Co. to the Bankers Roundtable warned that "many institutions are moving billions of payment dollars from FedWire to CHIPS to avoid overdraft charges."[7] Under these circumstances, the Fed definitely did not wish to impose a requirement for collateral in connection with daylight overdrafts–especially as this collateral would have to be drained from the banks' capital, and that was too shallow a pool already.

In the end, then, seeking risk reduction, the Fed and the Bank for International Settlements recommended an emphasis on bilateral netting between participants in the markets rather than multilateral netting through the clearinghouses. This was a surprise, and not a pleasant one. No article of faith is more tenaciously held in the community of finance economists and central bankers than the belief that diversification diminishes risk. Moreover, the clearinghouse as a collective has both the incentive and the capacity to police the condition and behavior of its members, while the individual bank is poorly placed and poorly motivated to judge its counterparties—especially in a world where central banks have installed an implicit safety net under every bank of any size. The London Metals Exchange, which permitted sellers to extend credit to those who bought from them, virtually collapsed when the tin market crashed (and later cost Sumitomo Bank more than $1 billion because copper trades could be executed with nobody the wiser), while New York's Comex commodities and options clearinghouse sailed through the greater disaster of the Hunt brothers' silver speculations simply by changing its rules.

As the Long Term Capital Management fiasco of 1998 was to demonstrate, the narrower base of bilateral settlements gives rise to complacency even as a trusted counterparty expands its lists of lenders to avoid creating concern among those already supplying its funds. "Correspondent banking" had been the norm before the creation of the Federal Reserve, and had been profoundly unstable, a source of the crises that rocked the markets. Now, in a late-twentieth-century context, with the exciting, mathematically complex, and highly leveraged world of derivatives instruments taking over as a source of risks and returns for the largest banks, the Federal Reserve helped create an operational infrastructure that diminished the amount and quality of information available both to the market and to the regulators. It *felt* safer, because the raw numbers of monies passing through the clearinghouse were lower, but in real life two-party netting and the reduction of flows through the clearinghouse would eventually become a threat to the system.

This was done on Alan Greenspan's watch, sometimes with and sometimes without his personal support. In the end, this willingness to have the banks conceal their risks behind over-the-counter bilateral settlements may prove to be the peril point of Greenspan's otherwise constructive legacy, and a major cause of financial crisis.

Looking back from the year 2001, Alan Greenspan's long reign as chairman of the Board of Governors, including the longest peacetime economic expansion in American history, seems a tale of placid progress, disturbed only by a need to repair the follies of foreigners. In fact, a lot of decisions had to be made, the gates were often strait, and 20/20 hindsight perceives that an astonishing percentage of the monetary policy decisions were right. Revisionist history will say Greenspan was lucky, and he would be the last to deny it. But Pasteur's comment that chance favors the prepared mind applies here as elsewhere. Those of us who were skeptical at the start owe him an apology. Writing in my *American Banker* column about the announcement that Greenspan would succeed Volcker, I said snottily that Volcker's "successor, while doubtless qualified, is a much more political fellow, and the record of our time is that when the Fed chairman is a political fellow–a Thomas McCabe, an Arthur Burns, a William Miller–we get inflation."[8] And I shouldn't've. Bill Clinton's tribute when he reappointed Greenspan for a fourth term in early 2000 was the correct evaluation: Greenspan led the Fed, Clinton said, "with a rare combination of technical expertise, sophisticated analysis, and old-fashioned common sense."

Greenspan also deserves credit, though I did not give it to him at the time, for his management of the severe downturn in the banking industry in 1989–91, when the profitability of the middling-sized bank fell from its traditional 1 percent of assets to something like 0.6 percent and most large banks would have been in the red if anybody had enforced honest accounting and valuation standards on them. The problems were bad in lending to "developing" countries, worse in loans to the merger-and-acquisition business, worst of all in commercial real estate, where a frenzy of construction in the second half of the 1980s had put American banks in competition with Japanese banks and American S&Ls (newly liberated by the Reagan "reforms" to lend in this area) for the privilege of financing an oversupply of office buildings and shopping malls. The S&L industry in its entirety had a negative net worth, and only a minority of the nation's larger thrifts were solvent.

Through the agency of the Federal Savings and Loan Insurance Corporation, a dependency of the regulatory Federal Home Loan Bank Board, the government had guaranteed the repayment of the deposits tens of millions of Americans had put into the S&Ls. The insurance fund was broke, and with the mounting publicity about this disaster after the 1988 election (both parties had agreed not to talk about the subject during the campaign, there being much blame for both), people were beginning to think about taking their money out. One of the gimmicks the bank board had used to keep thrifts afloat was the issuance of FSLIC notes. The S&Ls could then take these notes to their district Home Loan Banks and get cash by pledging them against loans from those banks. As early as 1987, there had been $100 billion of these FSLIC notes in the vaults of the district Home Loan Banks. Each of these banks had its own regional directors responsible for its performance, and they had grown itchy about taking FSLIC notes as collateral. It was clear that at some point Congress was going to have to appropriate large sums (the best guess in early 1989 was $150 billion) to build up the assets in the S&Ls to the point where their value matched the deposit liabilities–and clear, too, that Congress hated the very idea, and was in no hurry to act. During its first month in office, with heavy publicity, the Bush administration introduced legislation "to clean up the S&L mess."

In early February 1989, L. William Seidman of the FDIC told Manuel Johnson, then vice chairman of the Fed, that thanks to all the bad publicity there might be a run on the S&Ls over Presidents Weekend in 1989. They would need fresh loans. Seidman's suggestion was an arrangement under which 45 percent of the money would come from the Federal Home Loan Banks, 45 percent from the Federal Reserve Banks, and 10 percent from FSLIC's not-yet-drawn-upon $750 million statutory line of credit at the Treasury. Under the 1980 Depository Institutions Deregulation and Monetary Control Act, the district Feds had the authority to lend money at the discount window to the S&Ls in their region. Greenspan was holed up in a hotel, writing his semiannual report to Congress on employment and money, perhaps the most challenging political task a Fed chairman has, and didn't want to touch this one with a pole. Johnson arranged a telephone meeting of the presidents of the twelve district Federal Reserve Banks, and told them that in this emergency it was necessary for them to appoint him as their lending officer de facto to make advances to the S&Ls, regardless of the quality of the collateral. Three of the presidents objected, saying they had to consult with their boards, but the other nine went along.

The major resistance came from within the Home Loan Bank system. William McKenna, who was a loyal Republican but had been involved as a young lawyer in drafting the original Home Loan Bank bill in Roosevelt days, had become chairman of the Federal Home Loan Bank of San Francisco. (He had also been chairman of Ronald Reagan's National Commission on Housing.) He felt he had fiduciary responsibilities, and he knew perfectly well that the S&Ls that would apply for these loans did not have suitable collateral to secure them. The bank board deposed him as chairman, but he remained on the board, where his influence was primary, and the San Francisco Home Loan Bank, located where the greatest fraction of the loans would have to be made, refused to sign on until one of the members of the bank board flew out from Washington and warned that if thwarted, the administration could tear down the Home Loan Bank system. This played out in the press as purely a Home Loan Banks story, but at Greenspan's testimony the week after, Representative John LaFalce, into whose ear a little birdie had put a little information, asked the chairman about the plan, receiving a white-faced reply that it was too sensitive to discuss in public. In the end, to Greenspan's fury, the only S&L to receive these emergency loans was Charley Keating's Lincoln Savings & Loan, on its way out.

The people–like me–who had opposed Seidman's plan and were outraged by the Fed's participation in it were right in principle, but Greenspan in tolerating it was right in practice. Our fear was that Congress, given any excuse to do nothing, would fail to stanch the bleeding in the S&Ls, which were in fact losing money at a rate in the billions every month. A couple of failed S&Ls, with infuriated depositors told they might have a long wait for their money, would light what we saw as a necessary fire under the seats of the mighty. But under the surface of the S&L problem was the larger problem of the real estate collapse that had already devastated the Texas banks and was about to strike in New England, collapsing once and for all Michael Dukakis's "Massachusetts Miracle." The country was in fact well served on this as on other occasions by Greenspan's dislike of anything violent or irrevocable.

Where Greenspan got lucky was in the aftermath of the 1990–91 recession, which the Fed fought by throwing previously unimaginable amounts of money into the markets. The visible component of the problem was the fact that the banks weren't making commercial loans. Net private borrowing in the United States fell from $389 billion in 1990 to $198 billion in 1991; the non-financial business sector, which had borrowed $124 billion in 1990, repaid $36 billion net of new borrowings in 1991. This phenomenon could, of course, have causes on either side: there could be a "credit crunch," or companies were not borrowing. Greenspan testified several times before congressional committees about the "headwinds" that were preventing the economy from progressing. Interest on Fed Funds was brought down to 3 percent, below the rate of inflation, to encourage borrowers and to create a steeply sloping yield curve (long rates were affected more by the inflation rate than by Fed rate cuts, and, indeed, the rate cuts at the short end of the spectrum were an argument for demanding more interest to lend long). Because banks borrow short and lend long, a steeply sloping yield curve improves their profitability–and encourages them to lend.

A favored explanation of the banks' lassitude was that their loans had been classified and written down by the bank examiners–especially those from the FDIC, where Bill Seidman wanted to be absolutely sure he could never be subjected to the criticisms of laxity that had bombarded the bank board after the carelessly examined S&Ls collapsed. My own explanation was that the accounting firms that audited the banks had also audited the S&Ls, and were actually being sued for large sums of money for their failure to spot the fraud. They, not the examiners, were compelling banks to recognize loan losses. I buttressed my argument with extensive quotes from a letter sent to all accounting firms that had bank clients by A. A. Somers, chairman of the Public Oversight Board of the American Institute of Certified Public Accountants, warning that if they were not tough on the banks, they risked the end of their profession as they had known it.[9]

The Fed poured money on the banking system. M-1, the total of cash and checkable deposits, rose 12.6 percent between December 1991 and December 1992, the fastest one-year growth in history. In fact, the economy did slowly turn during the course of the year–but not fast enough to keep George Bush from being clobbered by Clinton operatives under the banner "It's the Economy, Stupid." Greenspan's Fed was left with the problem that the growth in the money supply had far outstripped the growth in what had been that year, at best, a slowly reviving economy. He could not and did not pull on the reins: the recovery was too fragile for that. He could comfort himself with the knowledge that M-2, including repurchase agreements, small savings accounts, and bank-based money market funds, had risen less than 2 percent while M-1 was soaring, but there were an awful lot of transaction dollars out there, ready to buy when the national mood changed.

Greenspan's luck was that the possessors of that extra cash bought securities instead of goods and services. Instead of a consumer price inflation, the United States got an asset price inflation–more conventionally described as a stock market boom. And

Greenspan's belief in the prescience of markets turned out to be justified: while the exponential rise in stock prices cannot be explained without some reference to herd behavior, the truth is that much of the rise in the stock market would later be validated by an increase in capital's share of gross domestic product, by the gigantic investment opportunity created by technological progress in the areas of telecommunications and computing, and by the easing of inflationary pressures as the federal budget moved toward balance.

There remains a mystery to haunt the dreams of central bankers, because nobody knows why monetary stimulus becomes consumer price inflation in one country and asset inflation in another. For the followers of Milton Friedman, the strikingly successful result of monetary policy in the United States in the early 1990s has a bittersweet taste, for the Master had always insisted that monetary stimulus inevitably showed up (perhaps after a lag) as an increase in consumer prices. And inflation in America remained dormant.

There is an explanation at hand, especially impressive because it predates the time in question. James Tobin in the 1980s developed the "*q* theory of investment," neatly stated by Steven Kamin, Philip Turner, and Jozef van 't dack of the Bank for International Settlements: "With an easier monetary policy stance, equity prices may rise, increasing the market price of firms relative to the replacement cost of their capital. This will lower the effective cost of capital, as newly issued equity can command a higher price relative to the cost of real plant and equipment. Hence, even if bank loan rates react little to the policy easing, monetary policy can still affect the cost of capital and hence investment spending. Policy-induced changes in asset prices may also affect demand by altering the net worth of households and enterprises. Such changes may trigger a revision in income expectations and cause households to adjust consumption."[10] There are two stimulants: the fact that market valuation exceeds the costs of actually building the enterprise persuades entrepreneurs that investment will be profitable, and the steady rise in the asset side of the consumer balance sheet (what Greenspan called "the wealth effect") leads people to spend more freely for goods and services.

The other side of Tobin's theoretical statement, however, is that a subsequent fall in asset prices could dangerously brake both economic growth and consumer spending. To the extent that Greenspan put credence in Tobin's theory (and he may have done so; they are totally opposed politically, but Greenspan as chairman did not think politically until George W. Bush needed him in 2001), pushing interest rates back up would seem dangerous. Nevertheless, in 1994, the Fed made a preemptive strike against euphoria. In February of that year, the Fed Funds rate was 3 percent. In February 1995, the rate was 6 percent. The first increase was only 25 basis points (one-quarter of 1 percent), but it shocked the market.

In 1994, mathematically inclined analysts were selling large foundations and hedge funds on the proposition that their computers could promise a return on investment in different "tranches" of collateralized mortgage obligations whether the market for such instruments went up or down. Among the most adventurous but popular tranches were the IO (for Interest Only) and PO (for Principal Only) pieces of a group of mortgages. IO presumably produced a relatively steady stream of income, worth more, like any stream of income, if interest rates on new instruments dropped. PO was presumably a long-term investment that would pay off in a distant future when people sold the house or paid off the mortgage. If interest rates dropped substantially, however, as they did in 1990-92, people might *refinance* their mortgages, which would produce sooner and greater income than originally calculated for the PO and lower returns on the IO. Of course, to the extent that people with high-rate mortgages did not refinance, the relative returns on the IO would rise when interest rates declined. It was a very complicated calculation, and the people who could do it were gurus. When you brought the guru together with the salesperson, the customer had a tendency to forget that human behavior cannot be predicted to high standards of reliability.

The mathematicians and strategists had not expected the Fed to raise rates in February 1994. Some large houses with heavy CMO portfolios took immense losses (most notably Kidder Peabody, which had been the largest player in this market; Joe Jett, the Treasury strips trader whose positions were revealed to have been misreported at about the same time, argued that the firm came after him to conceal the much greater losses in the securitized mortgages department). One "hedge fund," Granite Capital, went under completely, taking with it $50 million of Rockefeller Foundation money.

When the CMO market collapsed, the Treasury 10-year note went south, fast. The average mortgage lasted about twelve years, and the mathematical fund managers hedged their CMO exposures with 10-year Treasury notes as the closest liquid instrument. H. L. Mencken once wrote three laws of politics; the second was "When the water reaches the upper decks, follow the rats." Dynamic hedging is a modern expression of that insight, transferred to finance. The way to protect a position, the mathematicians say, is to analyze covariances until you find an instrument that moves in the same direction as the instrument you own, up when it goes up and down when it goes down. Then you can protect the value of your position when the market collapses by selling in that comparable market, where, presumably, the panic has not yet hit. So as the prices declined on the CMOs, more and more money managers ran to the 10-year Treasury market to sell and protect themselves.

Normal expectation in the Federal Open Market Committee is that a rise in the Fed Funds rate will reduce the gap between the short-term rate and the long-term rate, if only because the central bank's willingness to raise short-term rates encourages investors in longer-term paper to believe that inflation will be kept in check. In February 1994, the Fed's little 25 basis-point rise had the opposite effect because it ricocheted off the CMO portfolios to the 10-year note and then to the 30-year bond as the mathematicians found ever more imaginative ways to hedge. The upward march of the stock market stopped for a year, and the feared price escalation did not occur.

Though he has denied it, I will argue that this experience was the push that moved Greenspan to a belief in "transparency"–in letting the money markets know much more about what the Fed was doing and wanted to do, and about what the banks were doing and its impact on the value of their portfolios. Alan Blinder recalled in a talk at the London School of Economics shortly after his return to private life that Greenspan in 1989 had told Congress that "it would be ill-advised and perhaps virtually impossible to announce short-run targets for reserves or interest rates when markets were in flux," and that even in normal times, "a public announcement requirement also could impede timely and appropriate adjustments to policy."[11] After the immense "announcement effect" of the 25 basis-point move in 1994, Greenspan I think changed his mind and decided that increasing the information content of a Federal Reserve decision would strengthen the impact of that decision.

In any event, the customs changed. Rather than letting the market draw its own conclusions about the FOMC decision from what the open market desk did in New York, the Fed began a custom of informing everybody during the FOMC's periodic two-day meeting in Washington not only what Fed Funds rate the desk would seek in the weeks ahead, but what the committee's expectations were for future changes in the rate. In fact, the market's understanding of the "information content" of the first, explosive 25 basis-point rise in 1994 had been correct—there were to be many more increases behind it. But nobody had prepared the players, so the change in the participants' mind-set occurred in twenty seconds rather than over a course of weeks.

Only a few years ago, Greenspan told Congress first that no records were kept of what was said at FOMC meetings, then that yes, the meetings *were* taped, but the tape was recorded over once the authors of the summary had heard it, and then, very reluctantly, having learned that Arthur Burns had left to the University of Michigan Library his transcripts of the tapes of the meetings when he was chairman, that in fact transcripts did exist. Now they are on the Fed's Web site (www.federalreserve.gov), only three months after the meetings. The new policy of announcing the change or stability of short-term rates during each FOMC meeting has been a spectacular success, smoothing price changes in normal times and heightening the "announcement effect" of an unexpected change in interesting times, like October 1998, when Greenspan put on the magic show with which this book began. It was hard to recall, watching Greenspan in action then and the effects of that action, that decisions to change rates had not long before been clutched tenaciously in the bosoms of the participants in the meeting. Speaking to the Economics Club in New York in early 2000, Greenspan celebrated a new willingness to indicate in the public FOMC statement whether or not the group had any bias toward changing rates at its *next* meeting. There might be times when surprise had a value, he said, but as an ordinary matter the Fed would function most efficiently by fulfilling the expectations it had created. The announcement of future bias also, of course, increased the opportunities for the chairman to change interest rates between meetings of the FOMC. On January 3, 2001, Greenspan jumped the last barrier, announcing a ½-point drop in the rates at 2:15 P.M, panicking short-sellers and rocketing prices.

In 1999, the Fed slowly took back the 75 basis-point cut from the Fed Funds rate in the 1998 crisis, each time carefully warning the markets with Delphic statements some weeks in advance to avoid a recurrence of the debacle of February 1994. The only fly in the ointment, and it was a big fly, was the failure of talk from the Fed, by the chairman and some of the governors, to slow the miraculous levitation of prices in the stock market. An additional percentage point added to the rates in the first half of 2000 did persuade the stock market to stop and think. In his testimony to Congress in summer 2000, Greenspan said he thought that the 175 basis points of increase in the Fed Funds rate, which the Fed had imposed on the money market, might well have brought to the famous soft landing the Icarus-like elevation of the national product. As the last half of this increase was ignored in the market for long-term paper, the challenge for Greenspan will be to explain how in a world where banks do a minor share of the financial intermediation, the Federal Reserve by increasing the rates they must pay for overnight money affects the course of the real economy.

Chapter 11

Internationally

[T]he Treasury certainly can instruct the Federal Reserve Bank of New York, wearing its hat as agent of the Treasury, to use Treasury money to buy or sell dollars, or marks, or yen, to affect the relationship between our currency and the currency of other nations. What it does not have the authority to do is to instruct the Federal Reserve to spend its own money and take the attendant risks. . . . The net result is a kind of mutual veto that in practice gives the last word to the agency that is most reluctant to intervene. Historically, that typically has been the Treasury.

–Paul Volcker (1992)[1]

THE INVOLVEMENT OF THE FEDERAL RESERVE in international financial matters was originally a New York thing, as Ben Strong of the New York Fed and Montagu Norman of the Bank of England set up a diumvirate to rule the world, bring back the gold standard, and keep politicians from debasing their countries' currencies. The gold standard meant that the value of one currency in terms of another was set automatically, by the gold that backed each of them.

Strong died in 1928, the economy crashed in 1929, and the United States sank into a sullen high-tariff isolationism. Britain (which meant the entire British Empire) abandoned the gold standard in 1931. In 1933, Franklin Roosevelt torpedoed an international monetary conference in London (where the United States was a participant) by unilaterally raising the price of gold from $20.74 per ounce to $35 an ounce while Congress prohibited the ownership of monetary gold by Americans. Experience with inconvertible currencies in the 1930s was highly unsatisfactory–every nation tried to do deals that devalued its currency to make exports cheaper and imports more expensive and create jobs for the unemployed. The exchange value of the currency was a politically sensitive decision, to be taken by finance ministries and treasury departments, not by central bankers.

The profits from the revaluation of the official gold stock were taken into the Treasury as an Exchange Stabilization Fund, to be used at the discretion of the Treasury to reduce, maintain, or increase the exchange value of the dollar. The Fed was out of this loop. It had already been denied authority to accept the two seats held open for the United States in the new Bank for International Settlements. This was a European central bankers' club formed in Basle to manage the payments involved in yet another effort to sort out German reparations and World War I debt, just in time to watch the international monetary system go to hell. (Its first major action was to advance money to Austria's Credit-Anstalt, which collapsed anyway with reverberations worldwide.) The American shares in the BIS were ultimately bought by National City Bank of New York and First National Bank of Chicago, and the United States never officially participated in the BIS until Bill Martin agreed with New York Fed president Alfred Hayes that John Kennedy's former prep-school roommate Charles Coombs, a vice president of the New York Fed, should go to the December 1960 monthly meeting of the BIS board to discuss the drain of gold from the United States.

In 1960, the wounds of World War II still crippled many national economies, and most of the world's currencies were convertible one to another only by prearrangement, as part of a transaction. At the Bretton Woods Hotel in New Hampshire in 1944, the Allied powers on the brink of victory had established a new framework within which currencies could be exchanged. That framework was a gold-dollar standard, pegging the price of gold at $35 for eternity and pegging the price of other currencies to the dollar. The United States agreed to sell any government dollars for gold or gold for dollars, at that price. Other countries would declare the value of their currency in terms of dollars, and under the rules of an International Monetary Fund created by the treaty would endeavor to manage their affairs so that for purposes of trade (*not* necessarily for purposes of investment flow–the difference is between "current account" and "capital account") their currencies would become convertible to the dollar. A central piece of the Marshall Plan in the early fifties was the $350 million donated to a European Payments Union to enable the holders of different European currencies to trade with each other by converting back and forth to dollars. The rules of the IMF permitted only a 1 percent variation from the fixed value of each currency in terms of dollars. Countries kept their reserves in dollars, which were more useful than gold (you got interest on your dollars, and the gold was sterile as well as price-fixed). And the gold hoard in the United States guaranteed the value of the dollar. In IMF terms, a gold dollar bought 888.6706 milligrams of fine gold, which translated to $35 an ounce.

Over time, this system could not work. The Belgian economist Robert Triffin, who was a research staffer at the Board of Governors and the IMF before becoming a Yale professor, published the demonstration in the most brilliant work of economic analysis in the postwar period, *Gold and the Dollar Crisis*.[2] (Among his other qualities–he was a great, burly charmer (where are the Triffins and the Henry Wallichs now, when we need them?)–Triffin had a sense of humor: his book opens with a "*Warning* . . . that the views expressed in this book do not necessarily reflect the opinions–if any–held by the official organizations with which he has been, or is now, associated.") His central thesis was that if the world economy was to grow at a good pace, which everyone wanted, it would need increasing amounts of a reserve currency to finance the resulting trade and investment. Industrial and jewelry use ate all the newly mined gold at $35 an ounce. To keep the Bretton Woods system going, then, the United States had to supply dollars to the commercial world through grants, loans, and a huge trade deficit. As the dollars piled up in the vaults of those with the trade surpluses, they would necessarily become less valuable, which meant that more and more of the accumulators would wish to use their dollars to buy gold at its fixed price. The American reserves, which could be held only in gold, would melt away.

Some years later, Milton Gilbert, the acerbic American "economic adviser" to the BIS, who wrote its brilliant annual reports, noted irritably that the American government was offering to buy gold at the same price it had paid in 1934. There wasn't anything else in the world you could buy in the 1960s for the same price you had paid in 1934; why would gold be an exception?[3]

The role of the BIS was a sore spot. It had done some banking services for the Germans in World War II, and the Bretton Woods delegates in establishing the IMF had forbidden governments to use the BIS. But central banks were not part of "government" (the Federal Reserve Bank of New York, after all, is owned by its member banks, who bought stock in it), and a pan-European financial agency was sorely needed in an age of inconvertible currencies. When the Marshall Plan set up the European Payments Union in 1949, the BIS came back into its own as manager, and thereafter flourished. Coombs was the first American to occupy either of the American seats at the table (the private commercial banks had been permitted to buy the stock but not to participate in the BIS). An elegant man with excellent manners, he was welcomed enthusiastically by central bankers eager to work more cooperatively with the Fed. His memoirs note that he could go to the monthly BIS meetings only as an observer, as the Fed was not a stockholder. "Nevertheless, I was extended the great privilege of an invitation to the governors' Sunday evening dinner, the inner sanctum from which all lower ranking officials were normally excluded."[4]

For fifteen years, through the administrations of four presidents (for Eisenhower was still in office when he went the first time), Coombs was the American liaison to the BIS and the European central banks. He took early retirement in 1975 when Volcker became president of the bank; for reasons I have never known or, really, wished to know, he and Volcker disliked each other intensely. He must have hated the idea of going to Basle with Volcker, who wouldn't have cared much for the dinners (his idea of a gourmet meal, a Fed staffer once said with some affection, "was mustard on the hot dog he bought from a street vendor"). Coombs's memoirs devote a chapter to the crisis of 1973, when George Shultz presided over a second devaluation of the dollar and Volcker as his Père Josef flew around the world in a private jet, trying to keep himself inconspicuous as he got out onto the tarmac, all six foot eight inches of him. But Coombs doesn't so much as mention Volcker's name. "[T]he Treasury," he writes about Volcker's travels, "had reached a decision . . . to dispatch its Undersecretary for Monetary Affairs to Tokyo, Bonn and Paris."[5]

The fact is that central banks—including the Fed—are deeply nationalist institutions. Their responsibility is the value of their own money and the growth of their own economy, and everything else is extraneous. When the full effect of the first oil price increases rippled through the world's economies in 1974, President Gerald Ford called together his economics team—Treasury Secretary William Simon, Council of Economic Advisers chairman Alan Greenspan, friend L. William Seidman, and Fed chairman Arthur Burns—to consider what help the United States could give to the countries that could not pay for the oil they needed without imposing enormous sacrifices on their people. There was general agreement that American banks, deluged with money from the oil-producing countries that had quintupled their prices, should "recycle" the deposits through loans to the needy nations. Arthur Burns sat on the couch in the Oval Office and said, "You call it recycling; I call it bad loans." These loans were in dollars, on variable interest rates, and when Volcker tightened in 1979, the borrowers went broke. In 1981, a visitor to Volcker's office suggested that he couldn't possibly keep it up.

"Why?" Volcker barked aggressively, having stubbornly taken the pain of an anteroom stacked with two-by-fours sent to him by enraged property developers who couldn't borrow the money they needed to build houses.

"Because you're bankrupting the Third World [a consequence of the recycling loans], and you're destroying the European cross-rates." In other words, foreigners seeking dollars to get the benefit of Volcker's superhigh rates were selling French francs rather than German marks to buy their dollars, which meant that the French franc came to be worth less and the German mark came to be worth more regardless of economic conditions in those two countries, each the other's most important trading partner. Though nobody ever said so, the need to defend intra-European trade and prices from the vagaries of the dollar was the prime mover economically in the decision to merge all the currencies into a Euro.

"Other people," Volcker said stolidly, "have their problems. We have our problems. I am hired to take care of our problems."

When a currency is freely convertible to other currencies (in practice, the world holds its reserves in dollars, Euros, and yen, and what convertibility means is that this currency can be sold on the market for one of those), the central bank's decision to raise or lower interest rates necessarily influences its price. Bagehot knew about this, too, noting that in a crisis, "we must look first to the foreign drain, and raise the rate of interest as high as may be necessary. Unless you can stop the foreign export, you cannot allay the domestic alarm."[6] In countries where businesses borrow in currencies other than the one in which they earn their revenues, a falling currency can be disastrous, because the earnings no longer service the debt. But there are no simple answers to these questions. In 1998, the yen, which had been in a state of near collapse because the Japanese economy was in the tank and the Bank of Japan had reduced interest rates to a minor fraction of 1 percent, soared through the crisis despite the almost invisible interest rates, because the gamblers who had borrowed yen to buy American and European paper had to cut their leverage and pay back their yen-denominated loans, *presto possibile*.

On occasions when foreign policy concerns overpower domestic concerns, the central bank can be left out. The decision to balloon the German monetary supply by exchanging East German Ostmarks for West German Deutschemarks at a one-for-one rate after the fall of the Berlin Wall was taken by Chancellor Helmut Kohl and Foreign Minister Count Otto von Lambsdorff without giving the president of the Bundesbank so much as a chance to object. (And it was announced to the amazed American *and* German financial communities through a talk given in New York at the Council on Foreign Relations by von Lambsdorff.) We live in an interdependent world, and however powerful a central bank may seem domestically, the fact is that the government and not the central bank controls relations with foreigners.

What put the Fed into the international business in a big way was the growth of the "Eurodollar" market, a full-fledged banking system outside the United States that made loans and investments and paid bills in American dollars. As the United States had both a large trade deficit and a grants program that spent dollars abroad, there were plenty of dollars that could be domiciled in foreign parts if bankers developed practical uses for them. The market was developed by bankers in London (the Brits didn't care what financial business you did in London so long as it didn't involve the pound), largely in response to the "interest equalization tax" of the Kennedy administration. The tax had been designed to diminish the attraction to American banks of lending to foreign borrowers, who were willing to pay higher rates than American borrowers paid. What it did was to create a separate dollar market insulated from the American dollar market by the equalization tax as well as by American reserve requirements and deposit insurance, neither of which applied to Eurodollars. When needed to meet commitments the banks had made at home that the Fed was trying to discourage, however, the Eurodollar could be repatriated, as it was in 1969. Thereafter, the

Fed could not completely neglect international considerations in its deliberations.

In 1974, the collapse of Germany's Bankhaus Herstatt, owing considerable money to American banks on foreign exchange contracts, stimulated negotiations at the BIS on who should be responsible for what in banks that operated internationally. In 1975, largely in response to Herstatt, the BIS negotiators reached agreement that when a bank established branches or subsidiaries abroad, the home country regulator, which saw consolidated results for the enterprise in all its countries, should take ultimate responsibility for them. But the American bank examiners could examine the branches of the American banks only in Britain, Japan, and Germany, not in Belgium or Switzerland or Austria, let alone the tax-haven jurisdictions like Jersey, Luxembourg, Netherlands Antilles, or Cayman Islands.

Then Banco Ambrosiano failed in Luxembourg, and the Italian government refused even to talk about compensation for its defrauded depositors, on the grounds that while chartered in Italy the bank was really owned by the Vatican . . . This is very tricky, and may tear the safety net of comity off the relations central banks cultivate with each other. As Ernest Patrikis, then still first vice president of the New York Fed, told a Group of Thirty conference on international insolvency in 1998, "When faced with the prospect of bankruptcy at a multinational bank, it is the solemn duty of each bank supervisor to do all that can possibly be done to ensure that the adverse financial effects fall on no customer or counterparty of the bank. But failing that, they should fall in another jurisdiction."[7]

The international alarums and excursions of the 1960s and 1970s were far more the concern of the Treasury than of the Federal Reserve. Though the Fed had established "swap lines" with most of the central banks that had currencies in widespread use, enabling the banks to come to each other's aid if somebody started a run on a currency, the lines could be activated only with the consent of the Treasury. When Britain fell into the slough of despond in 1976, it was Treasury Secretary William Simon and Undersecretary Ed Yeo who dealt with Prime Minister Harold Wilson and Chancellor of the Exchequer James Callaghan. The negotiations over new IMF Articles of Agreement to adjust that organization to the realities of floating exchange rates was done by that same Yeo with Jacques de Larosière, then the head of the French *Trésor*, later to be head of the IMF itself and Paul Volcker's ally in trying to rescue the multinational banks from the disastrous miscalculations that had led to the "debt crisis" of 1982, et seq.

Banks follow trade, and American banks had been active abroad under full domestic authorization since the Federal Reserve Act of 1913. (Before then, of course, domestic authorization had not been necessary: Morgan started in New York as a branch of a British operation, and Brown Brothers Harriman was half-owned in England before there was a Fed.) In 1919 another act, sponsored by Senator Walter Edge of Florida, removed geographical restraints on branching by "Edge Act" subsidiaries that were dedicated to financing foreign trade. Foreign banks could own subsidiaries in the United States or open branches with the approval of the state chartering authorities, which led to the anomaly that Barclay's could have offices in both New York and California, which was forbidden to American banks. Not until 1978 did the International Banking Act give federal agencies authority over foreign banks, and then the purpose was mostly to enforce rules that the foreign banks receive "national treatment" (i.e., follow the same laws that applied to American banks), and that our banks receive national treatment abroad (i.e., follow the laws applying to the banks of the country in which they had branched). Interstate branching by foreign banks that had already happened was grandfathered, however, as was their power to engage in securities activities forbidden to American-owned banks. As of 1994, when Congress finally lifted interstate branching restrictions on American banks nationwide, no fewer than seventy foreign banks had interstate branching privileges.[8]

In 1979, the Fed took the lead in forming an Interagency Country Exposure Committee (ICEC) with three members each from the FDIC, the OCC, and the Fed itself, to rate "country borrowers" with loans from American banks. The ICEC met three times a year, and apparently filed its reports in files, classifying them as so confidential that not even the bank examiners could see them, let alone the banks. The years 1979–82 saw the orgy of apparently profitable "recycling" lending to less developed countries, at fantastically high interest rates that could make sense only if continuing inflation drove down the burdens of repayment. By then the SEC was in the act, demanding that bank holding companies, which were subject to SEC accounting rules, detail in their annual reports the extent of their lending to public and private borrowers in foreign countries. The Fed angrily opposed. De Saint-Phalle noted in his book that "the nine principal money-center banks in the United States have made loans in just two Latin American countries–Mexico and Brazil–in excess of their combined capital. How can this be adequately explained by the Federal Reserve Board?"[9]

Among the changes made possible by the International Banking Act was the creation of an offshore banking arrangement within the territorial United States. The first International Banking Facility (IBF) opened in New York in 1981, and gave both domestic and foreign banks access to the tax shelters of "shell branches" in offshore havens. Banks operated through these "facilities" (there was no physical presence, just as there is no physical presence other than a lawyer's office behind the brass plates in the Cayman Islands, et al.) under the benignly astigmatic eye of the Fed, which had no way to know what foreign banks and branches were doing in such venues, and not much information about what the American banks were doing. Like the Eurodollar market in London, activity in the IBF was not of immediate domestic interest–loans could be made from such facilities only for use abroad.

One would think that the recurrent currency ruckus of the 1970s and early 1980s would have put questions of foreign economic and currency developments front and center in the deliberations of the Federal Open Market Committee. But Volcker firmly denies that he turned the screws on the money supply in October 1979, and loosened his grip in August 1982, for reasons related to lectures from or problems in foreign countries. Steven Axilrod, who became chief economist for Nikko Securities after sitting in the Fed's magnificent conference room for two decades as a central aide-de-camp to Arthur Burns and Paul Volcker, told a meeting of the Economic Policy Committee of the American Association for the United Nations in the early nineties that in all those years he never heard a discussion of the impact of Fed interest-rate decisions on other economies or on the exchange rate of the dollar—or an international reason for moving American interest rates up or down. Scott Pardee, apparently a plain blunt man, the clever, intellectual, soft-spoken solid-citizen head of the foreign exchange desk through the 1970s, would make a presentation of foreign exchange developments to the FOMC as Peter Sternlight, the stolid-looking but crafty head of the open market desk, would present the domestic market picture. But the debate among the members of the committee was about American matters. After the 1980 election, when primitive Friedmanites took over the White House economic offices, Pardee quit because he had nothing to do and went off to Discount Corp. as vice chairman.

Greenspan has unquestionably been more closely attuned to developments elsewhere in the world, though he punished Argentina and made the task of the European Central Bank much harder when he began his frontal attack on the markets in the spring of 2000. Ordering the magical quarter-point drop in interest rates between FOMC meetings in fall 1998, he said explicitly that he did not think American prosperity could survive a significant downturn in the rest of the world, and that was one of the reasons he had to move. In Greenspan's time, the sections of the research staff that look at developments abroad have had more time and attention than ever before. Operationally, moreover, the Pardee and Sternlight jobs have been combined in Peter Fisher, a young, casual, curly-haired, terrifyingly smart senior v.p. at the New York Fed. But as Paul Volcker observed at an IMF conference while he was still president of that bank, "It is not easy for any domestic policymaker, particularly in the larger countries with relatively smaller external sectors, to make a lot of allowance for the external effects of its policy and to work with other countries toward achieving some consistency and compatibility, in the interests of a broader stability."[10]

The Federal Reserve first became significantly involved in supervising the activities of branches of foreign banks after the passage of the Foreign Bank Supervision Enhancement Act of 1991, itself a reaction to the discovery that nobody had really kept an eye on the Bank of Credit and Commerce International, a worldwide enterprise run by Pakistanis but headquartered in Luxembourg (and sustained by the sheikh of Abu Dhabi). The American subsidiary was called First American, and was chaired by no less than Clark Clifford, Harry Truman's most cherished counselor and a big-time Washington lawyer. Bert Lance, who had been Jimmy Carter's budget director, was also involved. The bank was a criminal enterprise (it was founded originally to skim the float on the wages of Pakistani laborers in the Gulf, whose salaries would be paid through BCCI and would take a long time to get to their loved ones). I knew one person who worked there, and quit in horror after a couple of months, but would never talk about it. Ernest Patrikis has spoken admiringly of the Fed's supervisory work on BCCI matters, but Harry Albright, the former New York State banking superintendent who spent eight years liquidating First American, had other views. BCCI, he wrote in his final report to the court, "was born of a combination of international competition by laxity of regulation and bank secrecy laws. Both remain rampant."[11]

Banking supervision, like counterintelligence, is hard to judge from the outside, because the success stories don't get told and the failures are on the front pages. The 1991 act returned New York to center stage, because most foreign branches are chartered by New York State and located not far from the Renaissance palazzo of the New York Federal Reserve Bank, an expansion of Rome's Farnese Palace. The number of bank examiners at the New York Fed has tripled since 1991, and most of them are involved in examinations involving international matters. "National treatment," which was strongly emphasized in the 1991 act, means that the foreign banks must give American examiners access to what the branches in America do in America. It is understood that any troubles host country supervisors find in the branches of foreign banks should be communicated immediately to the home country supervisors, though the question of how home country supervisors inform the examiners in the host country of home country problems is a little less established. The third possibility—that home country supervisors will find something the host country examiners had failed to find in their own examinations—blew up in the Fed's face in 1995 when the Japanese Ministry of Finance discovered a billion-dollar loss from trading irregularities in the New York branch of Daiwa Bank and concealed the problem from American regulators for more than six months. Inflammatory things were said. If a senior official of the Japanese ministry had committed suicide in the aftermath, the general belief in New York would have been that somebody from the Fed had handed him the snicker-snee.

In the 1980s, American bankers were worried about low-priced competition, especially from Japanese banks, which had virtually no capital requirements and bought their way into markets by giving away stand-by guarantees for commercial paper and the like. The Basle capital accord, requiring banks active in international lending to maintain 8 percent capital, half of it equity, grew to a large extent out of such concerns. Some branches have been especially active in the derivatives market. Union Bank of Switzerland admitted to the largest single loss from the Long Term Capital Management crash. Such matters are presumably run on the home office credit rating, and ultimate authority rests with the home office. It is not clear how much the Federal Reserve looks at such matters.

The GAO found that 67 percent of the funding for foreign branches and agencies came from interbank loans and loans from the bank's own affiliates, with 47 percent of the assets in the same category. Thus the net impact of foreign bank operations in the United States appeared to be an inflow of funds. They have made a major contribution not only to their countries' investments in the United States, but to the oiling of the American financial system. In December 1992, which will probably remain the high-water mark, 24 percent of all outstanding commercial and industrial loans in America were on the books of foreign branches and agencies.

Increasingly, foreign involvement in national banking systems–in Europe and Latin America as well as in the United States–has come from the purchase of banks in one country by banks in another. Citibank and Hong Kong Shanghai (HSBC) have built consumer franchises all over the world. Deutsche Bank has noisily acquired Bankers Trust; ABN Amro, which owns European-American in New York, has quietly created a major franchise through the Midwest, based on Chicago's LaSalle Bank; Spain's Santander is a major presence throughout Latin America (having done well in the United States, where its cautious $300 million investment in preferred stock in First Fidelity of New Jersey transmuted profitably into a significant stake in First Union). As the Euro has become the instrument for finance in Europe, banks have been virtually forced to create pan-European entities. Given the dominance of the dollar, all such giant banks must have a foothold in the United States too, either through separately capitalized subsidiaries or through active branches. The supervision of American banks active abroad is presumably easier, in part because consolidated books must be kept in the United States, in part because the concentration is awesome: Greenspan told a House committee in 1990 that four American banks do half of all the international business done by American banks. "The international role of the banks," he added, "has changed from one of simply extending credit to one of facilitating transactions."[12]

How to regulate and supervise such "Large Complex Banking Organizations" (LCBOs) is one of the great practical questions of our time. The Basle Commission on Banking Supervision, chaired by William McDonough of the New York Fed, has turned out its "core principles," and subcommittees have made recommendations about disclosure. The accountants as a profession are working to set up international auditing standards (which they will then as individuals–hey, one has to make a living–find ways to evade). The International Monetary Fund has written "data dissemination standards" and invited central banks to post on the IMF Web site a description of the data about their condition that they publish on their own Web sites. With the World Bank, IMF has organized a Financial Standards Assessment Program to help national central banks get a grip on what goes on in their own banking systems. The heart of the program has been regional conferences to spur and control the development of "modules" that apply internationally acceptable Standards and Codes.

BIS with the help of the central banks of the G-7 nations has spawned a Financial Stability Forum (the G-7 are the United States, Canada, Japan, Britain, Germany, France, and Italy). The OECD has a committee trying to write rules to prevent the use of multinational banks for tax evasion, and the world's major finance ministries have a task force seeking to prevent money laundering in some thirty or so offshore "financial centers," from Jersey to Gibraltar to Lichtenstein to the Cook Islands to Aruba, that live off money-laundering. The U.S. Treasury Department under Secretary Larry Summers was remarkably ambitious in seeking to abort opportunities for malfeasance. Meanwhile, American supervisors, both at the Fed and at the OCC, hope against hope that the risk management cadre in the giant financial services institutions knows what it's doing and has the authority within the firm to control what happens–and that the market will sense trouble early enough to give the supervisors a head's-up.

Sir Andrew Large, formerly chairman of the Securities and Investments Board in Britain, writes that

> Work along these lines is already underway in various countries and is being pursued globally by the Group of Thirty, which proposed an industry forum to propose a set of standards in its report entitled 'Global Institutions, National Supervision and Systemic Risk.' Under this plan, supervisors would ask the firms themselves to develop proposals and, once they felt comfortable with them, supervisors would

monitor and supervise the firms based on their adherence to the standards. A key problem in carrying out this procedure will be to avoid even the impression that industry is calling the shots. That would obviously be unacceptable, and supervisors must clearly be in the driving seat.[13]

Susan Krause of the Comptroller's Office, who chaired the Basle committee on disclosure and transparency, says, "Using the information banks use for their own risk management would be best, of course, but that conflicts with harmonization. From a policy point of view, it has to evolve."

Nobody knows how much time remains for this evolution to be accomplished. The lesson of 1997 and the "contagion" from the Asian crisis is that the emergence of new markets for new instruments in new places has placed a great strain on the supervisory capacities of all banking regulators, who must know what is going on in faraway places because their own banks are likely to be involved. In Thailand, it turned out that the central bank had used its dollar reserves to purchase forward contracts on the Thai baht, as the cheapest and most effective way to maintain the current exchange rate and help local businesses manage their dollar-denominated debt. It is, perhaps, worth exploring what this means. In spring 1997, the forward price of the baht in dollars was the same as the spot price, but interest rates on the baht were into double digits, while 90-day loans of dollars to high-rated borrowers were at about 6 percent and 90-day loans of yen were under 2 percent. A lender could borrow dollars at 6 percent, use them to buy baht, lend the baht to a bank for 90 days at 12 percent, and sign a forward contract entitling him to buy his dollars back at the end of 90 days. His return was guaranteed and (since he had almost no money of his own in the deal) virtually infinite. The player in this game who was sure to run out of money some day was the buyer who guaranteed the forward price of the baht in dollars—which had to be the Thai central bank. But the only people who knew what was going on were the currency speculators who were winning the game.

In Korea, the central bank had turned over the national reserves to the commercial banks, to make a better return on the assets. (Greenspan has proposed that all countries keep reserves sufficient to pay for their imports for a year, but that's a losing proposition for the countries, because the interest rate they must pay on their borrowings is much higher than what the reserves can earn kept in short-term U.S. Treasury paper, which is where they are supposed to be.) Korean banks became the largest holders of the bonds Brazil had issued as part of the deal that ended the 1980s debt crisis, and when Thailand got in trouble and people began worrying about Korea, the bonds had to be sold, adding 8 percentage points to the cost of borrowing money in Brazil and stripping Brazil of one-quarter of *its* reserves in a single month. Then it turned out that Korean banks had other interesting involvements with international finance. J. P. Morgan had set up a company in Malaysia that sold a Korean bank derivatives on which the Koreans would make money if the Thai baht retained its value with reference to the Japanese yen, and lose money if the baht lost value with reference to the Japanese yen. Morgan—other individuals, of course—was meanwhile acting as adviser to the Thai central bank and recommending a devaluation of the currency. We know about this because the Koreans lost $350 million very quickly and refused to pay, and when Morgan sued, the New York law firm of Skadden Arps put the story in its brief for the defense.

At a lunch in Geneva, I noted that the word on Wall Street was that 70 percent of Korean reserves in 1997 had been turned over to the country's commercial banks to prop them up and yield the Korean government a better return. An adviser to the Korean Finance Ministry denied vigorously, even bitterly, that 70 percent of the reserves had been so imperiled. "Maybe 60 percent," he said finally, "but not 70 percent." One should note in passing that such behavior is no longer permissible: the IMF's new Standards and Codes prohibit a nation from counting as part of its reserves any funds deposited in its own banks.

Because central banks tend to be trusting souls, and because markets rather than banks now set the price of money and judge the creditworthiness of the players, the world outside the United States has been placing financial regulation and supervision functions in other hands. The recent congressional decision to give the Federal Reserve umbrella supervision over financial institutions in America has more resonance than the Fed itself–still a highly nationalist institution–can realize. What will be needed in the years ahead is a regime of disclosure. Giving the lead role to a central bank that has historically drawn its authority from its control of information cannot make the financial architecture more stable; it may prove a source of additional instability.

PART FIVE

The Day Jobs

Chapter 12

The Payments Franchise

A number of visitors to Bank Indonesia during the early 1990s brought with them the concept of a national payment system. Literature started arriving from various quarters which contained references to the "payment system," and staff at Bank Indonesia sought to understand what was meant. Needless to say, there were many views on the subject once it became a topic of discussion.

—Adolf Latuhamallo, deputy director, Bank Indonesia[1]

AMONG THE TASKS OF THE FEDERAL RESERVE SYSTEM from its beginning was arranging the payments system so that checks written in dollars on any bank in the United States would be honored "at par"—full value—at any other bank in the United States. It was a very old problem. Prior to the Civil War, when most banks made loans by issuing banknotes to their borrowers, enforcers were necessary (the Bank of the United States at its many branches or the Sheffield Bank in Boston for New England) to make sure that there was gold behind the banknote. Without a seal of approval from such a "correspondent," banks found that at any distance from their office, people (and other banks) might accept their notes in payment only at a discount

247

from their face value. The origins of financial journalism in the United States can be found in the few surviving issues of various *Bank Note Reporters* advising businessmen and bankers of the status of the paper monies issued by various banks.

When "demand deposits" and checks took over from the local banknote, the habits of discounting persisted. Local checks cleared at par at the local clearinghouse. Out-of-town checks would be credited to the payee's account for a percentage point or two less than the amount for which they were written—and in many cases not credited for some time, to make sure that the local bank would not be the loser if the faraway bank bounced the check. (To this day, big-city banks accepting for deposit a check drawn on an out-of-town bank for a sum larger than $7,000 will reserve the right not to give credit for *seven* business days. This is down from ten days in the New York–San Francisco interchange at the turn of the twentieth century, but less of an improvement than would seem indicated in the light of the drastic changes in communications.) Intercity clearance was done mostly through patterns of correspondent banks, which kept deposits with each other and finalized payments through changes in correspondent balances. Because banks competing for correspondent business might give credit to their correspondents for what were still uncollected funds (even where the correspondents did not give credit to their depositors), no small part of the reserves of banks that were not members of the Federal Reserve System was fictitious.

If ever there was a government activity that was constitutional under the commerce clause, it was a law to force the acceptance of checks for their face amount regardless of the geographical location of the bank on which they were written. The demand deposit system had become, in effect, the national currency, and the national currency had to be accepted everywhere. But the Fed as originally organized was essentially a correspondent bank where members kept balances (required balances, called reserves—and, indeed, non-member banks were entitled under state law to consider as their "reserves" the balances they kept at correspondent commercial banks). The first significant competition between the Federal Reserve Banks and the commercial banks came with the decision by the banks, acting individually in the 1920s, to accept "clearing balances" from non-member banks that wished to collect through the Fed the checks their customers received—and make it possible for others to collect on the checks the customers of those banks had written. The only weapon the Fed had to police "non-par collection" was a refusal to make its own clearing facilities available to banks that did not give full credit to the checks they put into the system. It was a pretty blunt weapon to use, because the Fed had no way other than rumor to know whether or not a non-member bank was paying other people's checks at par—and because FedWire, which moved money at the speed of electricity, was originally an internal operation, available only as a way to transfer gold balances among the Federal Reserve Banks themselves.

Banks were reluctant to give up discounting of checks as a source of profits, and it took two generations before the last non-member banks, mostly in the South, signed the pledge not to clip the currency. In 1969, Howard H. Hackley, the Fed's general counsel, estimated that there were still about six hundred banks that did not give full value for checks drawn on out-of-town accounts, and were thus barred from the use of Federal Reserve check-clearing facilities.[2] Since 1980, *all* banks and credit unions and savings associations that offer checking accounts under any name have had to keep reserves at the Fed and most (to the disgust of the large correspondent banks) thus have found it more convenient to clear their out-of-town checks through their local Fed. Control over "presentment schedules"—the times at which various instruments must be presented at the Federal Reserve Bank to get credit today or tomorrow—gives the Federal Reserve System a powerful weapon to deep-six potential competitors. One of the key facts about the system is that check processing—moving the paper, verifying the "cash letters" the receiving banks send with the bundles of checks drawn on each paying bank—constitutes the largest single occupational category of the people who work for the Federal Reserve (outside Washington, of course, their employer is their local district bank, not the system).

George White, who organized the first Chase Bank involvement with retail electronic payments and then went out on his own to become a consultant and conference organizer in all areas of funds transfer, once observed that the major roadblock the Fed has thrown in the path of electronic payments has been its steady and remarkable improvement in the quality of check processing. As late as the early 1960s, checks were processed by hand, with armies of clerks in green eyeshades slotting the paper into pigeonholes. By 1974, when I came around to the back offices of the banks with an introduction from my friend the lieder singer Senior Vice President Tom Waage of the Federal Reserve Bank of New York, the check-processing business had been significantly automated with the imprinting of information in an MICR (magnetic ink character recognition) code on every check.

I followed a check I had written on my account at Manufacturers Hanover in New York City to Jake Piccozzi's gas station on Shelter Island, New York, through the hands of the tellers at the Shelter Island branch of the Valley National Bank (who credited Jake with the total amount of all the checks he was depositing), through the keypunching clerks at the East Hampton branch (who printed MICR numbers for the amount of money on the check below my signature on the lower right-hand corner of the check), through a large processing room in Valley Stream (where my check was bundled with other checks Valley National would present to the New York Fed for credit to its account), through the Federal Reserve Check Processing Center in Jericho, New York, through the main office of the Federal Reserve Bank of New York downtown on Maiden Lane (where my check became part of the "cash letter" that the Federal Reserve Bank of New York would present to Manufacturers Hanover for credit), through the New York Clearing House on Broad Street, to the Manufacturers Hanover processing center in downtown, and eventually to the "till" at my branch at Forty-third Street and Fifth Avenue where Manny Hanny stored the checks I had written for delivery back to me at the end of the month. From Jake Piccozzi's deposit of my check to its arrival in the till took forty-three hours; the check passed through the hands of about two dozen people (including couriers) and half a dozen times through the wondrous long, clattering industrial machines that read the routing codes and account numbers and amounts, and dropped the pieces of paper into the slots that said where they should go next.

The story of the Piccozzi check was magnificent, but even in 1974, to quote the French general observing the Charge of the Light Brigade into the valley, it wasn't war. For all the imagination and money put into the machinery, checks were a slow and expensive way to pay bills. By 1974, the credit card had risen from the muck of its clumsy introduction—when banks dropped cards from the skies and then tried to collect from the people to whom they had been sent, whether or not those people had ever seen the cards—and was becoming a significant payments medium, lavishly supported by annual fees from cardholders, substantial commissions from merchants, and monthly interest payments from users. The flimsy slips customers signed to signify their acceptance of charges, which the merchant then deposited at his bank with the day's intake of checks, were clogging up the transmission media available to the banks in the consortia that issued the cards. They came to the Fed for help, asking for a way to blend their credit card slips with the checks for processing, and the Fed told them to get lost. They were thereby forced to develop the first large-scale electronic payments system, which operates without paper all the way from the merchant's cash register through the continuous netting of payments between banks, without any input from the Fed.

Payments and their clearance and settlement are the essential infrastructure of the modern economy and of all markets. It is the fact that FedWire gives instantaneous transfer of the ownership of Treasury paper as well as cash that makes possible the use of repurchase agreements to finance the mathematically calculated speculation that shows up as swaps and futures contracts and options. But the payments world, necessarily, is also a world of legacy systems, because the adoption of new payments procedures happens very slowly, over periods measured in decades rather than years, and the providers of the existing processes have a great stake in the continuing use of the old machinery.[3]

In the year 2000, something more than 68 billion checks were written in the United States. At the 1998 "bank structure" conference of the Federal Reserve Bank of Chicago, David Humphrey of Florida State and Lawrence Pulley of the College of William and Mary estimated the costs of the checking system in 1996 at $204 billion, $1,050 per adult, more than 2 percent of the gross domestic product. Something more than half of this expenditure is quite unnecessary, reflecting missed opportunities for lower-cost electronic payments and ritualistic nonsense like the rental of aircraft to fly canceled checks around the country every night at a cost of roughly $50 million a year, so that the information taken from them by reader/sorter machines in the cities where they were presented by payees can be separately taken again by reader/sorter machines in the cities where the payors have their bank accounts. Paul M. Connolly, first vice president of the Fed of Boston, who became the system's point man on electronic payments in 1994, told a conference of business editors in 1995 (after a stronger than usual disclaimer to "emphasize that I am giving you my own views, not any official pronouncement of the Federal Reserve") that "we *should* be heading for a cashless society, because our payments system is dominated by the use of cash and checks, which work, but impose huge expenses on us, embody lots of inefficiencies, and carry considerable risk."[4]

As early as 1988, Humphrey and Allen N. Berger, then both on Fed research staffs, identified the persistence of the checking system at the center of the payments business as a "market failure. . . . Decisions made in a market setting reflect only the private costs faced by market participants. . . . [O]ne cannot expect market participants to make decisions that best reflect resource use for society as a whole unless the prices observed in the market reflect the full social (instead of private) cost impact of products or services being sold or produced."[5] With billions of dollars sunk into machinery and tens of thousands of jobs at risk, and an institutional structure that dares not risk the loss of function in the outer reaches of the empire–after all, what would the Federal Reserve Bank of Minneapolis or the Federal Reserve Bank of Philadelphia *do* if they didn't have checks to clear— the Fed has stood as a bulwark against the substitution of electronic payments for checks, using its powers as banking regulator to that end. One gets remarkable actions by the Fed to maintain the current situation. In late 1996, carrying support from inefficient banks, the Fed even petitioned the Congress to change the law that now requires banks to give credit to depositors no more than two business days after they deposit a check drawn on a local bank. Instead, the Fed suggested that in our age of instantaneous electronic communications, banks should be permitted a three-day "hold" during which the money may be available to the bank but not to the depositor.

The checking system is a "debit transfer" system—that is, what moves is a claim against the payor. The first step in the payment is the crediting of the money to the account of the recipient (who may or may not get the prompt use of it, according to the quality of her relations with her bank). And it is only after the check has been processed at the bank on which it is drawn that the money is deducted from the payor's account. If the payor can delay the arrival of the check at his bank, he continues to have the use of the money. Thus "cash management" is taught in the business schools, and magazines will pay authors for articles with checks drawn on banks far away. (I was once paid for a talk at the University of Southern California Business School with a check drawn on a bank in Durham, N.C.) The bank that has sent the check out gets credit from the Fed for "cash items in process of collection" before the bank that must send the money even hears about it. This is "Federal Reserve float," and in 1979, when high interest rates made it really worthwhile to accelerate collection on one side and delay payment on the other, Fed float topped out at $6.7 billion a day.

Congress was unhappy about this, and as part of the negotiations for the Monetary Control Act of 1980, the Fed promised to do something about it. Among the attempts was what Governor Lyle E. Gramley in a letter responding to criticisms by the General Accounting Office called "a large effort to design procedures for the collection of large dollar-value checks electronically—electronic check collection (ECC). . . . Progress to date [April 10, 1981!] has been very encouraging."[6] One does not know whether to laugh or cry at the information that in 1983 the largest check that could be "truncated" in this system was $1,500—or the news that in the year 2000 the Federal Reserve Bank of Minneapolis had just launched a large-scale experiment in electronic check presentment.

In 1983, the California Clearing House Association sought to initiate a "Cashwire" system to be settled at the end of each day on the books of the Federal Reserve Bank of San Francisco. A letter from R. B. O'Donoghue, assistant vice president of the Fed of San Francisco for electronic payments, informed Norma Blackmore of the Wells Fargo Bank that "Each Reserve Bank has been advised by the Board of Governors that we are not to enter into any new net settlement agreements without approval from the Board. If the Clearing House Association wishes to make a formal request, it should be forwarded to me and I will see that it goes promptly to Washington. I do feel that gaining approval for such a request is likely to take some time. . . ."[7]

Two electronic payments devices were developed by the Fed itself and are still in use. The big-league one was FedWire, which went back to 1918 as a Morse code communications device between district banks, and grew into a system for the instantaneous payment of large sums. The minor-league operation was the Automated Clearing House, for much smaller, usually consumer-related payments.

FedWire is a barebones transaction from bank to bank, and the message about which account is to be credited for what comes separately, through the Society for Worldwide Interbank Financial Telecommunications (otherwise SWIFT), a private organization based in Belgium which also has the management contract to operate the European Central Bank's Target payments system for Euros. FedWire transfers roughly $1.5 trillion a day; SWIFT messages carry instructions to transfer about $2.5 trillion a day.

FedWire is a credit transfer system: what moves is the actual money, from the payor to the payee. If the payor doesn't have the money in his account, presumably the payment does not go through, but as noted in the last chapter, the Fed offers "daylight overdrafts" by which payors can borrow from the Fed without going through the nuisance of the discount window to pay their bills on an intraday basis. It should be noted also that such borrowings are necessary only after a bank has exhausted its reserve account, and that the credit extended by the Fed to the banks during the course of the day is much larger than the total reserves the banks maintain at the Fed overnight–$60-odd to $120 billion as against total reserves of less than $40 billion, of which only about $6 billion is in fact on deposit at the Fed, the rest being cash in ATM machines, which can be counted as reserves. In the classic European Real Time Gross Settlement systems, borrowing to make final payments by wire transfer is done in the private sector–or, in the case of Target, from the national central banks that clear their client banks' payments to the European Central Bank.

The European central banks demand that such loans be collateralized, that is, that the banks using the system keep on deposit assets of undoubted quality, like paper issued by their own governments. The Fed has refused to make such demands on American banks, on the grounds that they already have to collateralize deposits of government agencies, their transfers through the New York Clearing House, and some of their positions in the derivatives markets. William McDonough, president of the Federal Reserve Bank of New York, is a little shamefaced about this system: "these overdrafts," he said in a BIS symposium, "still serve as an example of an unintended legacy of a payment arrangement designed many years ago at a time when the potential for growth in payment volumes and the risk implications of intraday exposure were not fully appreciated."[8]

Bruce Summers, the Fed's point man on electronic banking through the 1980s, is now director of the Fed's experimental automation programs (the FRAS project, for Federal Reserve Automation Systems, very hush-hush) based in the Federal Reserve Bank of Richmond, Virginia. He argues that lending by the central bank is necessarily safer than lending from the private sector, because the

Fed "has fuller information concerning the creditworthiness of its counterparties than does any other correspondent bank or clearing-house. . . . [T]he institutional feature that most distinguishes central banks as payment system operators is their access to privileged supervisory information about the condition of commercial banks."[9]

FedWire was not, really, a competitor to the checking system. People receiving very large payments by check had never put the check into a clearing process; they hired a courier to take it to the bank on which it was issued, and present it directly for immediate credit. But the Fed did get involved in the creation of an electronic consumer payments system, the Automated Clearing House(ACH), which was designed to facilitate direct deposit of payrolls.

What was wrong with the ACH was that it was a payments process that could be initiated only by organizations. Bills could be paid through the ACH only if the recipient of the money had arranged to receive ACH payments. Even then, the customer's bank had to make the investment in hardware and software to link the customer's account to the ACH. The district Feds ran all but three of the ACHs in the early years (the exceptions were the New York Clearing House; a "cactus switch" spun off from the Valley National Bank of Phoenix by a sharp middle-aged techie named Paul Finch; and a Hawaiian venture expressing Hawaii's resentment that the Fed had no presence on the islands). Apart from direct deposit, which was popular with government agencies like Social Security and the U.S. Air Force as well as some manufacturing corporations eager to be released from obligations to deliver cash in individual envelopes to the factory door, the largest single use of the ACH was as a way to pay insurance premiums. Chase Bank ran a service for the insurance companies, arranging automatic debits from policyholders' accounts on premium date. Banks and S&Ls which ventured into telephone banking were also users of the ACH.

It was a clumsy system. To submit its depositors' payments through the ACH, a bank had to prepare a reel of magnetic tape registering the payor, the amount, the payee, and the account to which the payment was to be made. Originally, the system was local to San

Francisco (with another ACH in Atlanta, where the Atlanta Fed had run its own preparatory study). This tape then had to be driven to the ACH offices just as though it were a cash letter of checks going to a clearinghouse or Fed check-processing center. At each ACH, other reels of magnetic tape had to be prepared for delivery to the receiving bank, which would blend the information on that tape with the credits claimed from the checks delivered to the clearinghouse. In 1974, the four existing ACHs (St. Paul, Minnesota, and Boston had started their own) organized a National Automated Clearing House Association to develop rules for interchange among them. The Board of Governors had to approve, and did not do so until 1978, at which point the ACHs (there were now thirty-two of them) managed to persuade the Fed to give them a fifteen-minute window onto FedWire at the close of day (6:00 P.M. New York time) so they could clear interdistrict payments electronically and stop shipping reels of tape around the country.

In the early 1980s, General Electric Capital, which had become a large-scale issuer of credit cards, decided there was money to be made in delivering electronic payments, opened a headquarters-cum-planning operation in Rockville, Maryland, near Washington, and opened for business as an ACH in San Francisco. This was not well received at the Fed. FedWire closed in those days at 6:00 P.M. EST. To make the fifteen-minute window after six, Pacific Coast banks had to get the ACH tape to the San Francisco Fed by 2:00 P.M. local time, leaving the Fed an hour to massage the incoming tapes and turn them into outgoing tapes. GE as a private-sector ACH would do all this work itself, and deliver to the Fed for transmission reels all ready to go. Nevertheless, on orders from Washington (I have the letter), the San Francisco Fed told GE that it would have to get its fully processed tapes in to the Fed's ACH at 2:00 P.M., just like the banks delivering their unprocessed tapes. That meant that GE had to close its gates, turning away customers who wished to deliver information closer to the Fed deadline, well before 2:00 P.M. Moreover, GE would have to pay the Fed for the processing work GE had already done for itself and its customers.

Today's Fed payments division admits that perhaps its predecessors played a little rough back in the bad old days, but then points out that GE's private-sector ACH on the west coast was taken over finally by Visa ("a more suitable processor," said a Fed lawyer smugly). Visa, however, has the same problems GE used to have. A 1998 submission from the three major private-sector ACH operations—the New York Clearing House, Visa, and the American Clearing House in Phoenix—echoes GE's old complaints:

> The Federal Reserve's pricing practices impede fair competition. Private-sector ACH operators exchange entries with each other at no charge, with each operator charging its customers for either the origination or delivery of the entries. In contrast, the Federal Reserve charges the private-sector operator's customers for entries exchanged between the Federal Reserve and the private-sector operator, while the private sector operator cannot charge the Federal Reserve's customers. . . . The Federal Reserve charges a monthly fee of $25 for each routing number a customer of a private-sector operator has on the Federal Reserve's master file. . . . By charging financial institutions for inter-operator item exchanges and routing number maintenance, the Federal Reserve artificially increases the costs for any institution that chooses to use a private-sector operator, thereby placing the private-sector operator at a disadvantage. . . . Private sector operators have the same final file submission deadlines as any financial institution. This requires the private-sector ACH operators to impose earlier deadlines for the financial institutions that they service, while those financial institutions that use the Federal Reserve may enjoy later deadlines.[10]

The Fed's advantage in "presentment" times merely carried into the electronic world its long established position in the checking world, where the district banks enjoy what Jeffrey M. Lacker and

John A. Weinberg of the Federal Reserve Bank of Richmond call "the six-hour monopoly." Barring special arrangements between the parties (which are common for high-value checks but not for routine items), a bank depositing a check at another bank must get it to the window by 8:00 A.M. to assure payment the same day. But the Fed can present a check any time up to 2:00 P.M. for good funds for itself on the same day. This monopoly constitutes a subsidy to the Fed; the authors note that "an organization that is not fully subject to market discipline could make wasteful investments designed to hold on to market share."[11]

In 1996, as part of the budget compromise that reopened the government, Congress passed a law requiring that from January 1, 1999, the federal government had to make all its payments by electronic funds transfer rather than by paper check. Making a paper payment cost the Treasury 43 cents and the cost for an electronic payment was 2 cents. Treasury's first cut at rulemaking under the law, in September 1997, explained the reasoning. Electronic payments could

> bring into the mainstream of the financial system those millions of Americans who receive Federal payments and who currently do not use the financial system to receive funds, make payments, save, borrow or invest. . . . Agency records indicate that recipients are 20 times less likely to have a problem with an electronic payment than with a paper check. Unlike check payments, electronic payments are not susceptible to being lost, stolen, or damaged in transit. In those few cases where an electronic payment is misrouted, it can be traced and rerouted to the recipient, usually within 24 hours after a claim of non-receipt is received, compared to an average of 14 days for a check. Further, electronic payments are far less susceptible to forgery or alteration than checks. Each year, the Government handles claims relating to approximately $60 million in forged checks, $1.8 million in counterfeit checks, and $3.3 million in altered checks.[12]

The Fed was not impressed. During the 1990s, the Fed's ACH had been greatly improved, eliminating reels of tape and concentrating the processing in three centers (down from forty-two). But the Fed never mandated that banks equip themselves to receive ACH payments, which crippled efforts to move the United States along the path to direct deposit already perfected by every other industrial country—and now put the Fed on a collision path with the new law, which apparently could not be obeyed without great expansion of the ACH. Instead, the Fed commissioned Bottomline Technologies, a Portsmouth, New Hampshire, consulting firm specialized in improving check security, to create a program that would allow banks not equipped for ACH to receive payments in paper form for their customers who were beneficiaries of federal benefits or purchases. An article in the *Federal Reserve Bulletin* worried that poor people lured into using the same financial system as richer people might lose "the informal financial market—that is, family, friends and social organizations—[that] is also a significant source of credit and financial services to lower income families."[13]

"We all have opinions about payments," David Allerdice of the Chicago Fed condescendingly told a meeting of the Financial Services Technology Consortium. "It's like all dogs have fleas. . . . Consumers do not think or care about how they pay for things." The Fed rejects systems that are Not Invented Here the way a sick man with a rare blood type rejects transplants. The list of rationales is extraordinary. People worry, we are told, that their phone bills will go up if they pay bills through a personal computer hooked to a phone line. "When you talk about electronic payments," says Brian Mantel of the Cleveland Fed sorrowfully, "you assume the money is in the account. What convenience means to people is, how certain am I that it's error-free?"

Alan Greenspan himself, speaking by videophone to the annual conference of the National Automated Clearing House Association in spring 2000, put the kibosh on all electronic ventures, musing that people prefer checks because they assert a tangible connection between them and their wealth, and that people regard checks as more *private* than electronic accounts. "Tampering with money has always had profoundly political implications," he said. "It took many generations for people to feel comfortable accepting paper in lieu of gold or silver." He did, however, think well of systems that would permit people to use debit cards to make purchases on the Internet, which "would clearly expand electronic payment capabilities . . . to those with bank accounts who do not hold credit cards." Given the infinitesimal size of the cadre of people with bank accounts who don't have credit cards—and the danger of loss of privacy and money in Internet purchases associated with debit card information—the argument should qualify whatever staffer wrote the speech for early retirement.

"As we look forward," Greenspan began his peroration, "the Federal Reserve recognizes that whatever innovations develop, the check will likely be with us for many years . . . we continue to modernize our check-processing systems. . . . In a period of change and uncertainty, there may be a temptation, and a desire by some market participants, to have the government step in and resolve the uncertainty, whether through standards, regulation or other policies. . . . Only consumers and merchants will ultimately determine what new products are successful in the marketplace. Government action can retard progress, but almost certainly cannot ensure it."[14] The "almost certainly" is vintage Greenspan.

One should note in passing that there is one electronic payments system to which the Fed has given wholehearted cooperation: CLS, the Continuous Linked Settlement system for foreign exchange trading, to be operated by the world's largest banks in London. Launch date has slipped several times, and may still be slipping: it's a very tricky technical problem. Payments in foreign exchange trading have been concentrated at the New York Clearing House Interbank Payments System computer, not at the Fed, and the business to be moved into the new institution presumably comes from CHIPS, not from FedWire. Someone very senior at the Federal Reserve Bank of New York said that the efforts of the New York Clearing House to become the center of electronic check presentment in the United

States were in reality a "death rattle" of an institution about to be fatally injured by CLS.

Unfortunately, these are serious matters. Joined together in the Financial Services Information Technology Secretariat, twenty-three of the nation's twenty-five largest banks have agreed to create services designed to eliminate checks in this first decade of the century. For banks to be the largest providers of these services, the Fed must indicate whether, to take the most obvious analogy, they are to drive on the right or the left side of the road. The absolute refusal of the Fed to participate–it has never sent so much as a vice president of a district bank to a meeting of the Data Interchange Standards Association, which is the central organization bringing together the creators of electronic information systems and also the liaison between the American National Standards Institute and the UN's EDIFACT group in Geneva–dooms not only the Fed itself but possibly the banking system to a marginal role in future payments systems. Already a number of industries–automobiles, chemicals, aircraft manufacturers, travel, steel, oil–have established their own protocols and platforms for ordering, selling, invoicing, and paying through the Internet. Even within the financial sector, more and more transactions are being settled through correspondent banking, in a process of bilateral netting that the Fed has shortsightedly promoted to mitigate the possible damage from its refusal to regulate the over-the-counter derivatives markets.

In 1999, after Alice Rivlin resigned as vice chair of the Fed to resume scholarly studies at the Brookings Institution (and devote more time to the city of Washington, where she served as chairman of the Control Board Congress had installed to oversee the financial affairs of the District of Columbia), Roger Ferguson succeeded her both as vice chair and as supervisor of the system's efforts in payments. Rivlin had chaired a "Commission" reporting on the future of electronic payments, which the staff had made into a brief defending the Fed's repeated sabotage. Everybody, the report said once again, is happy with checks; it would be a mistake to set standards that would limit the options of the market or even to participate in the work of groups like the Data Interchange Standards Association (who are we to tell people to drive on the right when there are possible systems that would involve driving on the left?), ending with the placatory declaration that nevertheless the Fed should take "leadership." Ferguson asked the staff to define what "leadership" might mean in this context, met privately with leaders of the outside groups trying to move toward electronic payments, and has sought to create an atmosphere in the building conducive to the idea that the Fed–even the Fed–might have something to learn. No small part of the future of the American financial system rests on how successful he is.

Chapter 13

Supervisions

A regulatory climate that does not appreciate that the financial develop-
ments over an extended period of good times will tend to breed the financial
environment that leads to the likelihood of crisis and hard times will not
serve this economy well.

–Hyman Minsky (1975)[1]

THE SECOND LARGEST GROUP OF EMPLOYEES of the Federal Reserve
System, perhaps four thousand altogether, work on aspects of the examination function. As noted in chapter 2, this is a more controversial
activity than the public knows, or the Fed likes to admit. To begin
with, there is no generally accepted job description or statement of
purpose. The most basic argument for bank examination is that banks
are special institutions that invest other people's money without
telling them where it is invested, and therefore must be policed by the
chartering authority to make sure the money isn't squandered or
stolen. The second argument is that the liabilities of the banks are
most of the money supply of the country, and there is thus an overriding public interest in making sure that the value of the assets purchased by those liabilities is indeed sufficient to cover them, with

something ("capital") left over. The "safety and soundness" of the individual banks determines the safety and soundness of the system.

Historically, the bank examiner's purpose was to determine that the value asserted for the assets by the bank management was reasonable. But it was and is hard to close banks, even badly run banks, when some minor adjustment will allow management to claim that the real value of the assets is indeed larger than the nominal value of the liabilities–hard even today, when Congress has enacted a law requiring "prompt corrective action" in dealing with banks with asserted capital below 2 percent of assets; much harder before 1992, when the banking supervisors had full discretion. "Market discipline" is supposed to be helpful, but the ethos of this situation is that the examiner stands *in loco mercatis,* so to speak; the law forbids publication of information derived from a bank examination. Depositors and lenders to this bank have thought it was safe or their money wouldn't be there, and it is indeed one of the reasons it's so hard to close down a bank that the public having learned this one is bad may flee others.

Bank secrecy makes the systemic situation worse, which adds to the burden on the examination process. "Supposing that, owing to defects in its government," Walter Bagehot wrote in England 150 years ago,

> one even of the greater London joint stock banks failed, there would be an instant suspicion of the whole system. One *terra incognita* being seen to be faulty, every other *terra incognita* would be suspected. If the real government of these banks had for years been known, and if the subsisting banks had been known not to be ruled by the bad mode of government which had ruined the bank that had fallen, then the ruin of that bank would not be hurtful. The other banks would be seen to be exempt from the cause which had destroyed it. But at present the ruin of one of these great banks would greatly impair the credit of all. Scarcely any one knows the precise government of any one; in no case has that government been described on authority; and the fall of

one by grave misgovernment would be taken to show that the others might as easily be misgoverned also. And a tardy disclosure even of an admirable constitution would not much help the surviving banks: as it was extracted by necessity, it would be received with suspicion. A sceptical world would say, "Of course they are all perfect now"; it would not do for them to say anything else.[2]

Every failure[3] is an embarrassment to the supervisory authority that was supposed to know how this institution was run, and didn't—or knew and chose to cut the offender some slack. Nancy A. Wentzler of the OCC told a Levy Institute conference in the spring of 2000 that the cognoscenti of these matters now feel that the greatest danger to the world's big banks is "operational risk"—the danger that behind the magnificent facade of the financial services holding company, nobody knows what's going on, and some of what management thinks is happening is not happening. Bank consultant Ed Furash says that the typical organization of a modern bank active on many fronts is a "silo" system, where each activity has its own staff and direction and expertise, and when significant risks pop up, the designated risk controller is a one-armed paperhanger. But in sufficiently complex institutions, supervisors may choose to trust the prominent and highly paid *grandi ufficiali* who run the place, and make only the most general determination that the people in charge of the bank seem to know what they're doing.

The belief here is that the reason why the Federal Reserve Bank of New York engineered the rescue of the Long Term Capital Management hedge fund in September 1998 was fear that the collapse of the fund would have exposed to public view the sloppy performance of the world's great financial institutions—and the careless, trusting supervision that had permitted this overconfident crowd of Ph.D. economists, mathematicians, and gamblers to carry positions in excess of $100 billion, and derivative contracts with nominal values over $1 trillion, on a capital base of less than $2 billion. I had occasion six months after the rescue to describe what they were doing for scholarly publication. They were "selling volatility"–that is, they were betting that prices in the option markets, and in markets where assets were valued according to their "optionality," overcharged the buyers of options by assuming greater volatility than was probable from the historical record. It was thus safe for people smarter than the market to sell options, especially when they could be paired in ways that paid off whether the market rose moderately or fell moderately. Because the gains per trade from these apparently sure things were very small, the game had to be played with enormous quantities of borrowed money. If markets moved further than mathematical probabilities said they were supposed to move, however, the losses from an inability to cash the winning positions in a single day of tight credit might eat up years of profits. The Chicago futures exchanges have a saying that exactly covers the LTCM case: "Traders who sell volatility eat like chickens and shit like elephants."[4]

John Meriwether, chairman and principal strategist of LTCM, had first come to public attention in Michael Lewis's *Liar's Poker*, where he was alleged to have responded to the challenge of a million-dollar bet on the serial numbers of dollar bills in their wallets uttered by John Gutfreund (chairman of the bond house then known simply as Salomon) by upping the ante to $10 million, at which point Gutfreund walked away.[5] Only a few days before the New York Fed felt it had to intervene to save Meriwether from losing his hedge fund, Alan Greenspan had testified to the House Banking Committee that "hedge funds were strongly regulated by those who lend the money."[6] The belief that Alan Greenspan knew whereof he spoke, a central tenet of the Fed's status, had been put in hazard.

The party line was that the failure of LTCM would have thrown onto the market all the collateral the hedge fund had used as security for its loans from the big international banks and investment banks, and would have endangered the banking system as the price of the collateral fell. The veteran banking commentator Carter Golembe had his doubts: "[T]he 'falling sky' scenario . . . had to be reported and could not be denied; this is the great value of using the prospect of imminent disaster to justify a particular action because, once taken, one will never know whether it was really needed. . . . Obviously, there had been a serious regulatory failure, by which I mean failure by bank examiners and their supervisors."[7] *The New York Times* reported that one of the unanswered questions that triggered Fed of New York intervention was the discovery that the examiners did not know how much LTCM owed the banks. Golembe commented, "That the Fed had no idea, or at least no good idea, how much Meriwether had been loaned by its banks (and possibly even had to resort to asking Meriwether) was mind-boggling." Henry Kaufman asks, "Where were the bank examiners? . . . And what about the senior managers at the institutional lenders? Were they aware of the magnitude of the risks their institutions had undertaken?"[8]

There was a systemic risk–not reverberations from the losses that might or might not have been imposed on the banks under the Fed's supervision (Chase, Bankers Trust, and J. P. Morgan domestically, plus the branches of Barclay's, Deutsche Bank, Credit Suisse First Boston, Union Bank of Switzerland, Paribas, and Société Général), but loss of public confidence in the U.S. government supervisors of the banks. Bagehot's point. The regulators had to save themselves. Because John Meriwether knew that, he was able to face down William McDonough as years earlier he had faced down John Gutfreund. The story of the endgame is splendidly told, with sympathy for all sides, in Roger Lowenstein's book *When Genius Failed.*[9] Meriwether gave McDonough a choice of theoretical scandal (for McDonough's action to push banks toward a rescue of LTCM played badly with members of Congress, bankers, and academics; Greenspan made it clear to the House Banking Committee that the decision had been McDonough's and not his) or of real scandal from the revelation that the world's biggest banks had been played for patsies under the nose of a New York Fed that was supposed to be supervising them. McDonough, fearful of raising the ante, herded the banks together into a "consortium" that found $3.6 billion to refinance LTCM. The annual report of the Bank for International Settlements noted disconsolately that "the inference to be drawn from the

Long-Term Capital Management affair is that the regulatory authorities as well as the principal creditors considered that a non-bank financial institution was too complex to fail."[10]

The Comptroller's Office enjoys pointing out that none of the
banks on the LTCM victim list was nationally chartered or examined
by the Comptroller's National Bank Examiners–they were all either
state-chartered or foreign-chartered, and thus by law wards of
the Fed. One nationally chartered bank did participate eventually
in the negotiations. John Reed, then co-chairman of Citigroup, told
the story as luncheon speaker at an OCC conference in Washington
in fall 1999. He had been in San Francisco, he said, when McDonough called him and told him he was needed in New York at the
meeting on what to do about LTCM. He remembered that he had
told McDonough he had no interest in that. Citibank had no exposure to LTCM. On the plane going back to New York, however, he
thought to himself that Citi was the lead bank to Goldman, Sachs
and to Morgan Stanley, both of which were in up to their eyeballs.
There was no way he could escape involvement.

In the early years, the district banks relied on information from their
discount windows as the indicator of how soundly their member
banks were conducting their operations. Anywhere from one-fifth to
two-thirds of the required reserves of the banking system were borrowed at the window until the Great Depression and the Great War
loaded the banks with Treasury paper, and the vice president of the
district bank who ran the window could *see* the quality of the paper
that was being offered for rediscount. There is a school of thought
that the information at the discount window was better information
than what comes out of bank examinations. Hyman Minsky, who
worked at the Fed and taught at Berkeley and Washington University in St. Louis before becoming resident scholar at the Levy Institute–and who served on bank boards to see what it looked like from
the other side–wrote in the 1980s:

If the Federal Reserve acts as a normal-functioning supplier of funds to banks through the discount window, then as long as banks value this source of funds they will conform to business and balance-sheet standards set down by the Reserve banks. On the other hand, if Federal Reserve credit is supplied to banks by means of open-market operations in government securities, then the customer relationship between a member bank and the Federal Reserve loses its power to affect member-bank behavior. The power of the Federal Reserve to affect member-bank behavior through normal banking relations was much diminished after World War II. This diminution of Federal Reserve clout, to use a concept drawn from Chicago politics, was not offset by an increased sophistication of Federal Reserve examination and regulation of banks. . . . Bank examination is largely perfunctory—the domain of accountants who look for proper procedures, documentation, and obvious fraud—rather than an inquiry into the economic viability and the exposures to risk of banking organizations.[11]

Minsky believed strongly that central banks must have authority to examine and supervise banks—not only because monetary policy cannot be made properly without an intimate knowledge of what the banks are doing, but also because the central bank "needs to know the results of *regulations and of monetary policy upon the viability of the regulated units*" (italics in the original).[12] But even Minsky worried about the inflationary impact of new bank reserves created by the central bank to keep bad banks from sinking: "As a result of the need to offset consequences of the inability of bank regulators or market organizations to prevent pre-crisis situations from developing, rates of growth of bank reserves that are not warranted by the potential growth of output are forced upon the Federal Reserve."[13] Robert Litan of the Brookings Institution testified in 1991 that the best way to keep the Fed from overlending to the banks it supervised was to "make the Fed pay for it. . . . The Fed is stingy. It doesn't like to lose money. It seems to me that if it knew it was on the hook for a loss, it would be in very early at the door of the FDIC and/or the Comptroller saying, you are not going to ever put the Fed in a position where it is going to have to shell out a dime."[14]

The Office of the Comptroller is responsible for individual banks; the Federal Reserve Board is responsible for the banking system. Historically, OCC examiners had been trained to freeze the institution (to the point where the examiners, arriving without warning early in the morning before the opening of the bank, counted the cash in the tellers' tills prior to the arrival of the day's first customers); Fed examiners had always looked at the ongoing enterprise. With nationally chartered banks owned by holding companies, the Fed does not examine the bank, and without an invitation from the Fed, the OCC examiners have no authority to examine anything but the bank. Most people believe that the FDIC examiners can visit anything that is funded with insured deposits, but in fact the Fed and the OCC traditionally kept the FDIC away from troubled situations, fearing that the insurer would go his own way. William Isaac, who was FDIC chairman from 1981 to 1985, complained about the Continental Illinois situation that "the eighth-largest bank in the country was going down, and the FDIC had never been in the door before."[15]

From the OCC's point of view, examiners from the Fed sat around in conference rooms with the high muck-a-mucks of the holding company, while the national bank examiners were down in the bowels of the building pulling loan files and seeing whether the bank was keeping tabs on the businesses where its money was employed. As the big banks became what it is now fashionable to call "complex institutions," the OCC too began to stress the larger questions of strategy and control and the capacity of the officers of the bank to carry out the strategies they proclaimed. Indeed, OCC examiners are now stationed permanently, year-round, in the bigger banks, receiving the more important reports that come up the pipeline through the bank's "management information system." One notes that the OCC charges banks for the cost of their examination, while the Fed does the job for free, at a cost of about $400 million a year. Every year, regardless of which party holds the job, the Office of Management and Budget in the White House urges Congress to charge the state-chartered banks a fee for examination services by the Fed, and every year the Conference of State Bank Supervisors beats it off at an early stage in the legislative process. One notes also that the consolidation drive in banking has put the independence of the OCC at risk, because a decision by Bank of America to switch its status from nationally chartered to state-chartered would today deprive the OCC of one-tenth of its total revenues. In June 2000, SouthTrust, a bank with headquarters in Birmingham, Alabama, and six hundred offices in eight states, converted to state charter.

Ed Furash, who has now sold his firm, was the proprietor of the most influential bank consulting business (he set up the Bankers Roundtable, where CEOs of big banks do indeed meet to discuss common problems, commission the studies Furash thinks have to be done, and occasionally issue blasts from on high). He likes to contrast the examinations done by the different federal agencies. "The Fed as a regulator," he said, "adores ambiguity. The OCC will say, seeing a bank that is buying collateralized mortgage obligations then putting them out for repurchase and using the cash to buy more collateralized mortgage obligations, 'The level at which you are doing dollar rolls into CMOs [the term of art] is not justified by your capital.' The Fed will say, 'You should look and see whether your dollar rolls are compatible with safety and soundness.'

"Some bankers love it because they get more wiggle room. Others say, 'Furash, will you tell me what the hell these guys really want.'"

And then, of course, there are the others that just don't care. William Isaac noted that it is "very tough to do—to go into a major bank before it has obvious problems and say, you guys are making a lot of real estate loans and we are really worried about it and we think you ought to slow down. I've seen it, I was in Security Pacific on behalf of that board of directors, looking at what happened and why. The Comptroller of the Currency actually was calling the thing at Security Pacific five or six years before it happened, before it blew up. They kept on saying, you're doing this, you're doing that, and Security Pacific would write back and say–we appreciate your kind note, but frankly, we are Security Pacific–you don't seem to understand that–and please keep in touch. That was the end of that. What are you going to do about it?"[16]

Testifying before the Senate Banking Committee in 1991, E. Gerald Corrigan, then president of the Federal Reserve Bank of New York, complained that his examiners (there were only two hundred of them at that point) were paid less than the New York State and Comptroller's examiners. "Their average tenure," he said, "is eight years. Their average salary is $50,000. And these two hundred people are responsible for the inspection of 7 of the 15 largest bank holding companies in the United States. . . . We've got to work like the devil to upgrade the professional skills and abilities of these bank examiners." But when he was asked why he didn't have more and better-paid examiners, he replied, "My inherent fiscal conservatism."[17] Under his successor, some of that has gone. The New York Fed in 2000 had about seven hundred examiners, and personnel in Washington said that good men with degrees from good schools cost $125,000 a year. The great expansion of the force reflects congressional decision to give the Fed a far more extensive role in the examination of the branches of foreign banks. The turnover rate remains something more than 10 percent a year. The fact that examiners working in some big banks keep running into former colleagues–and senior colleagues, at that–is a matter of concern among the regulators, but there isn't much they can do.

The job is different from what it used to be. Examiners still give a bank a "CAMELS" rating, the initials standing for Capital, Assets, Management, Earnings, Liquidity, Sensitivity (to changes in interest rates: this last is new). The Fed in examining foreign branches and agencies started with an AIM rating (for Asset quality, Internal controls, and Management capability), and switched to ROCA (for Risk management, Operational controls, Compliance, and Asset quality). For bank holding companies, the acronym is BOPEC, for Bank subsidiaries, Other nonbank subsidiaries, Parent company, Earnings, and Capital adequacy. Each factor is graded on a five-point scale, and a composite rating is awarded. All such ratings are still great secrets; telling anybody a bank's rating is a crime, and examiners don't talk. (So much, perhaps, for "transparency.") But pretty much everyone now believes that the lesson of the 1980s and 1990s is that bank examination must be "risk-focused." When the examining team comes into a large bank these days, nobody counts the cash, and if anybody pulls the loans from the file drawers to see if they are "performing," it's a junior member of the team. It's much more important to know the Value at Risk from interest-rate swaps, whether the bank is still on the hook for loans that have been securitized and sold to the market ("recourse"), or which "tranche" of the collateralized mortgage obligation the bank has kept for itself (residual or "Z" tranches, which the OCC has forbidden banks to hold, are known on Wall Street as "toxic waste").

The question of what to do with a bank that has stunk it up has no obvious answer. FDICIA tells the supervisors that a bank with less than 2 percent capital should be closed down, the logic of that being that there is no longer enough cushion of its owners' own money to protect the deposit insurance fund from having to pick up its losses. The determination that a bank has fallen below the risk-adjusted capital floor is left to the Fed, which never wanted it. George Kaufman and George Bentson were the authors of the original Structured Early Intervention and Resolution (SEIR) plan that underlay FDICIA, and Kaufman was not happy with what the Fed did. "[R]egulators vigorously opposed the enactment of a strong SEIR and have been dragging their feet since. . . . [R]egulators have moved slowly in introducing market-value accounting. They have also adopted numerical definitions of adequate-capitalization for prompt corrective action on a book-value basis that are both far too low for ensuring safety, particularly in relation to either the riskier portfolios banks have selected in recent years or the more volatile . . . and considerably lower than at the banks' uninsured 'unregulated' competitors [i.e., finance companies]."[18] Though the Fed cannot pull a bank charter because it does not create one, it can when angry issue a cease-and-desist order to put a stop to a course of conduct it feels will make a bank unsafe. More usual is the negotiated "Memorandum of Understanding," by which a bank agrees to consult with its examiners before carrying out its plans; such a document may include, as one at Bank of America in the mid-1980s did, an insistence that the top officers of the bank be replaced. The MoU with Citibank in 1990 required the bank to raise more capital, and if a subsequent examination of Chemical had produced a more favorable impression could conceivably have compelled the sale of the bank. It should be noted that examiners at any time have the right to insist that they (or their bosses) present their findings and concerns to the board of directors of the bank.

For the large international banks, where the financial stability stakes are high, currency exposures—assets or debts denominated in foreign currencies, forward contracts to acquire or deliver currencies—are a significant area for the examiners. So, of course, are derivatives, instruments that draw their value from the price movements of other financial assets. Unfortunately, many of these instruments cannot be valued as one values loans or bonds; some, indeed, cannot be priced in any market and have only a "probable" value.

In dealing with "Large Complex Banking Organizations" (LCBOs), American bank examiners have moved from pinning down the condition of the bank at the moment of its examination to judging continuously whether the risks in the portfolio of a financial holding company cast doubt on its future viability. The OCC keeps a small group of examiners in a big bank every day all year long, with quarterly conferences to review what seems to be happening. The Fed has not yet at this writing installed permanent teams in the holding companies (though it projects doing so at some time, despite "concerns that such a presence could undermine examiners' independence"). If you live every day with one bank's risk management model (and its risk managers), you are likely to think that is the way to go. Instead, the Fed has monitored with off-site questioning, some of people and some of computers, and with "point-of-time" visits by examining teams. But the teams are not doing the sort of "transaction testing" that characterized traditional examinations; they are looking at the risk models.

The district banks hire the examiners, subject to the board's "commissioning requirements." Most of them come out of the banking schools or the business schools of the best universities. (In 1990–91, when most of the big banks were in big trouble and were merging to downsize, the Fed was able to hire experienced bankers as examiners, but most of the time the job offers are not competitive for the people you would like to have.) The district banks give them four to six months of "core training," leading to a national "proficiency exam" created by the board for the entire system. Much of this training is done collaboratively by the district banks, which make policy for themselves acting through their standing Conference of Presidents and (more operationally) their Conference of First Vice Presidents. Both in Washington and elsewhere, the Fed operates through committees and subcommittees: the 1996 GAO report on the Fed lists seven each of committees and subcommittees, and the list doesn't include temporary groups like the continuing Financial Services Policy Committee formed by all the banks, or SCRIM, the Subcommittee on Credit, Reserves, and Risk Management, headed by the presidents of the Federal Reserve Banks of Chicago, Kansas City, and Minneapolis. A good deal of time and money gets spent trying to make sure that the system is reliable–that different examiners will take the same approach to the same instrument.

There are six risks in the Fed's lexicon: credit risk (including the danger of default by counterparties in various deals as well as borrowers), market risk, liquidity risk (the danger that a borrower's failure to pay its loan or a derivatives counterparty's failure to perform on expiration will coincide with the need for that money), operational risk (snafu in the information systems), legal risk (unenforceable contracts), and reputational risk (loss of business through bad publicity). To these, Ernest Patrikis when first vice president of the New York Fed added intellectual risk (the danger that the one person in the organization who understands the position gets hit by a bus). I like to think of a combination of reputational and intellectual risk, which is the danger that the one person in the organization who is reputed to understand the position really doesn't. "Examiners are challenged," a GAO study said gently, "to avoid being overly influenced by banks' risk management systems while relying on those systems and other data furnished by the bank to make their assessments."[19]

For some years, it has been fashionable to argue that nobody starting from scratch could conceivably design a system of financial services regulation that looks anything like what the United States has. Equally true is the proposition that nobody starting from scratch would ever come up with the financial services supervision system we have. Key questions about the obligations of auditors to the examiners (and examiners' obligations to seek elucidation from the bank's auditors) have never been fully thrashed out. Since 1979, when it was called into existence by the Congress, a Federal Financial Institutions Examination Council has met at regular intervals to keep all the supervisory services reading as much as possible from the same page, and over the years it has issued a number of emollient statements; but its function clearly is to make policy rather than determine the details of action, and it gave no help to the beleaguered Home Loan Bank Board during the S&L crisis.

A degree of comparability in examination standards has been achieved internationally, with the adoption of the Basle Accord in 1988, requiring minimum levels of capital for internationally active banks. The required capital was 8 percent of risk-weighted assets, with at least half of that in the form of equity. At bottom, a capital requirement is a way to assure that banks have their owners' money– not just depositors' money and the money they have been able to borrow–at risk in their ventures. The risk weightings assigned for the first decade of the agreement were pretty crude, and in some ways dangerous. All commercial loans were assigned a 100 percent weighting; all loans to governments that were part of the Organization for Economic Cooperation and Development (OECD) were assigned a zero weighting. Interbank loans to banks in OECD countries got a 20 percent weighting (which is one of the reasons Korean banks were able to borrow too much); government guaranteed mortgage paper of the FNMA and FHLMC variety in the United States also got a 20 percent weighting (though whole mortgages had to be counted at 50 percent), which meant that when the banks were in trouble in the early 1990s, they loaded up with mortgage paper. With loans to strong companies and loans to weak companies carrying equal capital allocations, banks were tempted to lend to weaker companies, who would pay more for the money. And banks became adept at setting up "Special Purpose Vehicles" financed by people who would otherwise buy loan packages from them, which could originate loans with guarantees from the banks, and greatly reduce the required capital allocation against credit risk.[20]

The worker bees in trying to flesh out Basle's twenty-five "Core Principles for Banking Supervision" have been a Committee on Banking Supervision chaired first by Peter Cooke of the Bank of England and more recently by William McDonough of the Federal Reserve Bank of New York. The struggles have been over the acceptance of banks' own models to determine the risks in derivatives positions and the creation of more sophisticated risk weightings in the credit area. In summer 1999, the committee decided to use the ratings of borrowers as published by the independent ratings agencies—Moody's, Standard & Poor's, and ICBA/Fitch—as measures of the capital banks should have to set aside against bond holdings, individual loans, or rated packages of loans. This was widely recognized as a doubtful proposition, creating a positive feedback loop—that is, a situation where the optimism of the lending officer was reinforced by the good cheer of the ratings agencies in good times, and the pessimism of the lending officer was buttressed by the gloom of the ratings agencies in bad times. (John Heimann says that the function of ratings agencies in a crisis is to go out on the battlefield and shoot the wounded.) It was endorsed, probably, because J. P. Morgan had published a mathematical exegesis of credit risk weightings based on published ratings, and the generation that thinks the name "Morgan" means quality and care still holds leadership positions in banks and government agencies.

There are other forces for uniformity. In response to the 1987 market crash, President Reagan established a President's Working

Group on financial markets, composed of the secretary of the treasury and the heads of the Fed, the SEC, and the Commodity Futures Trading Commission. It was the President's Working Group that recommended the "circuit breakers" that halt trading in stocks and derivatives on stocks after an extraordinarily large move in stock prices. Revived by Lloyd Bentsen in 1994, this is a more active body than is generally realized, with regular meetings including a biweekly conference call among senior staffers at all the agencies plus the Federal Reserve Bank of New York. The Fed is usually represented by a governor. Its most important function in the late 1990s was as a device to crush the intelligent proposal of Brooksley Born of the CFTC that over-the-counter derivatives be subject to greater disclosure and perhaps regulation, a word with which the Clinton Treasury did not wish to be associated. Wall Street widely but erroneously (and from Alan Greenspan's point of view infuriatingly) believes that the Working Group has mysterious behind-the-scenes relations with the big securities houses, and rescues the stock market as an empowered Lone Ranger with secret accounts in the Chicago pits that buy up stock index futures whenever prices drop *too* dramatically.

Most large banks today organize participations in their large loans by other banks and insurance companies from day one. (This is known in the trade as "blowing it out of the bank.") To reduce duplication, the Fed and the OCC have developed a Shared National Credit program through which examiners from both agencies can compare their views of big syndicated loans. Fed programs "target" activities across district lines to perform comparable inspections of similar activities at large banks in "Coordinated Supervisory Exercises." The three such mentioned by Richard Spillenkothen, director of the Division of Banking Supervision and Regulation, were "credit risk modeling, emerging markets trading activities, and liquidity risk management."[21] Findings from such investigations are entered on a National Examination Database available to the full examination staff. In spring 2000, the database was enhanced and extended by a Banking Organization National Desktop that placed results and analyses of the results on the examiners' PCs.

Still, most Federal Reserve examinations continue to be divided by district, with regional and national banks supervised in the jurisdiction that contains their headquarters. This has been a headache, especially when a North Carolina–based entity, NationsBank, takes over Bank of America, which had always been run from San Francisco. People speak delicately of the effort–"we brokered a deal"–to establish functional lines of examination that would permit the people who examined the "wholesale bank" to remain on the west coast while the supervision of the holding company and the retail bank moved, inescapably, to Richmond.

In June 1999, Washington sent orders to the supervisory staff to make sure that a senior supervisor is appointed as the "Central Point of Contact" between the examiners and the LCBO. In New York, that individual is supposed to "spend all day every day at Morgan or Chase or Citi," and there are quarterly meetings coinciding with the issuance of the corporate 10-Q reports required by the SEC, "to study the strategy that drove the profits or failed to drive profits. And to ask for the track record on follow-up to problems auditors have raised." Four months later, the board decided to create a "senior staff level position" in Washington to coordinate staff resources for banks that did not have enough big-bank business to maintain the necessary specializations. Districts are to some extent encouraged to develop specialists, who can be loaned across the lines to help embattled examination staffs in other districts. Washington clearly feels that nationwide banking will eventually require the Board of Governors itself to take direct control of the examination process. The district banks, already threatened with the loss of full-time employees from the movement to electronic banking, have taken a stand like Horatius at the bridge.

But the problem is larger than that. Classical bank examination, "transaction testing," was potentially an adversarial affair, with the examiner looking for problems and assuming that there might well be problems not previously revealed to him. "Risk-focused" examinations are forward-looking, and work on the assumption that the bank's leadership knows the truth and tells the truth about what it is doing and what it plans to do. And of course most bankers most of the time are quite trustworthy—it is the psychological fundament of the business. I have met a number of them, and as Joe H. Palmer wrote of the New York Jockey Club half a century ago, you could not get better men if you set a bear trap in the aisle of a cathedral. But people under pressure see the world a little differently, and in banking in recent years the pressures have grown increasingly heavy. Some humility is in order. Publishing the report of its Study Group on Accountants, Bankers, and Regulators after the 1990–91 constriction of the banking systems around the world, the Group of Thirty stated flatly that "For many institutions that failed or found themselves in serious financial difficulty, everyone's assessment of asset quality was wrong. Confidence in supervision and financial reporting was badly eroded."[22]

To the extent that the examination does have an adversarial component, it rests on the fact that the examiner's task is to form a view of whether in fact the bank can carry out its plans as presented. Who are the counterparties for the "credit derivatives" which save the bank from defaulting borrowers? How much funding will be lost with a decline of value in the bonds temporarily owned by those with whom the bank has "repurchase agreements"? What protection does the bank have against severe fluctuations in the value of long-dated currency options? *Will the models work?* "I called a big bank and asked to speak to their expert on Korea," Treasury Secretary Robert Rubin said at a conference six months after the East Asian crisis, "and we were astonished to find out how little they knew." What is the responsibility of the examiner to find out whether his hosts whose models are to determine the risk weighting of the assets really know the resiliency of their positions under stress?

A good deal of what is necessary remains common sense. "If the State Department wants you to do Chad," John Heimann said reminiscently, "you take reserves against that loan immediately." E. Gerald

Corrigan of Goldman, Sachs, who co-chaired the bank/investment bank study of instability in 1998, says that in July of that year it was already too late to protect yourself against the disaster following the Russian default in August because the market had priced the hedges so high. "In a world of collateralized credit," says Christine Cumming, vice president specializing in derivatives for the "supervisory group" in New York, "liquidity risk can be desperate." *The problem is never that the borrower or the counterparty can't pay; the problem is that the lender or the winner on the derivatives contract can't afford not to be paid.* As the technology improves and information spreads, banks need the profits gained from creating tight articulations of cash flows, and the system can become vulnerable without anybody on the inside noticing the escalating risk. "The business has changed so quickly," says Cumming, "that the homogeneity is gone, the understanding of fundamental risk is gone."

Alan Greenspan's fear of ordering participants in a private market to follow imposed standards has limited the Fed's role in risk reduction as it has limited its participation in electronic payments. To the extent that every large bank has its own proprietary model for judging risk, even specialist examiners have to fall back on trust. For a while in the mid-1990s, the Fed played with the idea of a "Pre-Commitment Approach," by which a bank would specify "the maximum potential loss it could suffer on its trading portfolio over a regulator-set horizon. Explicit in the PCA is a bank commitment to contain losses within its pre-commitment amount. Should a bank incur trading losses in excess of its capital commitment, it would be subject to penalties. Although the penalty structure has yet to be determined, penalties may take the form of fines, capital surcharges, or perhaps other more intrusive regulatory discipline."[23] This would have changed the nature of risk control: instead of the bank worrying about the trader who hid the slips, the supervisor would have to worry about the entire institution hiding the slips. Especially when looking at derivatives that are "marked to model," the option of denying the loss would be pretty irresistible.

The Value-at-Risk model promoted by Morgan in the early

1990s failed in 1997 in the Asian crisis and then self-destructed in 1998 after the Russian default. But it is still in use. The recommended supplement is a "stress test," that presumably permits the risk manager to simulate the impact on his bank's capital under varying assumptions. There are two ways such simulations can be used. One is to make plausible assumptions and measure the results; the other is to look at the assumptions that would make the bough break and come to a judgment of whether they are plausible. The latter use of stress testing is rare. And the Federal Reserve Bank of New York has found that banks resist the idea that an examiner can submit his own list of assumptions and ask that they be used in the bank's stress test. Among the powers of the modern examiner surely should be the authority to require a bank to use assumptions other than its own in testing the risk of exotic instruments.

One comes back to the simple truth that leverage is dangerous, whether it is excessive margin in the stock market or inadequate capital in banks or daisy chains of repurchase agreements that monstrously enlarge the structures that can be raised on small foundations. John Reed, then co-chairman of Citigroup and much experienced of course as chairman of Citicorp before that, told a luncheon at an OCC conference on risk in 1999 that "Our problem in 1991 was that we didn't have the capital. Chase took a three billion dollar write-off on real estate, and the market saw in a nanosecond that we couldn't do that because we didn't have the capital. My rule of thumb is that a loss will be twice as big as any of the models say. And my decision is to be better than the regulators' minimum capital *after* you take your losses." Alan Greenspan told the same meeting that keeping more than the minimum capital reduces the return on equity–"but so does the purchase of fire insurance."

John Heimann, after training bank supervisors all over the world as head of the BIS Financial Stability Institute, feels that reliance on detailed examination is hopeless. What you get, he says, is "bloodhounds tracking greyhounds." (Mike Moussa, chief economist of the IMF, says this may not be as bad as it sounds, because the greyhounds run around in circles.) "The question," Heimann adds, "is how you can move to qualitative supervision–you can't quantify this." A very senior Fed examiner says with concern that "the way exposures are related is an area where people are coming up the learning curve." For the time being, BIS suggests that banks allocate capital for triple the loss that their V-a-R models tell them should be required. But in the political nexus of bank examination, such rules are abstract, faraway, and hard to defend. The old system of requiring "haircuts" on less secure assets may be historically oriented and bottom-up rather than risk-focused and top-down, but in the absence of market-value accounting, it's easier for all concerned to see what's happening. And in the end the salvation of the supervisory system can come only from the creation and publication of information that can easily be used by the markets.

Chapter 14

The Fed and the Poor

FED Governor Lindsey made a casual remark questioning why banks with the highest C[ommunity] R[einvestment] A[ct] ratings generally had the lowest safety and soundness ratings. While that remark seemed to evoke a positive reaction from the bank and thrift industry representatives (there were a lot of smiles and nodded agreements), the author felt impelled to speak up and disagree based on research . . . that showed absolutely no relationship between CRA ratings and proxies for safety and soundness.

–Kenneth Thomas (1998)[1]

A THREAD THAT RUNS THROUGH AMERICAN BANKING for its entire history is the fear that the money center banks–from Bank of the United States to J. P. Morgan–will vacuum the money from the American people and spread it out on Wall Street for use by city slickers. The twelve Federal Reserve Banks stand as monuments to the wistful national desire to create separate money markets in different parts of the country. As time passed and the role of government grew, the regional hopes to seize shares of the allocation of credit and the universal insistence on money for mortgages were mostly satisfied by government guarantee and subsidy. But there re-

285

mained a great social disparity. Banking had never been a democratic activity. Prior to World War II, banks did not offer consumer
credit, though they might lend to finance companies that did. Nationally chartered banks were forbidden to lend on the security of
real estate–the only significant asset ordinary people had–until the
McFadden Act of 1927, and even then their authority to write resi-
dential mortgages was very limited. Mutual savings banks and S&Ls
grew out of cooperative actions by individuals who by income–or
race or color or creed–did not qualify for credit from a bank. Some
immigrant communities were effective at such organization, and developed closely knit institutions, forming a security blanket many
could clutch. Other communities–and especially the African-Ameri-
can community–were simply left out.

As the population exploded out of the cities after World War II,
the ethnic communities left behind a ragtail of black and Hispanic
dependencies. Urban renewal chased the better established out of
what homes they had, and further concentrated the poor. These decaying neighborhoods were systematically deprived of investment
and credit by both banks and insurance companies, which often
drew lines on the map to make sure lending officers did not commit
their institution's money in the wrong places. The process was called
"redlining," because a red crayon was the instrument of choice for
marking up the map. There had never been many banks or bank
branches in these neighborhoods; now the banks that were there
consolidated or shut down, transferring deposits to another branch.

Before all of us who witnessed it are gone, testimony should repeatedly be given to the monstrous discrimination that was a casual
unexamined fixture in American life before the civil rights movement
of the 1960s raised consciousness and conscience. Bank examiners
were supposed to assure the safety and soundness of the banks, and
to that end they would discourage banks from lending to blacks and
the lesser breed of ethnics, even in some instances when the loan re-
quested was an FHA-insured or VA-insured mortgage. Banks participated in steering blacks away from neighborhoods where they had
made loans to white homeowners, for fear that the presence of a

black face in a neighborhood would lower the value of the home as collateral. There were very few blacks working in banks, and virtually no successful black banks. (This is a continuing problem: the introductions to white vendors and potential customers that a white bank can arrange are much more valuable to a black businessperson than anything a black bank can do.) When I went looking for a prosperous black-owned bank in the early 1980s, I was repeatedly directed to the same institution, a bank in Durham, North Carolina, which had good relations with one of the few successful black insurance companies, based in the same city. And even this bank was worried, because NCNB (predecessor of today's Bank of America) had just installed one of those newfangled ATM machines in the Duke hospital, and the convenience of depositing one's paycheck and drawing cash where one worked was luring depositors away.

Absence of credit in poor neighborhoods meant declining valuations, declining tax revenues for cities, fewer jobs, more crime. Gary A. Dymski of the University of Massachusetts points out that quite marginal differences at the beginning can exponentiate with time:

> [E]conomic units in communities receiving lower credit flows will become relatively less creditworthy as the relative value of their properties lags behind values elsewhere. Areas with lower credit flows and declining values, in turn, will appear less attractive to depositories seeking borrowers. So some communities accumulate extensive bank branch networks and, in turn, job and business opportunities, while others languish and fall behind. Units in communities with robust credit flows and active asset resale markets can more readily build up equity than units in stagnating neighborhoods. . . . Because of these unstable dynamics, slight initial differences in areas–which may be based on racial perceptions or on unequally distributed bank branches–will eventually rigidify into material differences. . . . *Unrestrained competition will deepen credit-market segmentation and social inefficiency* (italics in the original).[2]

Virtuous or vicious circles begin with the presence or absence of banks. Dimitri Papadimitriou, Ronnie J. Phillips, and L. Randall Wray of the Levy Institute add the proposition that "Government action in this area is entirely appropriate because of the increase in social costs of a deteriorating community. This is made readily apparent by empty and decaying buildings found in some neighborhoods, but the costs in human capital are equally enormous, even if they are not so visible. Empty homes and closed businesses mean unemployment with concomitant losses to the individuals and to society."[3]

A significant pressure point was the fact that the losers, including, after all, city governments, had deposits in the local banks. When the civil rights movement began to roll, the first proposal was to banks that had deposits from these busted neighborhoods or from citywide institutions. Demands were made that these banks find ways to help revitalize the dying neighborhoods. In Illinois, a state law required banks to break out their loans by location, and the First National Bank of Chicago was publicly discomfited when the newspapers publicized the fact that despite its advertised support for revitalization in and around the University of Chicago neighborhood, it had completely redlined the district in its lending policies. The result of the publicity was the cooperation of the bank in the structuring of South Shore, the mother bank of community development lending in the United States.

Agitation by community groups bore national fruit in 1977, when Senator William Proxmire, chairman of the Senate Banking Committee, sponsored and shepherded through Congress the Community Reinvestment Act (CRA). The act rests on a congressional "finding" that regulated financial institutions are "required by law to demonstrate that their deposit facilities serve the convenience and needs of the communities in which they are chartered." (So much for the incessant call of the industry, with the support of the Fed, that "banks are not public utilities.") It applies only to institutions that take insured deposits, another illustration of the assertion that deposit insurance constitutes a subsidy to the banks that receive it. To certify that the banks and thrifts are in compliance with community reinvestment, the regulators are instructed to add to their usual examination for safety and soundness an examination assessing the institution's "record of meeting the credit needs of its entire community, including low- and moderate-income neighborhoods." To pass CRA tests, a bank must have a policy statement that its directors believe what the law says, a fairly high loan-to-deposit ratio, a record of having made loans to low- and moderate-income applicants, and a program to reach out to the community for borrowers.

The Federal Reserve, to quote William Schwenck Gilbert on the House of Lords,

> *throughout the war*
> *Did nothing in particular*
> *And did it very well.*

Discrimination against low-income people in lending operations was a subject guaranteed to be of no interest to the Federal Reserve System. The Fed could never be the agency of choice for a program to compel banks to invest in the ghetto. But it was there, and among its roles was the approval or denial of bank mergers, and of plans for bank holding companies to acquire new banks. Seeking to force banks to behave better in the less favored areas of their neighborhoods, the Congress wanted to be sure that any snakes under these rocks would not affect the public view of the safety or soundness of the institution in question, so the punishment for failing to serve minority borrowers had to be the denial of something the bank badly wanted that the public didn't care about. The OCC was involved when a nationally chartered bank wanted to open a branch in a state that permitted branching, and the FDIC might be involved when a holding company wanted to open a new bank and needed deposit insurance. But most of the time, the petition that would be accepted or denied was one sent to the Fed.

Kenneth H. Thomas, a Wharton School lecturer on finance and consultant to banks who has written two large and dramatic tomes about CRA, says that the Fed tried to strangle the legislation at birth, but then dutifully staffed the job, with a CRA compliance officer appointed in each district bank and as many as seventy examiners detailed to perform CRA examinations during the normal bank exams. The Fed's immediate responsibility was only for state-chartered member banks, and in dealing with national banks or state banks that were not Fed members but parts of holding companies, it was bound to give great credence to the CRA reports from the Comptroller and the FDIC. Other subsidiaries of the holding company, like mortgage banks and credit card banks, were not subject to CRA examination: the case for CRA rested on the government's deposit insurance. Like the rest of the bank examination, the CRA ratings were secret. Thomas believes that there were occasions when the Fed persuaded the other regulators to goose up a rating from "Substantial Noncompliance" so that the board could approve an application it wished to approve. The first time the Fed announced that a merger had been denied because the acquirer had an inadequate CRA rating was 1989, when Continental Illinois was forbidden to close its purchase of Grand Canyon State Bank in Scottsdale, Arizona. Continental was still partly owned by the FDIC when the ruling came down; it had no branches; and as a big-business bank, it made virtually no loans to any neighborhood. The bad CRA rating was probably a convenient excuse for something the Fed would have done in any event.[4]

Reports of bank examinations are held in the *sancta sanctorum*, where nobody but the directors of the bank can ever see them. But there was no reason why a negative CRA rating should raise doubts about the soundness of the bank, and the Congress in its punitive mood after the S&L disaster voted in 1989 to make each bank's CRA file–complaints, responses to complaints, examiner reports, and the banks' reaction to the examiner reports–available to the public. (In 1991, still annoyed with the banks, Congress included in the FDIC Improvement Act a requirement that when CRA examiners find an actual violation of the Equal Credit Opportunities Act, they *must* refer the matter to the Department of Justice.) Appeals that the bank may have taken against its rating are not part of these files, and Thomas reports that the Fed does not keep such records itself. "Perhaps," Thomas suggests, "the Fed's appeals are handled in an informal and friendly atmosphere without the need for records? Or perhaps no one really appeals their CRA ratings, because the banks are always happy with ratings given by the easiest CRA grader in the business?"[5]

Bankers, regulators, and economists don't like CRA. When the Brookings Institution had a conference on the subject a few years ago, I was the only member of the economics ensemble in this allegedly liberal group prepared to say a good word for it. In the world of the academic economist, by definition, bankers make loans to promote the allocation of resources to their most profitable use. A government rule that says they must make loans they would not otherwise make is "credit allocation," which makes the system less efficient and from an economist's point of view less just. Banks that are reluctant to lend into urban slums or rural shantytowns have reasons other than prejudice, and it is doubtless more expensive in man-hours to find and nurse good commercial borrowers in bad neighborhoods. Inevitably, a law like CRA spawns an immense paper trail of regulations and forms and legal interpretations, and the paperwork burden gets worse every year as frustrated petitioners demand more "objective" valuations. Large banks can afford to donate a "compliance officer" to the pot of laborers in the vineyard of bank examination; smaller banks really can't. And even after all the paperwork is done, the resulting evaluation is almost inevitably rather subjective, sometimes an embarrassment for all concerned.

In addition to CRA, there are concepts of "fair lending" built into various housing and consumer credit legislation. Jess Belew, executive director of the Consumer Bankers Association (mostly large banks), noted that "CRA is neighborhood housing; fair lending goes to race and gender. We could live more easily with these things if we didn't keep getting mixed signals from Washington." Another player is the Civil Rights Division of the Department of Justice, which marches to its own drummer. Pursuing a discrimination case against Barnett Banks of California, the department refused to share its evidence with either the Comptroller or the Fed. The case failed in the courts. In the mid-1990s, Justice also went after Chevy Chase Bank, a suburban Washington bank that had amalgamated several S&Ls, one of which had been advised as to its CRA responsibilities by Ken Thomas, who was not pleased. Both the Comptroller and the Fed refused to delay a Chevy Chase merger on the evidence Justice showed them, but the bank signed a consent decree that committed it to an $11 million payout and new branches in neighborhoods where it had never had a presence.

It is fair to say that the Fed's compliance staff when asked about CRA matters takes a position that defends (a) itself and (b) the banks. Thomas reports that when he went to the district banks in 1996 for documents under the Freedom of Information Act, someone at the board sent out an order that all information for Thomas was to be routed through Washington; the letter of instruction was withdrawn three weeks later, but not all the documents that had been sent to Washington were in fact passed on to Thomas. (Seeking material for its own fair lending reports, the GAO found that each staffer interviewed showed up with a Fed lawyer.) More significantly, Thomas found major discrepancies between the "Performance Evaluation" (PE) rating that was published for each bank and the "Management Report" on the compliance examination that was submitted to the bank itself on the conclusion of the exam. In the 1994 examination of the Premier Bank of Wytheville, Virginia, for example, the PE said that "The institution is in compliance with the substantive provisions of antidiscrimination laws and regulations." The Management Report began, "The overall level of compliance with consumer and civil rights law and regulations is considered less than satisfactory."[6]

A visit by a community leader or a reporter to Griff Garwood, until recently director of the Division of Consumer and Community Affairs, was neither pleasant nor instructive. At issue when I visited was the question of how the Fed would cooperate with the new law that required the federal government to make all its payments by electronic funds transfer starting in January 1999. This would pretty much require a lot of poor people to get bank accounts, something the Treasury Department was eager to accomplish, to save money for itself and to bring the 10–15 percent of American households who lack such accounts into the mainstream of the payments system. This goal in turn would require the cooperation of the Fed, which was not forthcoming, though the board paid for the publication of a few pamphlets. The Fed lawyer most involved with the new law suggested to me that check-cashing shops were just fine for city slums, and noted that in the Fed's surveys a lot of the people who used check-cashing shops had bank accounts somewhere but preferred the convenience of the storefront shop.

It was not until a few months later, though the information was in no way surprising, that a community group from East Palo Alto testified in a hearing before Treasury Department officials that on an average annual household income of about $16,000, the residents of that slum averaged about $600 a year in check-cashing fees. Such burdens could be avoided if the government that sent them their Veterans or Social Security or welfare money arranged for a money-saving direct deposit to their accounts and access to the cash through the free use of ATM machines. Well, said a lady at the Fed meeting—a very senior personage, too—there aren't that many ATM machines in the urban slums, or in those backwoods rural counties. They need a check they can cash at the grocery. But the ATM card, as a debit card, can be used at the grocery, permitting the recipient to buy her groceries and take out cash. If it's a chip card, it can even keep the recipient's records on the card. That way she can leave most of the money in the account, and not have to walk around with full pockets. Well, said the lady at the Fed, think of all those people in the slums who buy at the bodega, and all those rural people where the local store isn't equipped to honor the debit card. But the Department of Agriculture, as required by law, is moving food stamps to a card chassis, and equipping these grocery stores and bodegas with card readers as part of the cost of getting away from the food stamps. Those readers will be able to handle all electronic benefits transfers–and all electronic funds transfers from Treasury.

Look at the Social Security Administration, said the lady at the Fed. It makes a lot of payments abroad, to people who emigrated, spent their working lives in America, then returned to the old country to retire. They need paper checks. But the fact is that the Social Security Administration has been remarkably successful–at an 85 percent or better level in some countries–in its drive to arrange direct deposit into bank accounts abroad, in the currency of the country, for recipients of benefits. The arrangements that have made this procedure possible have been worked out by the Federal Reserve Bank of New York. The staff in Washington either does not know about them or does not wish to talk about them.

Perhaps the most remarkable knee-jerk reaction from the Fed's Consumer and Community Affairs staff came in 1994, when Alicia Munnell of the Boston Fed published a study of discrimination in mortgage lending, with the conclusion that yes, Virginia, it is harder for dark-skinned people to get loans in New England. Several of the 250 researchers on the board's staff were sent off to beaver away and chew down Ms. Munnell's findings. The Clinton administration had intended to give Ms. Munnell what one of its occupants has called the girl seat on the board, but congressional opponents argued that her putative colleagues would be reluctant to serve with her.

In 1994, Congress ordered the Fed to establish definitions of discriminatory lending policy, to be used in CRA examinations. In 2000, after newspaper publicity about predatory practices in low-income communities, the Fed appointed a committee to look into the matter. "Abusive 'sub-prime' lending occurs all the time," says Peggy Twohig of the Federal Trade Commission, speaking very quickly from behind a desk piled high with paper. "Banks are out there doing this kind of stuff all the time, and you don't see federal regulators doing anything about it. The Fed has Reg B–Equal Credit Opportunity Act–and we're pretty much stuck with that; we have to go by whatever the Fed says even if we disagree."

Both publicly and privately, the Fed has always refused to acknowledge the existence of discrimination in any part of the American banking system. Bank examination–especially modern bank examination–is based on trust in the examined. The dynamics of the situation lead the staff to acceptance of pro forma declarations that may or may not be true, and thus resistance to the (often uninformed, often crude) allegations of the protestors. Where other agencies may find problems, the staff is doubly armed to resist. In early 2000, the General Accounting Office reported that in contemplating big mergers (the six biggest of the late 1990s), the Fed had not forwarded complaints sent to it to the Department of Housing and Urban Development (HUD) and the Federal Trade Commission, which had power to investigate fair lending questions. And the board had in January 1998 adopted a policy of not conducting consumer compliance examinations of the non-bank subsidiaries of a bank holding company when mergers were proposed, partly (exquisitely) because it would not be fair to the mortgage subsidiaries of a bank holding company to have to defend their practices when mortgage companies that were *not* subsidiaries of bank holding companies did not have to undergo such experiences.[7] Fairness to the bank holding company far outranked any questions of fairness to low-income consumers.

Greenspan himself undertook to defend the Consumer and Community Affairs Division in a long letter of reply to the GAO. "Enforcement of the fair lending laws, including the authority to determine compliance," he wrote (or signed),

> has been specifically granted by statute to various agencies other than the Board, except with respect to state member banks of the Federal Reserve System. . . . For example, Congress specifically granted the Federal Trade Commission, and not the Board, jurisdiction over the enforcement of the fair lending laws as they apply to nonbank companies; this includes all nonbank subsidiaries of a bank holding company. . . . We agree with the concept that the Board should

295

consider relevant information in the course of acting on a bank holding company application. But given the context in which we deal with fair lending concerns, we do not agree with that part of the recommendation that urges the board *to seek information about consumer complaints*–from the other banking agencies, the Department of Housing and Urban Development, and the Federal Trade Commission–during the application process (emphasis added).[8]

The pity of it is that most of the governors who have drawn the short straw that makes them the liaison between the Fed staff and the protestors have become enthusiasts for the program. Governor Laurence Meyer, the former economics professor at Washington University in St. Louis and proprietor of a successful forecasting service, calls CRA "incredibly effective, beyond expectations." A Treasury Department study mandated by the Gramm-Leach-Bliley Act found no less than $600 billion in loans to low- and moderate-income (LMI, in the jargon) borrowers and communities in the CRA territories between 1993 and 1998, with a follow-up study to come.

Even Larry Lindsey, a hugely self-confident, overweight young former Harvard professor who came to the board with doctrinaire libertarian attitudes and fought off efforts by Ludwig's OCC to strengthen the examination standards for CRA ratings, wound up a fan of *some* law along community reinvestment lines, at least in principle. Greenspan himself allowed Representative Maxine Waters, Chair of the Black Caucus, to take him on a tour of south Los Angeles. It is a very cheerful experience to tour a rescued neighborhood where the results of fresh money are visible in the lives of the neighbors. I made the rounds of the South Bronx a few years ago with Mark Willis, who was head of the community development program at Chase in New York, and can testify to the exhilaration in seeing the change that credit has made in the lives of the people who have had the full-court press. Willis, who had come to Chase from the mayor's office–and was among those missing after Chemical bought Chase and pruned staff–said his mission had been explained to him simply: he was not to lose money, but he didn't have to make any; the publicity value of the project covered the subsidy in the interest rates, and the senior officers of the bank liked the idea that their money had really revitalized a neighborhood. Chase still got a lousy CRA rating, by the way.

The last threat to Gramm-Leach-Bliley in the closing days of the 1999 Congress was Senator Gramm's insistence on saving the small Texas bankers from the pain and intrusion of CRA exams, and he got some of what he wanted, especially a decline in the frequency of such exams for banks with less than $1 billion in assets (and a rule that community groups agreeing to withdraw their objections should have to publicize their use of whatever grants and loans come their way as a result, which is not necessarily a bad thing). Community groups fought hard to keep the program and mostly won, in part because the big banks refused to rally round Gramm. Still, the activists were disappointed.

The financial holding company structure, Malcolm Bush of the Woodstock Institute wrote for the quarterly magazine of the Federal Reserve Bank of Minneapolis,

> establishes in the financial regulatory structure an automatic shrinkage of the CRA umbrella as traditional banking activities are increasingly offered in nonbank institutions. . . . Therefore, the growing body of businesses that exploit lower-income families, such as predatory mortgage lenders, payday loan stores and car-title lenders, will have less competition from regulated lenders and will continue their growing assault on that market. . . .
>
> The failure to modernize CRA also has consequences for low-income families' access to retail banking services and consumer credit. Just as the lack of CRA pressure creates a dual market in mortgage lending, so has the lack of that same scrutiny left many lower-income neighborhoods with only check cashing outlets, rent-to-own stores, and payday and car-title lenders for checking and credit services.[9]

What is especially unfortunate about the Fed's failure to take CRA seriously is the loss of the opportunity to design new and different products that would be of service to a community now largely excluded from financial services. The Clinton administration has stressed Community Development Financial Institutions, which may well be—though Thomas hates the idea—the best channel for bank contributions to the social fabric. Lending into low-income neighborhoods is an art. Thomas himself has suggested shared branches in the slums, to minimize the fixed costs banks must meet to serve such neighborhoods. Early in 2000, the Treasury unveiled a plan costing about $30 million, to pay banks to offer "lifeline" accounts to enable direct deposit to individuals by government or employers, and access to cash by those individuals (free for the first three uses each month) through ATM machines.

The truth is that after a generation of expanded retail banking services, the United States has been moving back toward the old days when people who didn't have much money would be served by high-margin cheapjacks who got their funds from banks that had no reluctance to accept their share of dirty money. The Fed's untroubled supercilious tolerance of these developments reminds us that there are people in high places who still believe government should not interfere with the freedom of contract between the loan shark and the needy.

PART SIX

What's Next?

Chapter 15

The Fed in Our Future

What has been done already has the sharp-edged reality of all the things which we have seen and experienced; the new is only the figment of our imagination. Carrying out a new plan and acting according to a customary one are things as different as making a road and walking along it. . . . Thought turns again and again into the accustomed track even if it has become unsuitable and the more suitable innovation in itself presents no particular difficulties. The very nature of fixed habits of thinking, their energy-saving function, is founded upon the fact that they have become subconscious, that they yield their results automatically and are proof against criticism and even against contradiction by individual facts. But precisely because of this they become drag-chains when they have outlived their usefulness.

–Joseph Schumpeter (1911)[1]

DAVID FROST WAS THE FED'S CHIEF OF STAFF in the 1990s. Like most government senior staff directors, he is a bulky white man in later middle age, who worked in shirtsleeves. He was Comptroller of the Navy before coming to C Street, and in that job he experienced the not uncommon Washington agony of being forced by Congress to spend money on things that he and his colleagues felt were a total waste, and being prohibited by Congress from spending money on the things that ought to get done. Nobody at the Fed cherished the agency's budgetary independence more than Frost. But he also had a larger loyalty. "You have your own views of the Federal Reserve," he said. "What I know is that the country *feels* better when it thinks well of the Federal Reserve." That's true, and while it's obviously circular–the country thinks well of the Federal Reserve when things are going well, which does not mean that things go well because people think well of the Fed–it's a point to be pondered by those of us who get irritated.

The Chinese, we are told, have a saying that you must be careful what you wish for, because you may get it. The Federal Reserve System in the year 2000 found itself the cock of the walk in American financial regulation. As part of the law that repealed Glass-Steagall, Congress had granted it "umbrella supervision" over everybody and everything. And now the system has to create relations with other regulators that had never previously been contemplated. Under the terms of the Gramm-Leach-Bliley Act, the Fed may even have to kowtow in the privacy area to state legislatures and to the Federal Trade Commission, which has joint jurisdiction and can mightily embarrass any Fed board that tries to defend misappropriation of customer data by the banks. "Regulatory authority was given to each agency, not only to the Fed," says Peggy Twohig of the FTC very cheerfully. "The Fed isn't used to that. Does a mortgage broker have a customer relationship that requires a privacy statement? The answer is Yes, and we published a document. The Fed's document is a little different. We do feel it's important for the Fed to coordinate and consult. But it's quite time-consuming."

The substantive problems are even worse. For the fact is that the Fed institutionally knows relatively little about securities, and even less about insurance. The relation of monetary policy to either is unknown in theory and very complicated in practice, passing as it does through the derivatives swamp. And "a dollar of risk in banking," says Vice Chairman Onno Ruding of Citigroup, "is not the same thing as a dollar of risk in insurance."

In the legislative process, moreover, the Fed lost some of its authority over the holding companies. Prior to March 13, 2000, a bank holding company that wished to launch itself into a new activity had to apply to the Fed for permission. After March 13, 2000, the financial holding company asserting that its new activity was "incidental" or even "complementary" to banking (a new phrase that must have been put in the law for a reason) merely had to inform the Fed, and if the Fed took no action within thirty days, the activity was legal–provided the bank in the holding company had a CRA rating of "satisfactory" or better (the sound you hear is the gnashing of teeth, not least at the Fed). The overall reduction of function was not unpopular within the Fed, which was getting tired of processing the stream of mostly plain-vanilla matters. One governor said not long ago that the largest single consumer of his time is the routine request by bank holding companies to add a bank or a branch or expand an ATM network. Law or no law, the Fed will retain its authority to insist that the other enterprises in the holding company be a "source of strength" to the company's bank.

The problem is that the new arrangements will require flexibility, and "this place," says a recent vice chairman, "is run by the barons of the staff." Under Bill Martin, who voted last when the board voted and might go along with a majority even if he disagreed (though he was usually careful to persuade a majority to be with him on any contentious issue before the meeting began), individual governors had staff people who worked essentially on their ideas and proposals. Under Burns, who always voted first (there was no reason, he once said, why the other members of the board should be wrong), the staff became an appendage of the chairman's office. By the time Volcker inherited, only Henry Wallich, who always wrote his own stuff, still had his own staff assigned to him. When Alan Blinder as vice chairman told a reporter he felt a need for his own lawyer to guide him around the labyrinth of the reg books, chief counsel Virgil Mattingly called to offer to second someone from his department.

Larry Lindsey, a right-wing Harvard professor appointed to the board by George Bush, was allowed an economist of similar views from the staff to be a personal assistant; and when Alice Rivlin was saddled with the payments issue, she was assigned a "generalist." But most board members have no more than a secretary.

It is understood that the staff works for the chairman. (Volcker remembered how shocked he was when he first visited the SEC and found that each commissioner has his own staff detailed to him; "we're much more collegial at the Fed," Volcker said, deadpan. If a governor wanted assistance at the Fed, he added, "a staff guy would make time for what he wanted done.") Still, in the old days, unanimity of view had not been demanded at the Fed. James Robertson could fight for years to get bank examination off the Fed's plate; the researchers of the Federal Reserve Bank of St. Louis could be the fount of monetarist analysis and advice; Frank Morris at the Federal Reserve Bank of Boston could warn publicly against real estate lending at a time when the Fed officially was against anything that looked like allocations of credit. Preston Martin as Volcker's vice chairman and Manuel Johnson as Greenspan's could even complain in public that monetary policy was too tight.

Now, in part because the press magnifies every statement that might be construed as off the page from which the chairman reads, every speech is vetted. "This is a great job," said Janet Yellen before resigning as a governor of the Fed to be chair of President Clinton's Council of Economic Advisers, "if you like to travel around the country and read speeches written by the staff." Vice Chairman Roger Ferguson, who came to the board from management consulting and knows all about stubborn staffs, is more positive. "You're no longer speaking as a private individual," he says. "You can say what's on your mind, but you have to do it in a way that isn't destabilizing. If you ask the staff a question based on readings you have done, you do get analyses that are on a high level and relatively neutral. The question is, are we up to speed on some of these emerging issues? Do we have people with the skill sets of the people on Wall Street?"

A staff-driven organization like the Fed has little flexibility. The staff cannot make changes on its own, and does not wish to make changes imposed from outside, a category that includes the governors. After two generations of fighting to centralize authority in Washington, the Fed has lost much of its capacity to delegate. A research staff of 275 at the board itself, with as many more at the twelve district banks, turns out much admired material. Congressman Barney Frank of Massachusetts, needling Greenspan at a hearing (it is a favorite occupation), commented that "the world's most powerful economists are clustered at the Federal Reserve." But these days papers arguing that the board may have got something wrong may not be permitted to reach the outside world. And the Washington staff insists on its right to see and its power to veto anything to be published by one of the district banks.

Many of the best researchers now have arrangements whereby they can teach (usually at business schools) or work part time at private-sector institutes, partly because people with their qualifications can make more outside than they can at the Fed, but partly also because a job outside the Fed permits them to say what they want to say in public. The Fed delicately and flatteringly co-opts its critics with invitations to Jackson Hole (Kansas City Fed) or Cape Cod (Boston Fed) or Miami Beach (Atlanta Fed) for conferences on weighty subjects. Jackson Hole, in late August when there isn't much news, gets headline attention; Blinder got into trouble when new to the board by making some anodyne comment about interest rates which reporters could take as a criticism of Fed policy.

In this atmosphere, it will be difficult for Fed staff to work with state insurance commissions on the determination of reserves in insurance companies, and with the SEC (where badly underpaid staff make a number of decisions and public appearances, too) on questions of accounting rules. As noted, there have long been major disputes with the Comptroller. In 1998, for the first time, the Fed interpreted Section 23 of the original Federal Reserve Act as meaning that nationally chartered banks in their relations with their own operating subsidiaries were bound to deal only at arm's length, with all loans collateralized. The legal authority for this maneuver was not easy to find, and historically the Fed had not applied such rules when banks made loans to their own real estate investment trusts. Discussing the matter at a conference of national banks and their supporters, Ivan E. Mattei of the law firm Debevoise & Plimpton said, "The Fed can do what it wishes, and it does."

Gramm-Leach-Bliley contains a tentative let's-try-it approach to merchant banking, giving banks temporary authority to make equity investments in non-financial companies with intent to sell once the company has been licked into shape. This had been something Ludwig badly wanted for nationally chartered banks, and his successor Jerry Hawke jumped on the bandwagon, announcing that only 5 percent of each such investment would have to be the bank's own money. The risks, Hawke argued, were no greater than those in a commercial loan, which in effect also requires 5 percent capital allocation. The Fed then announced, noting that the secretary of the treasury agreed (which was the first Hawke had heard of it), that if banks wished to do merchant banking either themselves or through their holding company, they would be required to allocate to each venture capital totaling 30 percent to 50 percent of the investment, making the business much less attractive. So much for "great deference" to the views of the functional regulator.*

---

*The OCC found several ways to take revenge in the next months, permitting nationally chartered banks to own stocks if they could make a plausible case that they were hedging an equity derivative, and allowing them to invest in mutual funds they were managing, though the funds' holdings were illegal for banks. This was done by sending letters to the banks involved, rather than by publishing new rules or standards. In the e-mails on the subject that were dutifully provided to the House Banking Committee by the Comptroller's Office, it was quite clear that the purpose of doing the deed quietly was to keep the Fed ill informed. Jim Leach, in his last days as chairman of the committee, blew his stack, calling for an investigation of the Treasury by the inspector general and writing a letter to Hawke: "I recognize that . . . the OCC argued that merchant banking should be done directly in a bank. . . . But Congress made a contrary determination. . . . [W]hen the OCC approves activities outside the law it . . . creates a rule structure that itself incentivizes risky bank behavior. . . . It is self-evident that once practices are established, however illegal, it is difficult to apply the brakes. That is why the law is so explicit in this area and why it is so important that an agency of the U.S. government not be allowed to flout its obligations to statute."[2]

"The role of the umbrella supervisor," says Governor Laurence Meyer, "is to protect the bank from risks taken elsewhere in the entity." And elsewhere, of course, includes "op subs" of the bank.

The worst aspect of the staff domination of the Fed is that staffs always and everywhere believe in secrecy (their power, after all, comes from their exclusive control of information). And the desperate need of the financial system looking ahead is for disclosure. What has made the bank examiner important is her authority to value the bank's assets, to compel "classification" and write-downs of loans she thinks may not be repaid according to contract. In the future, however, markets, not examiners, will effectively value the assets.

The most popular device for bringing market discipline to the aid of banking supervisors is the "subordinated note," which a large bank would be required to issue to the market to the extent of at least 2 percent of its liabilities. If the bank goes blooey, holders of the note can be paid only after all other creditors are satisfied, including, of course, the depositors. Stockholders in a failing bank may push management to gamble, as they will get the winnings if the gamble succeeds, but holders of subordinated notes can never receive more than the interest on the note and will oppose risky behavior. These notes would be traded, and if their price fell, increasing the yield, the regulators could take it as an early warning signal. Under no circumstances would any government body be permitted to pay off the holders of subordinated notes. Subordinated notes were promoted in the early 1990s by the General Accounting Office, and Governor Meyer has enthusiastically advocated them. Congress in passing Gramm-Leach-Bliley gave the banking regulators two years to report back on research they would all do to prove that the subordinated note would be a good thing or a bad thing.

The question is how much information the market will demand before pricing a bank's subordinated notes. "If banks would report every day to the Fed the same balance sheet they report to the CEO," says Gerald O'Driscoll of the Heritage Foundation, formerly of the Federal Reserve Bank of Dallas and Citicorp, "we could eliminate regulation. Then if you're doing business with a Korean bank you want the same report from him." The Bankers Roundtable has called for "market-incentive" regulation to replace the "mandates" of the regulators and supervisors. Its report quotes William McDonough of the New York Fed that "effective market discipline is not possible without meaningful public disclosure." Praising increased disclosure, the report notes that "This, of course, does not necessarily mean more information. . . . What market-incentive regulation does is to require the disclosure of relevant and perfecting information that can be used by participants for making informed and time-critical decisions."[3] And who will decide what is relevant and perfecting information, and what is not necessary? Why, the banks, of course.

Sir Andrew Large, former deputy chairman of Barclay's and chairman of the British Securities and Investments Board, gives the response: "When people who have been used to opacity get into financial difficulty, they do not want to tell the world about it. A major advance in transparency, and the cultural shift that goes with it, usually will not happen without the commitment of both the government and legislature–or, worse, a big crisis–to bring it about."[4] The fact is that large American banks keep four sets of books: one for the internal management information system, which hopes to keep the bosses informed of what's happening; one for the regulators; one for the Internal Revenue Service; and one for the stockholders.

Peter Fisher, who runs the desk that makes flesh of the Federal Open Market Committee words, says that "Every time somebody publishes a period-end balance sheet, required by the SEC, it's a lie. If instead every firm published its quarterly exposures–what we look at daily–at the end of each quarter–published the high, the medium, and the low–then we would know what the leverage is. All these guys went to school where you smooth the distribution." In his presentation to the OCC risk seminar in fall 1999, John Reed of Citigroup speculated idly about why the stock market awards bank stocks a lower multiple of earnings than almost any other industry. It might be, he thought, because people don't trust the numbers. Alan

Greenspan, testifying before a House committee in 1990, noted without making judgments that "Japanese firms issue the same report for tax purposes and for stockholders, so that their financial statements fully reflect the maximum deductions from earnings for such items as depreciation that can be taken for tax purposes; in contrast, U.S. firms issue different reports for tax purposes and for stockholders."[5]

Alexandre Lamfalussy while still managing director of the Bank for International Settlements suggested that "globalization, in combination with financial innovation (in particular of the off-balance-sheet type), has significantly increased the opaqueness of the financial markets. This lack of transparency has two facets. One is the difficulty of assessing the creditworthiness of individual market participants on the basis of publicly available information. Imaginative financial structures, spreading across borders, add to the confusion."[6] Greenspan, who was a fierce defender of bank secrecy in his first years at the Federal Reserve, has become a public proponent of greater transparency. (He offers a splendidly Greenspanian reason for his change: as recently as the 1980s, banks lived off the information they had that other people didn't have; information was costly, and those who invested the money to gather it had property rights, they were entitled not to have it taken away from them in the name of theory. Now, thanks to the march of information technology, information is cheap, and thus the benefits to the market from gaining it exceed the costs to the bank in losing exclusivity.) But the fact is that in the area where the activities of the banks are most opaque– over-the-counter two-party derivatives trading–the Fed has stood with the industry to fight off meaningful disclosure. Even disclosure to the examiners has been curtailed, as banks are permitted to determine the riskiness of their own portfolios for purposes of measuring capital adequacy.

A major reason why the banking system has become increasingly opaque is the regulators' encouragement of bilateral "netting" arrangements, by which two parties that have several derivatives deals with each other can simply compare their winning and losing positions and establish a net number for that moment in time. Such arrangements stimulate a return to old-fashioned correspondent banking, which means that growing proportions of the business banks do disappear from the realm of public transactions.

The credit card system, for example, barely impinges upon the Federal Reserve; the rolling settlement occurs at the Chase Bank, which has accounts directly or indirectly with all the banks that issue cards and arrange with merchants to accept the cards. A credit to a merchant's bank increases the bank's or its correspondent's account at Chase; a debit to a cardholder decreases *his* bank's account at Chase. The Fed's wire- and check-processing systems may be used to remove or supply cash to participants whose balances become topheavy, but as a normal matter the Fed is out of the loop. The development of B2B (business-to-business) internet-based systems in the various industries–oil, automobile, travel, and so on–means that payments flows will skirt the Fed, making an even greater hash of the measurements of monetary aggregates. In the next few years, a lot of the world's trade will be electronically ordered, invoiced, and financed on a correspondent banking basis, perhaps with the banks as the indispensable middlemen, translating one customer's messages to make them readable to another customer's incompatible processing platform, leaving clearinghouses and central banks none the wiser. It is by no means impossible, though I will give odds against it, that the participants in these well-marked enclaves can develop their own electronic money and their own method for assessing interest rates within their sphere, shaking off what they would consider the costly legacy systems of the Federal Reserve. "I don't think the Fed thinks enough about the future," says consultant Ed Furash. "Where do they spend their R&D money? They spend nothing on financial products."

The central banks' game should be multilateral netting through a clearinghouse for securities, derivatives, and currency transactions to keep a contemporaneous record of all events. Transactions should then be completed by Real Time Gross Settlement of payments. No doubt banks dealing directly with each other and with their customers in specialized industries can design swaps and options and swaptions and structured notes that more exactly meet the needs of the "end user." But for that very reason, such instruments are subject to Mayer's Second Law of Derivatives, that when you segment value, you also segment liquidity.[7]

Contracts create instruments. Standardized instruments are widely understood and easily traded. Special-purpose instruments are less liquid and are worth less to others if they are closely tailored to the needs of the immediate parties to the contracts. Exchange-traded derivatives, like futures and options contracts on interest rates and exchange rates, priced in public, cleared, and settled through clearinghouses that keep records of the large traders, can provide highly if not perfectly effective hedges for their users. They also provide the disclosures necessary if we are to have the market-compatible incentives that Greenspan and the IMF and the BIS and the Bankers Roundtable say we need.

In chapter 1, the thought was raised that the lack of transparency may have saved us in 1998; if people had known how bad it really was, we might never have got out of it. But the other side of that coin is the argument that if the Korean and Thai and Indonesian and Russian banks had been compelled to report their real condition on a continuing basis, the suppliers of the funds would have put on the brakes before there was a crisis. There is also a case to be made that the banks that piled on the dollar-denominated loans in Korea knew perfectly well that the banks to which they were lending were weak institutions; they simply assumed that some government, the Korean or their own, would step in when the loans were threatened and make everybody whole. And were right: moral hazard. But the reason government guarantees have been effective is that the governments have maintained control of the information, and in the West that control is rapidly eroding. All the money a bank has except its capital is borrowed, one way or another, and the people and organizations from whom it is borrowed have other places to put it. Banks and bank holding companies have stockholders, and the stockholders are advised by analysts. News travels fast.

And the repurchase agreement and the derivatives contract reduce the redundancy in the system.

"Many years of effort, both at the domestic and at international levels," writes William R. White, chief economist of BIS and former deputy governor of the Bank of Canada, "will be required on the part of central bankers as well as many others to ensure that the international financial system demonstrates the proper balance between efficiency and stability."[8]

So we return full circle, to the fact that central banks were designed for a time when banks provided much of the capital in an economy, and controlling the liabilities of the banks controlled the money supply of the country. Even then, the control of the money supply was a doubtful proposition, because credit could be substituted for money at the margin in many guises. Now, at a time of cash management accounts and home equity loans, when people can liquify not only their securities holdings but their homes, control of the money supply is virtually impossible; indeed, the notion that there is a generalized "demand for money" in the economy, which has sustained monetary theory from the start, has become a souvenir. We are dominated by market-based finance—of which, increasingly, banks are merely a subset, as they securitize and sell loans of all sizes, shapes, and maturities. The pricing genie is not out of the bottle, but a lot more economic activity is now in the bottle with him.

"Investment banks have become banks and don't have a credit culture," says John Heimann. "Banks have gone to market and don't have a market culture. Nobody can be on top of it."

Central banks can raise short-term interest rates by selling paper into the market or lower them by buying paper in the market. There is no question that selling short-term paper can push down the price of other paper, and that the reverberant effects of the loss of value in the paper that people and businesses have pledged against their loans can affect economic activity throughout the society. There is also no question that buying paper, pouring money into the economy, will produce results, an increase in the price either of goods and services or financial and other assets. "Capitalism," Hyman Minsky wrote in the 1980s, "leads to two sets of prices, one for capital assets and one for current output."[9] And nobody knows why a given monetary stimulus produces asset inflation rather than price inflation.

Yasushi Mieno, who as governor of the Bank of Japan in 1990 sold paper to prick the bubble in the Japanese real estate and stock markets, told the 300th anniversary conference at the Bank of England in 1994:

> In the late 1980s we encountered a third new challenge, the birth and expansion of asset price bubbles along with general price stability. In hindsight, asset price bubbles accelerated economic growth and eventually increased inflationary pressures. But with actual price developments remaining subdued, at least initially, monetary policy action was taken a bit too late. Of course, monetary policy should not be aimed at asset price stability. Yet we cannot ignore asset prices . . . given that any large fluctuation can have a serious impact on financial systems. I think the question still remains on how we should treat asset prices in formulating monetary policy.[10]

By then the Japanese stock market was down more than 50 percent from its peak in 1990, and nobody knew how far down the real estate market had gone, because there were no transactions. And the Japanese banks were bust, which made the recovery of economic growth all but impossible until they could be sewn together again.

Alan Greenspan was in the audience at this conference, listening to Mieno. Five years later, he told the Kansas City Fed gathering at Jackson Hole that "We no longer have the luxury to look primarily to the flow of goods and services, as conventionally estimated, when evaluating the macroeconomic environment in which monetary policy must function. There are important—but extremely difficult—questions surrounding the behavior of asset prices and the implications of this behavior for the decisions of households and businesses."[11]

The theoreticians have been arguing for several years about the extent to which central banks should pay attention to asset prices. The discussion is being conducted on a very high level, with very tenuous links to reality. But the truth of the matter is probably that asset prices are at the heart of what a central bank does as we open the new millennium. "Monetary policy," Charles Goodhart told a Levy Institute conference in 1999, "has its real effects by its influence on asset prices. But the effect of interest rates on asset prices is the result of a whole chain of attitudes, and the relations of interest rates to asset prices are highly uncertain."

Keynes's "liquidity trap" resulted from the expectations of possible bond buyers that attempts by central banks to inflate the currency in bad times would lead to higher interest rates, depressing the value of fixed-income instruments. If the instruments are long term, the loss in their market value will start at the first execution of such a policy, and will greatly exceed any gain the same investor can receive from higher rates when he buys new paper. Put another way, the rising interest rates that accompany increased expectation of inflation cannot make up for the investor's loss in the value of marketable fixed-interest long-term paper. Thus there will be a buyer's strike at low interest rates: people will prefer to hold cash rather than interest-bearing bonds that might later lose their value.

In the nineteenth century, when the Bank of England enforced a gold standard, most British government debt was in the form of "consols," which never matured, and thus there was no pull to the par of ultimate repayment to break the fall in their value when market interest rates rose. The depth of the drop in price became, as Marx wrote, an encouragement to foreigners to come buy the bonds, which resupplied the Bank with gold. One notes again that the mechanism by which the Bank maintained the gold standard was the impact of a rise in bank interest rates on the price of assets, the fixed-income paper that was the dominant form of financial asset at the time.

In our credit-soaked economy, there can be no Keynesian liquidity trap: the buyer's strike is against long-term instruments. A three-month Treasury bill or 90-day commercial note gives you back 100 cents on the dollar very soon, and if you've lost half a cent in total return because rates rose 2 percentage points the day after you bought the paper (and that's all you do lose), you're not suffering from it. An age of derivatives instruments makes it possible for people with a longer-term need for money to borrow in the short-term market, hedging their risk by swapping or by selling bond futures at a commodities exchange so that higher interest rates when the short-term loan must be renewed produce trading profits from the hedge large enough to absorb the interest costs on the rollover of the short-term loan. What seems plausible at this point—one wishes more people were studying these problems—is that these influences and attitudes and tactics still work through a banking system.

Nevertheless, the argument about whether the Fed "should" target asset values is now over: the Fed has no choice. It is not only a matter of "wealth effects" that promote excess consumption and thus create pressures on either the domestic price level or the trade deficit. In conditions of modern finance, cheap money from an escalating equities market can promote overinvestment and an eventual collapse in economic activity from the failure of previous investments to generate an adequate (or any) return. The effect of financial innovation has been to make the entire economy more like the housing market. *See* the Internet stocks in April 2000.

Banks, of course, were much more important in Japan than they are in the United States—or will be, looking ahead, in Europe—and in Japan itself once the contents of the postal savings system empty out into the markets. But as we have seen in Asia and in Russia—and my hunch is that a more careful unblinkered analysis of the Latin crisis would produce equivalent vision—it is the health or sickness of the banking system that determines the dimension of a crisis and its duration.

Howard Davies of the Financial Services Authority in Britain stated the case in an interview with Rosa Lastra in 1998:

When a securities firm collapses, you can liquidate both sides of the balance sheet and count the losses, as both assets and liabilities are marked to market. . . . When a bank collapses, you cannot liquidate it easily because loans are typically highly illiquid and valued at historical cost. . . . Perhaps in due course, when bank assets become perfectly securitized–a process which is likely to be difficult and lengthy–banks' specialty will fade away. However, for the time being . . . a crisis in the bank can generate a liquidity crunch, with the potential for systemic risk.

Furthermore, even when financial crises are triggered by institutions other than banks, they tend to show up in banks and typically are dealable through banks. In other words, if you need to supply liquidity to the market you know you will typically provide it through banks even if the origin of the problem was in a securities firm.[12]

Henry Kaufman puts it even more simply with the suggestion that in the modern world the banks are collectively the lender of last resort to non-financial corporations that normally get their money in the market, while the Fed backs up the banks. In operation today, as noted earlier, the Fed backs up the market and the FDIC rescues the banks.

Commenting some months later on the close call in 1998, Alan Greenspan suggested that the reason we had got out of it was a built-in redundancy in the American financial system: we had both banks and markets. When the markets pooped out, the banks picked up the slack. "Following the Russian default of August 1998," he told the World Bank Group and the IMF "program of seminars" on September 27, 1999, "public capital markets in the United States virtually seized up. For a time not even investment-grade bond issuers could find reasonable takers. While Federal Reserve easing shortly thereafter doubtless was a factor, it is not credible that this move was the whole explanation of the dramatic restoration of most, though not all, markets in a matter of weeks. . . . Arguably, at least as relevant

was the existence of backup financial institutions, especially commercial banks, that reply filling in some of the funding gap. . . ."[13] It
was the diversity of funding sources that saved us.

In fact, the banks did not pick up the slack until after the magic
show on October 15. And then it was because they followed the
markets, which popped 7 percaced the intermediation function of the
public capital markets. As public debt issuance fell, commercial bank
lending accelerated, effectivelent the next morning. In his analysis
here, as sometimes elsewhere, Greenspan is trapped by his unshak-
able philosophical bias that whatever is, is right. Still, unlike the
Japanese, the American banks were able to play their part because
after the scare of 1990–91–when John Reed learned that he wanted
to have more than the required minimum capital left on his books *after* taking the maximum loss his mathematicians said he could sus-
tain on his bank's trading positions–they were well capitalized and
able to acquire new business with the funds the Fed pumped in.

The need is for redundancy and care. Greenspan inferentially
warned the same conference to which Reed spoke that "risk managers need to . . . set aside somewhat higher contingency resources–
reserves or capital–to cover the losses that will inevitably emerge
from time to time when investors suffer a loss of confidence. These
reserves will appear almost all the time to be a suboptimal use of
capital. So do fire insurance premiums."[14] Cowed by mathematicians
they don't understand (by "risk models," quoting the chairman again,
"that essentially have only dimly perceived sampling characteris-
tics"), both the CEOs of the banks and the regulators have permitted
tighter and tighter articulation of the cash flows of the banking system and the markets, risking the danger that what Hyman Minsky
called a "displacement" can like the chaos theorists' butterfly in Indonesia start a tempest beyond their powers of intervention. Christine Cumming of the New York Fed, speaking at the same
conference, noted that "the risk management process has been
driven by the needs of the big financial institutions, not by the supervisors." It is hard to think of any action less suited to the needs of this
time than the Basle committee's decision to let banks set their own

risk weightings for their assets, a process guaranteed to make booms bigger and busts worse. The purpose of supervision should not be to increase the profits of the banking system in good times.

The self-interest of the central bank leads it to be solicitous of banking systems, but over time the venture is hopeless. Joseph Schumpeter pointed out almost a century ago that "the compensation for greater risk is only apparently a greater return: it has to be multiplied by a probability coefficient, whereby its real value is again reduced—and indeed exactly by the amount of the surplus. Anyone who simply consumes this surplus will atone for it in the course of events. Therefore, there is nothing in the independent role often attributed to the element of risk, and in the independent return sometimes connected with it."[15]

Applying this argument to the banking system, Jan Kregel writes that banking has profited historically not from risk bearing but "from its expertise in evaluating the risk and arranging for the hedging of the loan." In determining how this work will be done, "the line of demarcation between the market and the firm is set by the costs of organization. The costs of covering the risks of commercial lending are lower when organized through markets than when organized directly within banks. This is the competition the commercial banks are facing. It is a competition they cannot win."[16] The task of the central bank, then, is to develop alternative mechanisms by which it can fulfill its role as the arbiter of attitudes to money. We have a way to go.

One of the great men of the later twentieth century was a mathematician named Richard Hamming, who for years was the math department of Bell Labs (he wouldn't have anybody bossing him or working for him). He invented the simple "parity" checking code that lies at the heart of all computers. He was also as a young man the chief mathematician on the Manhattan Project that built the atomic bomb. One day Robert Oppenheimer, the director of the project, came by his office in Los Alamos and told him that the whole crew was going off the next day for White Sands, to set off the first nuclear explosion. Hamming declined the invitation.

"I can't understand that, Dick," said Oppenheimer. "You have three years of your life in this thing. Don't you want to see it become real?"

And Hamming said, "No. If I got the math wrong, none of you are coming back, and there ought to be somebody left who remembers what we did."

It is in that spirit that the modern financial world should be supervised. Communications are so quick, and positions so closely synchronized through the hedging processes in the derivatives markets, that a cascading collapse can begin in remote corners nobody is watching. This is not a joke: what distinguishes the developed from the developing countries is the redundancy of essential services in the industrialized world. The late John Holt, a teacher and self-proclaimed revolutionist, a good guy who was a student radical long after he had ceased being a student, wrote a piece in *The New York Times* in the late 1960s expressing his horror about how much damage he knew he could do to New York by dropping a bomb in a single well-chosen manhole. (It was more interesting that the *Times* ran it than that John wrote it.) But no one bomb in no one manhole can make that much difference in America: our world is, as it should be, full of alternative routings.

The task for financial supervision in the years ahead will be to assure redundancy as we complete and others begin the transition from a bank-dominated to a market-dominated world. The challenge to the Fed is to find its place in what will be a new financial system if not a new economy.

It was Greenspan's good fortune to have been chairman through many years when the simple-minded dichotomies–growth v. inflation, employment v. inflation–seemed to be real. The Bush tax increase of 1990 and the Clinton tax increase of 1993, together with a degree of restraint in spending, produced a considerable fiscal drag on the economy, creating cash surpluses each year, over and above the excess Social Security receipts which until the late 1990s had simply been expropriated by the government to pay current bills. Households could and did spend an ever higher proportion of their income because the government was saving.

The demand for information technology generated what were perceived worldwide as gigantic investment opportunities in the United States. Investment money–"capital account" money–flowed into the United States, matched by an unprecedented outflow of dollars–a "trade deficit" or "current account deficit"–by Americans buying goods and services abroad. According to the Bank for International Settlements, in 1999 foreigners bought American businesses, started businesses in America, and bought American equity securities to a total of $359 billion more than expenditures abroad for such purposes by Americans.[17] Meanwhile–the two numbers are chicken-and-egg, you never know which caused the other–there was an unprecedented outflow of dollars, $339 billion from Americans buying more goods and services abroad than foreigners were buying in the United States.

Note that despite all the hand-wringing about the size of the current account deficit, the net capital inflow more than matched the current account outflow. Because the demand for dollars to invest exceeded the provision of dollars from purchases abroad, the dollar remained strong, keeping import prices low. Under the eye of eternity, what was happening was that this generation of Americans was selling some of the productivity of the next generation to foreigners, to finance current consumption. But if today's investments more than paid out their servicing costs, the next generation would still see a net benefit even after deducting what had to be paid out abroad.

It surely has not been unreasonable for a Fed chairman to coast happily on such a tide. Low inflation expectations have kept wage increases low. Sharp and continuing rise in the share of the American GDP taken by corporate profits, and interest rates more than 2 percentage points higher than those in Europe (and 6 percentage points higher than those in Japan), have encouraged capital inflow without punishing domestic production, employment, or household income. What Greenspan and his successor have to dread is a reversed scenario, with profits and stock market prices declining, and autonomous investment inflows failing to cover what has become an institutionalized American preference for foreign merchandise, driving down the exchange value of the dollar and raising American prices for the imports Americans continue to consume. Meanwhile, loss of discipline in Washington winds down the fiscal surplus, leaving the debt creation in households and businesses to be financed by expansions of credit, putting further pressure on prices.

In this scenario, the Fed can forget about the kindly tug-of-war between growth and inflation; what's happening is a simultaneous loss of growth, loss of jobs, and acceleration of inflation: "stagflation," the story of the 1970s. With the loss of growth, banks find themselves with lots of bad loans and junk bonds default, discouraging investors. The slowing economy calls for interest-rate reductions, but the falling dollar and growing inflation call for interest-rate increases. And since we don't know *how*, let alone how quickly, interest-rate movements change real economic activity, the dilemma is painful beyond the relief of analgesics. The great comic Jimmy Durante had a closing routine built on the lines "Did you ever have a feeling that you wanted to go and still have the feeling that you wanted to stay?" One can imagine Alan Greenspan trapped in such sensations as early as 2001.

I think, myself, that it doesn't happen. Allowing for deflation of the market bubble, for the dishonest accounting practices now common in American enterprise that overstate profits and understate the claims that have been created on future profits, for substantial increases in energy costs, for the roadblocks to the advance of information technology created by a corrupt U.S. Congress that gave away needed spectrum space to broadcasters, for the normal tendency of the dumb things people do in good times to create subsequent bad times, there remains the power of innovation, the dimension of the changes to be expected from human extension of the mind itself, the long-cycle benefits of immense and persistent investment demand. We live in a time when the Pandora's box of capitalism, so feared for so long, releases mostly good things, and people will, as David Frost suggested, think well of the Fed.

Yet it can blow up. Greenspan's legacy is not only the conservative's desire not to fix what ain't broke but also the conservative's acceptance of institutional structures that support today's weight (and make money doing so) but may not support tomorrow's. The question one hears at Greenspan's Fed at the conclusion of serious dispute is always, "Can the government do it better?" It is an intelligent question, but when the subject is the fragility of the financial safety net and the weight that may fall on it, the answer must be one that convinces those who lack the faith. The truth is that liquidity, the only significant weapon remaining in the central bank's arsenal as decision making moves to the markets, will not necessarily go where you want it to go when you need it to go there. Having won supervisory control of the entire financial services industry, the Fed must bring into the light where the markets can see them continuously the now hidden maneuverings of the private banking empires, the derivatives dealing, the over-leveraging that accompanies overreliance on diversification and probability. And the Fed has never believed in sunshine as a disinfectant. The tragedy for all of us would be if the Fed's and the Treasury's and the Congress's reverence for people who make a lot of money left us unprotected against some sudden revelation of the truth that becomes obvious only in hindsight, that a lot of them don't know what they're doing.

Notes

Unless otherwise specified, all quotes in the text are from interviews with the author.

CHAPTER 1

1. Karl Marx, *Capital.* Vol. III, ed. Frederick Engels, trans. Ernest Unter-mann, first U.S. edn. (Chicago: Charles H. Kerr & Co., 1909), fn p. 575, added by Engels for this edition.
2. *Global Emerging Markets, Deutsche Bank Research,* vol. 1, no. 3 (October 1998), pp. 20–21.
3. Ibid., p. 38.
4. Ibid., p. 68.
5. William D. Falloon, *Charlie D.: The story of the legendary bond trader* (New York: John Wiley & Sons, 1997), p. 91.
6. Thomas L. Friedman,"Oh, By the Way," Foreign Affairs column, *The New York Times,* October 10, 1998, p. A-15.
7. Cited in Marvin Goodfriend, "Monetary Mystique: Secrecy in Central Banking," *Journal of Monetary Economics,* 17 (January 1986), p. 64.
8. Cited in Alan S. Blinder, *Central Banking in Theory and Practice* (Cambridge, MA: MIT Press, 1999), pp. 74–75.
9. Cited in Basle Committee on Banking Supervision, *Enhancing Bank Transparency* (September 1998), p. 8.
10. Cited in ibid., pp. 72–73.
11. Lowell Bryan, *Bankrupt* (New York: HarperBusiness, 1991), p. 224.
12. "Improving Public Policy Disclosures in Banking," Federal Reserve Staff Study 173 (Washington, DC: Federal Reserve Board, 2000), pp. 2, 4.
13. Opening statement of E. Gerald Corrigan at the Symposium on Risk

Reduction in Payments, Clearance and Settlement Systems, January 25, 1996, New York; unpaginated.

14. Paul Krugman, "We're Not Japan," *The New York Times,* December 27, 2000, p. A-21.

15. Ingo Fender, "Corporate Hedging: The Impact of Financial Derivatives on the Broad Credit Channel of Monetary Policy," *BIS Working Papers No. 94,* Basle, November 2000, pp. 19–20.

16. Henry Kaufman, *On Money and Markets* (New York: McGraw-Hill, 2000), pp. 56, 81.

17. Lester V. Chandler, *Benjamin Strong: Central Banker* (Washington, DC: Brookings Institution, 1958), p. 444.

18. Marriner Eccles, *Beckoning Frontiers* (New York: Alfred A. Knopf, 1951), p. 254.

19. Erik Hoffmeyer, *Thirty Years in Central Banking,* Occasional Paper No. 48 (Washington, DC: Group of Thirty, 1994), p. 13.

20. "New Challenges for Monetary Policy." Remarks by Chairman Alan Greenspan before a symposium sponsored by the Federal Reserve Bank of Kansas City, August 27, 1999; http://www.federalreserve.go/boarddocs/speeches/1999/1999087.htm

Chapter 2

1. *Independent and Accountable: A New Mandate for the Bank of England.* A Report of an Independent Panel chaired by Eric Roll (London, 1998), Executive Summary, p. xi.

2. Benjamin Haggott Beckhart, *Federal Reserve System* (Washington, DC: American Institute of Banking, 1972), p. 100.

3. Donald G. Simonson and George H. Hempel, "Banking Lessons from the Past: The 1938 Regulatory Agreement Interpreted," *Journal of Financial Services Research* (1993), pp. 253–54.

4. *Hearings on S. Res. 71, Operation of the National and Federal Reserve Banking Systems.* U.S. Senate Committee on Banking and Currency, 71st Cong., 3rd Sess. (Washington, DC: GPO, 1931), p. 1096. I am indebted to Ronnie J. Phillips of Colorado State University for this citation.

5. Ibid., p. 1069.

6. Thibaut de Saint-Phalle, *The Federal Reserve: An Intentional Mystery* (New York: Frederick Praeger, 1985), p. 80.

7. Martin Mayer, *The Bankers* (New York: Weybright & Talley, 1975), pp. 391–92.

8. Joan E. Spero, *The Failure of the Franklin National Bank* (New York: Columbia University Press, 1980), p. 142.

9. *Compendium of Major Issues in Bank Regulation.* Printed for the use of the Committee on Banking, Housing and Urban Affairs. U.S. Senate, August 1975, pp. 908–9.

10. Ibid., p. 926.

11. Charles Goodhart, *The Evolution of Central Banks* (Cambridge, MA: MIT Press, 1988), pp. 7, 8.

12. Editor's Headnotes, *Banking and Law Journal* (March 1983), p. 219.

13. Walter Bagehot, *Lombard Street,* 14th edn. (London: John Murray, 1968), p. 220.

14. *Modernizing the Financial System: Recommendations for Safer, More Competitive Banks.* Department of the Treasury, Washington, DC, February 5, 1991, p. 56.

15. Ibid., p. 68.

16. *Georgia Ass'n of Independent Insurance Agents* v. *Saxon,* F. Supp 802, 1966.

17. See *NationsBank of North Carolina, N.A.* v. *Variable Annuity Life Insurance Co.,* 115 S.Ct., 810 (1995), and *Barnett Bank of Marion County, N.A.* v. *Nelson,* 517 U.S. 25 (1996).

18. *Bank's Securities Activities: Oversight Differs Depending on Activity and Regulator* (Washington, DC: GAO/GGD-95-214, September 1985).

19. These comments are quoted from Chairman Greenspan's testimony to the Senate Banking Committee on March 4, 1994. I have taken them from Carter H. Golembe, *Key Banking Issues Entering the New Millennium. The Golembe Report,* Delray Beach, FL, 2000, pp. 73–74.

20. *CSBS Examiner* (Washington, DC), October 31, 1997, p. 1.

21. Martin Mayer, "Don't Bank on Reform," *Wall Street Journal,* March 28, 1997, p. A-16.

22. Martin Mayer, "Who Should Regulate the Banks?" *Barron's,* August 31, 1998, p. 44.

23. Testimony of William M. Isaac to the Subcommittee on Financial Institutions of the House Banking Committee, February 16, 2000.

24. There is no transcript of this–it was not part of Greenspan's prepared statement–but I was there.

25. Gibson, Dunn & Crutcher, "Memorandum Re: The New Financial Modernization Legislation, November 12, 1999." Cited in Golembe, "Financial Modernization Legislation: The End of the Beginning." *The Golembe Report,* vol. 1999–9, p. 8.

26. "Greenspan Claims Wider Powers Under Reform Act," *American Banker,* November 16, 1999, p. 1.

27. *The Golembe Report,* vol. 1999–9, p. 9.

28. Howard H. Hackley, "Our Discriminatory Banking Structure," *Virginia Law Review,* vol. 55, no. 8 (December 1969), p. 1470.

CHAPTER 3

1. Bagehot, *Lombard Street,* pp. 116–17.
2. Bray Hammond, *Banks and Politics in America from the Revolution to the Civil War* (Princeton, NJ: Princeton University Press, 1967), p. 61.
3. Beckhart, *Federal Reserve System,* p. 2.
4. Marjorie Deane and Robert Pringle, *The Central Banks* (London & New York: Viking Penguin, 1994), p. 146.
5. Sylvia Nasar, "Economy's Growth Keeps to Fast Pace, Up 4.5% in Quarter," *The New York Times,* May 1, 1999, p. B-14.
6. Henry Thornton, *An Enquiry into the Nature and Effects of the Paper Credit of Great Britain* (London: Hatchard, 1802), p. 60, in Goodhart, p. 18.
7. R. S. Sayers, *The Bank of England, 1891–1914* (Cambridge: University Press, 1976), p. 8.
8. Ibid., p. 397.
9. Goodhart, *The Evolution of Central Banks,* p. 161.
10. An interesting discussion of this situation in Roy Harrod, *The Dollar* (New York: W. W. Norton & Co., 1963), pp. 46–47, makes the point that the two-week settlement period for transactions on the London Stock Exchange was a considerable help to the Bank of England, which did not have to worry about the use of call money for securities trading.
11. Gerald T. Dunne, *A Christmas Present for the President,* Federal Reserve Bank of St. Louis, 1964, p. 1. Reprint from *Business Horizons,* vol. 6, no. 4 (Winter 1963), pp. 43–60.
12. Ibid., p. 15.
13. Lawrence F. Ritter, ed., *Selected Papers of Allan Sproul* (New York: Federal Reserve Bank of New York, 1980), p. 176.
14. *Congressional Record,* 72nd Cong., 1st Sess., vol. 75, 1932, pp. 9884–85.
15. Donald Bruce Johnson and Kirk H. Porter, eds., *National Party Platforms, 1840–1972* (Urbana, IL: University of Illinois Press, 1975), p. 171.
16. H. Parker Willis, *The Federal Reserve: A Study of the Banking System of the United States* (Garden City, NY: Doubleday Publishing Co., 1915), p. 68.
17. James Grant, *Money of the Mind* (New York: Farrar, Straus & Giroux, 1992), p. 144.

18. W. G. McAdoo, *Crowded Years* (Boston: Houghton Mifflin, 1931), p. 288.
19. *Federal Reserve System: Current and Future Challenges Require Systemwide Attention* (Washington, DC: GAO/GGD-96-128), p. 83.
20. *Annual Report,* Board of Governors, Washington, DC, 1914, p. 18.
21. Charles P. Kindleberger, *Economic Response* (Cambridge, MA: Harvard University Press, 1978), p. 118.
22. Chandler, *Benjamin Strong,* p. 434.
23. Jane W. D'Arista, *The Evolution of U.S. Finance.* Vol. I: *Federal Reserve Monetary Policy: 1915–1935* (Armonk, NY: M. E. Sharpe, 1994), p. 17.
24. Ronnie J. Phillips, p. 96.
25. See de Saint-Phalle, *The Federal Reserve,* p. 71.
26. Johnson and Porter, eds., *National Party Platforms, 1840–1972,* pp. 350–51.

CHAPTER 4

1. Chandler, *Benjamin Strong,* p. 314.
2. George Moore, *The Banker's Life* (New York: W. W. Norton & Co., 1987), pp. 113, 115.
3. In Rosa Lastra, *Central Banking and Banking Regulation* (London: Financial Markets Group, London School of Economics, 1996), p. 25 n.
4. Blinder, *Central Banking in Theory and Practice,* p. 55.
5. Eccles, *Beckoning Frontiers,* p. 254.
6. Letter from Sproul to Robert T. Stevens, Chairman, New York Fed, in Ritter, ed., *Selected Papers of Allan Sproul,* pp. 74–75.
7. Letter from Sproul to C. F. Cobbold, Governor, Bank of England, in ibid., p. 79.
8. Eccles, *Beckoning Frontiers,* pp. 488–89.
9. Ibid., p. 498.
10. Allan Sproul, *The "Accord"–A Landmark in the First Fifty Years of the Federal Reserve System,* first printed in the *Monthly Review* of the Federal Reserve Bank of New York; quoted here from Ritter, ed., *Selected Papers of Allan Sproul,* pp. 50–51.
11. Ritter, ed., *Selected Papers of Allan Sproul,* pp. 86, 87.
12. Ibid., p. 73.
13. Martin Mayer, *The Fate of the Dollar* (New York: Times Books, 1980), p. 171.
14. Robert Choate, "Bank on Transparency," *Financial Times* (London), March 2, 1998, p. 18.
15. Milton Friedman, "Should There Be an Independent Monetary Authority?" inserted in *The Federal Reserve System After Fifty Years.* Hear-

ings Before the Subcommittee on Domestic Finance of the House Committee on Banking and Currency (Washington, DC: GPO, 1964), p. 1172.

16. *Report of the Committee on the Working of the Monetary System* (London, August 1959), para 768 @ p. 273.

17. Joseph Kahn, "Era May End for Floating Currencies," *The New York Times,* January 2, 1999, p. B-4.

18. Chandler, *Benjamin Strong,* p. 197.

CHAPTER 5

1. *History of the Eighties: Lessons for the Future.* Vol. II, *Symposium Proceedings,* January 16, 1997 (Washington, DC: Federal Deposit Insurance Corporation, 1997), p. 90.

2. Michael D. Bordo, Bruce Mizrachi, and Anna J. Schwartz, *Real versus Pseudo-International Systemic Risk: Some Lessons from History,* Working Paper No. 5371 (New York: National Bureau of Economic Research, 1995), p. 36.

3. Andrew Sheng, "Role of the Central Bank in Banking Crisis," in Patrick Downes and Reza Vaez-Zadeh, eds., *The Evolving Role of Central Banks* (Washington, DC: International Monetary Fund, 1991), p. 197.

4. Andrew Sheng, ed., *Bank Restructuring: Lessons from the 1980s* (Washington, DC: World Bank, 1996), p. 54.

5. Report of the Committee on Interbank Netting Schemes of the Central Banks of the Group of Ten Countries, Basle, November 1990.

6. Marx, *Capital.* Vol. III, ed. Engels, p. 620.

7. "Discussion" by Jack M. Guttentag of a paper, *Problems of the Account Manager,* by Alan Holmes in *Controlling Monetary Aggregates II: The Implementation.* Proceedings of a conference held September 1972 by the Federal Reserve Bank of Boston, p. 76.

8. Marx, *Capital,* Vol. III, p. 693.

9. Sheng, "Role of the Central Bank in Banking Crisis," in Downes and Vaez-Zadeh, eds., *The Evolving Role of Central Banks,* p. 209.

10. Gerard Caprio, Jr., and Lawrence H. Summers, "Finance and Its Reform: Beyond Laissez Faire," in Dimitri B. Papadimitriou, ed., *Stability in the Financial System* (New York: St. Martin's Press, 1996), p. 406.

11. R. H. Timberlake, Jr., *The Origins of Central Banking in the United States* (Cambridge, MA: Harvard University Press, 1978), p. 223.

12. *Grant's International,* New York, October 15, 1999, p. 3.

13. *Grant's Interest Rate Observer,* New York, March 3, 2000, pp. 6–7.

14. Charles Kindleberger, *Manias, Panics and Crashes* (New York: Basic Books, 1978), p. 170, citing O. M. W. Sprague, *History of Crises Under the National Banking System* (New York: Augustus M. Kelley, 1968, reprinted from 1910).

15. Stephen Fay, *Portrait of an Old Lady: Turmoil at the Bank of England* (London and New York: Viking Press, 1987), p. 59.

16. William R. White, "Evolving International Financial Markets: Some Implications for Central Banks," *Bank for International Settlements Report* (April 1999), p. 21, n. 60.

17. H. Robert Heller, "Prudential Supervision and Monetary Policy," in Downes and Vaez-Zadeh, eds., *The Evolving Role of Central Banks,* p. 59.

18. Sheng, "Role of the Central Bank in Banking Crisis," in ibid., p. 198.

19. *International Insolvencies in the Financial Sector.* A Study Group Report (Washington, DC: Group of Thirty, 1998), p. 147.

20. Ibid., p. 146.

21. Fay, *Portrait of an Old Lady,* p. 63.

22. Victoria Robb, "The Genesis of Regulation," in *Financial Stability Review* (London), vol. 2, no. 2 (Autumn 1998), p. 30.

23. Fay, *Portrait of an Old Lady,* p. 59.

24. Ibid., p. 62.

25. Ibid., p. 89.

26. John Gapper and Nicholas Denton, "Danger Signals Ignored," *Financial Times,* October 20, 1996, p. 10; excerpted from their book *All That Glitters* (London: Hamish Hamilton, 1996).

27. *Report of the Board of Banking Supervision Inquiry into the Circumstances of the Collapse of Barings* (London: HMSO, 1995), chap. 12, para. 33.

28. E. Gerald Corrigan, "Luncheon Address: Perspectives on Payment System Risk Reduction," in David B. Humphrey, ed., *The U.S. Payment System: Efficiency, Risk and the Role of the Federal Reserve* (Boston: Kluwer Academic Publishers, 1990), pp. 129–30.

29. See *The Future of Futures: A Strategic Plan for the Chicago Mercantile Exchange,* Chicago, August 1987, p. 4.

30. Stephen Fay, *The Collapse of Barings* (London: Richard Cohen Books, 1996), p. 211.

31. Victoria Robb, "The Genesis of Regulation," *Financial Stability Review* (London), vol. 2, no. 1 (1997), p. 41.

CHAPTER 6

1. Chandler, *Benjamin Strong,* p. 88.

2. Carter Golembe, "The Deposit Insurance Legislation of 1933: An Ex-

amination of Its Antecedents and Its Purposes," *Political Science Quarterly* (June 1960), p. 181.

3. *Condition of the Federal Deposit Insurance Funds.* Hearings Before the Committee on Banking, Finance and Urban Affairs, House of Representatives, July 7 and August 3, 1988 (Washington, DC: GPO, 1988), p. 123.

4. *Financial Crisis Management: Four Financial Crises in the 1980s* (Washington, DC: GAO/GGD-97-96), p. 36.

5. Irvine Sprague, *Bailout* (New York: Basic Books, 1986), p. 153.

6. Ibid., p. 160.

7. Martin Mayer, "Deposit Insurance Weakness Worst of All Banking Problems," *Financier* (August 1985), p. 64.

8. Sprague, *Bailout,* p. 250.

9. *Condition of the Federal Deposit Insurance Funds,* pp. 122–26.

10. *Comments on Federal Deposit Insurance Reform.* The Conference of State Bank Supervisors, Washington, DC, March 9, 1990, p. 6.

11. Kenneth J. Arrow, *Essays in the Theory of Risk-Bearing* (Chicago: Markham Publishing Co., 1971), p. 142.

12. Sheng, ed., *Bank Restructuring: Lessons from the 1980s,* p. 3.

13. Bernard Shull, "The Limits of Prudential Supervision," in Papadimitriou, ed., *Stability in the Financial System,* p. 165.

14. *Condition of the Federal Deposit Insurance Funds,* p. 124.

15. *Follow-up Report on Financial Oversight at Stock Index Futures Markets During October 1987.* Commodity Futures Trading Commission, Washington, DC, January 6, 1988, p. 55.

16. Martin Mayer, *Markets: Who Plays, Who Risks, Who Gains, Who Loses* (New York: W. W. Norton & Co., 1988), p. 78.

17. *Report of the Presidential Task Force on Market Mechanisms,* January 1988, Study VI, Washington, DC, p. VI-40.

18. Quoted from the *Congressional Record* without footnote in *The Golembe Report,* vol. 1995-7, p. 12.

CHAPTER 7

1. Letter from Sproul to Robert T. Stevens, Chairman, New York Fed, in Ritter, ed., *Selected Papers of Allan Sproul,* p. 127.

2. William C. Melton, *Inside the Fed: Making Monetary Policy* (New York: Dow-Jones Irwin, 1985), p. 14.

3. In D'Arista, *The Evolution of U.S. Finance,* Vol. I, p. 222.

4. Bagehot, *Lombard Street,* p. 26.

5. Federal Reserve Act as amended, Section 13, #2.

6. Fischer Black, "What a Non-Monetarist Thinks," in Black, *Business Cycles and Equilibrium* (New York: Basil Blackwell, 1987), p. 95.

7. Harrod, *The Dollar,* p. 50.

8. Ron Chernow, *The House of Morgan* (New York: Atlantic Monthly Press, 1990), p. 313.

9. John Maynard Keynes, *Essays in Persuasion* (New York: Norton, 1963), p. 285.

10. D'Arista, *The Evolution of U.S. Finance,* Vol. I, p. 163.

11. Ibid.

12. B. M. Anderson, *Economics and the Public Welfare,* 2nd edn. (Indianapolis: Liberty Press, 1979), p. 264.

13. Eccles, *Beckoning Frontiers,* p. 130.

14. Ibid., pp. 131–33.

15. Moore, *The Banker's Life,* p. 101.

16. *Annual Report of the Federal Reserve Bank of New York for the Year 1938,* p. 69.

17. Eccles, *Beckoning Frontiers,* pp. 175, 170–71.

18. *70th Annual Report,* Bank for International Settlements, Basle, June 5, 2000, p. 4.

CHAPTER 8

1. Sherman J. Maisel, *Managing the Dollar* (New York: W. W. Norton & Co., 1973), p. 173.

2. Chernow, *The House of Morgan,* p. 539.

3. Maisel, *Managing the Dollar,* p. 115.

4. Ibid., p. 114.

5. Charles A. Coombs, *The Arena of International Finance* (New York: Wiley-Interscience, 1976), p. 71.

6. Beckhart, *Federal Reserve System,* p. 74.

7. Harold van B. Cleveland and Thomas F. Huertas, *The Bank for All: A History of Citibank, 1812–1970* (New York: Citibank, 1984), chap. 14, p. 19.

8. Ned Eichler, *The Thrift Debacle* (Berkeley: University of California Press, 1989), pp. 28, 29.

9. Kaufman, *On Money and Markets,* p. 56.

10. Sidney Homer, *The Bond Buyers Primer* (New York: Salomon Brothers & Hutzler, 1968), p. 89.

11. See "Mortgage Security Hedging and the Yield Curve," in *Federal Reserve Bank of New York Quarterly Review,* vol. 19, no. 2, (Summer–Fall 1994), p. 92 et seq.

CHAPTER 9

1. Mayer, *The Fate of the Dollar,* p. 3.
2. Maisel, *Managing the Dollar,* p. 107.
3. William Greider, *Secrets of the Temple* (New York: Simon & Schuster, 1987), p. 342.
4. "Adam Smith," *Supermoney* (New York: Random House, 1972), pp. 42–45.
5. Karin M. Lissakers, *Banks, Borrowers and the Establishment* (New York: Basic Books, 1992).
6. R. S. Sayers, *The Bank of England, 1891–1914* (Cambridge: University Press, 1976).
7. Melton, *Inside the Fed,* p. 51.
8. Paul Volcker and Toyoo Gyohten, *Changing Fortunes* (New York: Times Books, 1992), p. 170.
9. See ibid., p. 274.

CHAPTER 10

1. *70th Annual Report,* Bank for International Settlements, Basle, June 5, 2000, p. 66.
2. Bob Woodward, *Maestro* (New York: Simon & Schuster, 2000), p. 142.
3. *Report of the Presidential Task Force on Market Mechanisms,* January 1988, Study VI, p. 6.
4. Ibid.
5. Ibid., p. 66.
6. Paul Van den Bergh and John M. Veale, "Payment System Risk and Risk Management," in Bruce Summers, ed., *The Payment System: Design, Management and Supervision* (Washington, DC: International Monetary Fund, 1994), p. 100.
7. *Banking's Role in Tomorrow's Payments System.* Vol II: *Payments System Overview* (Washington, DC: Furash & Co., 1994), p. 51.
8. Martin Mayer, "The Pilot Bails Out," *American Banker,* July 7, 1988, p. 1.
9. Mayer, *The Bankers: The Next Generation,* pp. 32–33.
10. "Overview" of *The Transmission Mechanism of Monetary Policy in Emerging Market Economies,* Policy Paper No. 3 (Basle: BIS, 1998), p. 11.
11. Blinder, *Central Banking in Theory and Practice,* pp. 74–75, quoting Testimony Before the Subcommittee on Domestic Monetary Policy of the Committee on Banking, Finance and Urban Affairs, U.S. House of Representatives, October 25, 1989.

Chapter 11

1. Volcker and Gyohten, *Changing Fortunes,* p. 234.
2. See Robert Triffin, *Gold and the Dollar Crisis* (New Haven: Yale University Press, 1960).
3. The best discussion of these subjects, sparing my blushes, is in Mayer, *The Fate of the Dollar.* But also note Milton Gilbert, *Quest for World Monetary Order: The Gold-Dollar System and Its Aftermath* (New York: John Wiley & Sons, 1980).
4. Coombs, *The Arena of International Finance,* p. 27.
5. Ibid., p. 229.
6. Bagehot, *Lombard Street,* p. 56.
7. *International Insolvencies in the Financial Sector: A Study Group Report* (Washington, DC: Group of Thirty, December 1998), p. 84.
8. *Foreign Banks: Assessing Their Role in the U.S. Banking System* (Washington, DC: GAO-GGD-96-26, February 1996), p. 43.
9. De Saint-Phalle, *The Federal Reserve,* pp. 221–22.
10. In Robert A. Mundell and Jacques J. Polak, eds., *The New International Monetary System* (New York: Columbia University Press, 1977), p. 35.
11. "Dead and Buried," *The Economist,* April 15–21, 2000, p. 82.
12. *Federal Reserve Bulletin* (July 1990), p. 509.
13. Sir Andrew Large, *The Future of Global Financial Regulation* (Washington, DC: Group of Thirty, 1999), p. 26.

Chapter 12

1. *Managing Change in Payment Systems,* Policy Paper No. 4 (Basle: BIS, 1988), p. 72.
2. Howard H. Hackley, "Our Discriminatory Banking Structure," *Virginia Law Review,* vol. 55, no. 8 (December 1969), p. 1454.
3. A neat example of how the future gets hobbled by the past is the new Sacajawea gold-colored dollar coin, minted in hopes of erasing the failure of the Susan B. Anthony dollar of the 1980s. Among the reasons for the failure of the Anthony dollar was that its size was very close to that of the quarter, and people were annoyed whenever they paid a dollar instead of a quarter. But the machinery designed to take the Anthony dollar, from the Las Vegas slots to the post office stamp machines, would have had to be replaced if the new dollar coin were significantly different in weight or size. So the Sacajawea dollar was the same size and weight as the Anthony dollar, and different essentially in

that its edge was not milled. The Treasury argued that because people could feel the difference between the milled quarter and the smooth dollar in their pockets and purses, they would not mistake one for the other and would be willing to carry the dollar coin. They weren't.

4. "Headed Toward a Cashless Society? A Federal Reserve Perspective." Talk by Paul M. Connolly before the Society of American Business Editors and Writers Conference on Personal Finance, Boston, October 15, 1995.

5. David B. Humphrey and Allen N. Berger, "Market Failure and Resource Use," in Humphrey, ed., *The U.S. Payment System: Efficiency, Risk and the Role of the Federal Reserve,* pp. 46–47.

6. Letter from Governor Lyle E. Gramley to William J. Anderson, Director, General Government Division, U.S. General Accounting Office, April 10, 1981, pp. 2–3.

7. Letter from R. B. O'Donoghue to "Mrs. Blackmore," March 4, 1983. The reader should note that these documents are merely the tip of an iceberg; other similar letters exist but have not been made available to the author.

8. William J. McDonough, "Managing Change in Payment Systems," in BIS Policy Paper No. 4, *Managing Change in Payment Systems,* p. 12.

9. Bruce J. Summers, "Comment on Controlling Risk in Payment Systems," *Journal of Money, Credit and Banking,* vol. 28, no. 4 (November 1996), Part 2, p. 864.

10. *Fair Competition on the Automated Clearing House Payment System: A Private Sector ACH Operator Proposal,* Submitted by American Clearing House, New York Automated Clearing House, VISANet Automated Clearing House, June 2, 1998; unpaginated.

11. *Can the Fed Be a Payment System Innovator?* Federal Reserve Bank of Richmond Annual Report for 1997, p. 22.

12. *Federal Register,* vol. 62, no. 179, September 16, 1997, pp. 48713–26; www.wais.access.gpo.gov

13. Jeanne M. Hogarth and Kevin H. O'Donnell, "Bank Relationships of Lower Income Families and the Governmental Trend Toward Electronic Payments," *Federal Reserve Bulletin* (July 1999), p. 465.

14. Remarks by Chairman Alan Greenspan, *Retail Payment Systems,* April 10, 2000; http://www.federalreserve.gov/boarddocs/speeches/2000

Chapter 13

1. Hyman Minsky, "Financial Instability, the Current Dilemma, and the Structure of Banking and Finance," in *Compendium of Major Issues in Bank Regulation,* p. 329.

2. Bagehot, *Lombard Street*, pp. 250–51.
3. *International Insolvencies in the Financial Sector*, p. 147.
4. Martin Mayer, *Risk Reduction in the New Financial Architecture* (Annandale-on-Hudson, NY: Levy Institute of Bard College, 1999), pp. 17–19.
5. Michael Lewis, *Liar's Poker* (New York: W. W. Norton & Co., 1989), pp. 14–17.
6. *Long-Term Capital Management: Regulators Need to Focus Greater Attention on Systemic Risk* (Washington, DC, GAO-GGD-00-3, October 1999), p. 15.
7. *The Golembe Report*, vol. 1998–9 & 10, "The Bailout of Long-Term Capital Management: A Few Crucial Questions," pp. 9–10.
8. Kaufman, *On Money and Markets*, p. 207.
9. Roger Lowenstein, *When Genius Failed* (New York: Random House, 2000), p. 203ff.
10. *69th Annual Report*, Bank for International Settlements, Basle, June 7, 1999, p. 148.
11. Hyman P. Minsky, *Stabilizing an Unstable Economy* (New Haven: Yale University Press, 1986), pp. 46–47, 240.
12. Hyman P. Minsky, Introduction to Bernard Shull, *The Limits of Prudential Supervision* (Annandale-on-Hudson, NY: Levy Institute of Bard College, 1993), p. 10.
13. Minsky, *Stabilizing an Unstable Economy*, p. 241.
14. *Strengthening the Supervision and Regulation of the Depository Institutions.* Hearings Before the Committee on Banking, Housing and Urban Affairs, U.S. Senate, Vol. 1 (Washington, DC: GPO, 1991), p. 346.
15. *History of the Eighties, Lessons for the Future.* Vol. II: *Symposium Proceedings,* January 16, 1997 (Washington, DC: FDIC, 1997), p. 99.
16. Isaac quoted in ibid., p. 115.
17. *Strengthening the Supervision and Regulation of the Depository Institutions.* Hearings Before the Committee on Banking, Housing and Urban Affairs, U.S. Senate, Vol. 2 (Washington, DC: GPO, 1991), p. 1262.
18. George G. Kaufman, "The Current State of Banking Reform," in Papadimitriou, ed., *Stability in the Financial System,* pp. 196–97.
19. *Risk-Focused Bank Examinations: Regulators of Large Banking Organizations Face Challenges* (Washington, DC: GAO/GD-00-48, January 2000), p. 41.
20. *Capital Requirements and Bank Behavior: The Impact of the Basle Accord.* Bank for International Settlements, Basle, April 1999, p. 45 et seq.
21. Ibid., p. 52.
22. *Defining the Roles of Accountants, Bankers and Regulators in the United States* (Washington, DC: Group of Thirty, 1995), p. 3.

Notes

23. Paul Kupiec, *Bank Capital Regulation for Market Risks.* Paper for an
    IMF Research Department Seminar, 1996, p. 3.

Chapter 14

1. Kenneth H. Thomas, *CRA Handbook* (New York: McGraw-Hill, 1998),
   p. 50.
2. Gary A. Dymski, "Comment" in Papadimitriou, ed., *Stability in the Financial System,* p. 352.
3. Dimitri B. Papadimitriou, Ronnie J. Phillips, and L. Randall Wray, *A
   Path for Community Development* (Annandale-on-Hudson, NY: Levy Institute of Bard College, Public Policy Brief No. 6, 1993), p. 10.
4. Kenneth H. Thomas, *Community Reinvestment Performance* (Chicago:
   Probus Publishing, 1993), p. 4.
5. Thomas, *CRA Handbook,* p. 74.
6. Ibid., p. 103.
7. *Large Bank Mergers: Fair Lending Review Could Be Enhanced with Better
   Coordination* (Washington, DC: GAO/GGD/00-16, November 1999),
   p. 14.
8. Ibid., p. 45.
9. Malcolm Bush, "The Road Not Taken," *The Region,* Federal Reserve
   Bank of Minneapolis, Special Issue: Financial Modernization (Spring
   2000), pp. 30–31.

Chapter 15

1. Joseph A. Schumpeter, *The Theory of Economic Development,* trans. Red-
   vers Opie (Cambridge, MA: Harvard University Press, 1936), pp. 85,
   86.
2. Letter, James A. Leach to John D. Hawke, Jr., December 18, 2000,
   www.house.gov/banking
3. *Market-Incentive Regulation and Supervision: A Paradigm for the Future.*
   Report by the Subcommittee and Working Group on Market-Incentive Regulation of the Bank Regulation and Risk Management Committee, The Bankers Roundtable, Washington, DC, April 1998, p. 19.
4. Large, *The Future of Global Regulation,* pp. 29–30.
5. *Federal Reserve Bulletin* (July 1990), p. 510.
6. In Forrest Capie, Charles Goodhart, Stanley Fischer, and Norbert
   Schadt, *The Future of Central Banking.* Tercentenary Symposium of the

Bank of England (Cambridge: University Press, 1995), p. 336.

7. See Mayer, *The Bankers: The Next Generation* (New York: E. P. Dutton, 1997), pp. 323–24. The third law is the most important. It states that risk-shifting instruments will tend to shift risk onto those less able to bear them, because them as got want to keep and hedge, while them as ain't got want to get and speculate.

8. William R. White, *Evolving International Financial Markets: Some Implications for Central Banks,* Working Paper No. 66 (Basle: BIS, April 1999), p. 28.

9. Hyman P. Minsky, *Stabilizing an Unstable Economy,* p. 177.

10. In Capie et al., *The Future of Central Banking,* p. 251.

11. Remarks by Chairman Alan Greenspan, August 27, 1999.

12. "The City's Troubleshooter: Banking Specialist and Author Rosa M. Lastra Talks to 'Watchdog' Howard Davies." Parliamentary Brief, January 1998, p. 30.

13. Remarks by Chairman Alan Greenspan before the World Bank Group and the International Monetary Fund, September 27, 1999; http://www.federalreserve.gov/boarddocs/speeches/1999/199909272.htm

14. Remarks by Alan Greenspan before a conference sponsored by the Office of the Comptroller of the Currency, October 14, 1999.

15. Schumpeter, *The Theory of Economic Development,* p. 33.

16. Jan Kregel, *The Past and Future of Banks,* Quaderni di Richerche No. 21 (Milan: Bancaria Editrice, 1998), pp. 90–92.

17. *70th Annual Report,* Bank for International Settlements, Basle, June 5, 2000, p. 32 (table).

Index

ABN Arno, 239
Agricultural Adjustment Act of 1933, 160
Agriculture, Department of, 52
Akyuz, Yilmaz, 9–10
Albright, Harry, 237
Aldrich, Nelson, 67, 78
Aldrich, Winthrop, 78
Aldrich Commission, 108
Aldrich-Vreeland bill, 67, 68
Allen, Woody, 205
Allerdice, David, 260
American Council of Life Insurers, 51
American Express, 185
American Institute of Banking, 32
American National Standards Institute, 262
Anderson, Robert, 89–90, 92
Angell, Wayne, 203
Argentina, 96, 236
Aristobulo de Juan, 105
Arrow, Kenneth, 131
Aruba, 240
Asian crisis of 1997–98, 7–8, 11, 17, 27, 102–103, 109–110, 241, 282, 315
Automated Clearing House (ACH), 254, 256–260
Axilrod, Steven, 15, 235–236

Bagehot, Walter, 41, 55, 57, 67, 103, 106, 108–110, 147, 231, 265–266, 268
Bailout (Sprague), 124, 126
Baker, James, III, 200–203, 207, 208
Baker, Ron, 116
Banco Ambrosiano, 233
Bankers Roundtable, 214, 272, 308, 311
Bankers Trust, 137, 239, 268
Bank examination, 264–284, 289–290, 294–295
Bank for International Settlements (BIS), 5, 16–17, 20, 163, 205, 212, 215, 227, 229–230, 233, 240, 268, 283, 311, 320
Bankhaus Herstatt, 103, 233
Bank Holding Company Act of 1956, 36, 40
  amendments to (1970), 37
Bank Indonesia, 247
Banking Act of 1933, 76–78, 161
Banking Act of 1979 (United Kingdom), 114
Banking Organization National Desktop, 279
Bank Negara Malaysia, 103, 105
Bank Note Reporters, 248
Bank of America, 85, 112, 124, 126, 272, 275, 280, 287

Bank of Credit and Commerce International (BCCI), 112, 237
Bank of England, 5, 13, 30, 33–34, 55, 56, 59–64, 67, 68, 81–83, 93, 103, 108–109, 111–119, 151, 155, 168, 173, 314
Bank of Israel, 5
Bank of Italy, 81
Bank of Japan, 5, 6, 13, 56, 162, 231
Bank of Montreal, 135
Bank of Nova Scotia, 115
Bank of the United States, 247, 285
Banque de France, 5, 64–65, 82
Barclay's Bank, 234, 268
Baring, Peter, 117
Baring Bank, 116–119
Barnett Banks, 44, 292
Barry, Marion, 51
Basle Accord, 238, 277, 278
Basle Commission on Banking Supervision, 18, 239, 317
Beckhart, Benjamin Haggott, 32, 57
Belew, Jess, 291
Bell, David, 175
Bennett, Jack, 199
Bentsen, Lloyd, 208, 279
Bentson, George, 274
Berger, Allen N., 252
Berlin, Isaiah, 21
Black, Eugene R., 159
Black, Fischer, 149
Blackmore, Norma, 254
Black-Scholes model, 149
Blair, Tony, 30
Blinder, Alan S., 18–19, 84, 223–224, 303, 305
Blumenthal, W. Michael, 187, 188, 192
Bond Buyer's Primer, The (Homer), 179
Born, Brooksley, 279
Bottomline Technologies, 260
Brady, Nicholas, 207–208, 211
Brady Commission, 211
Brash, Donald, 80
Brazil, 7, 96, 235, 242
Bretton Woods system, 182, 183, 227–229
Brimmer, Andrew, 37, 184
British Financial Services Authority, 39
British Telecom, 137
Brookings Institution, 291

Brown, Gordon, 28
Brown Brothers Harriman, 234
Brunner, Karl, 15
Bryan, Lowell, 19
Bryan, William Jennings, 66
Bucher, Jeffrey N., 39
Bulgaria, 96
Bundesbank, 29, 56, 72, 84, 182, 192, 232
Bureau of Federal Credit Unions, 52
Bureau of the Budget, 75, 175
Burns, Arthur, 79, 93, 96–97, 144, 166, 182–184, 186–187, 198, 224, 230, 236, 303
Bush, George, 42, 201, 205, 211, 220, 304, 319
Bush, George W., 22, 156
Bush, Malcolm, 297

California Clearing House Association, 254
Callaghan, James, 234
Call money market, 66, 136
Calvo, Guillermo, 6
Capital (*Das Kapital*, Marx), 103–104
Caprio, Gerard, Jr., 105
Carter, Jimmy, 187, 188, 192, 194, 195
Catastrophe Bonds, 42
Cayman Islands, 7, 233, 235
Central banks, 3, 4, 14–17, 19–23, 26–27. *See also* Federal Reserve System
  beginnings of, 55–57
  independence of, 81–93
  societal differences, 58–66
  systemic risk, 101–119
  Truman administration and, 84–93
Certificates of deposit, 174, 176–177
Certificates of indebtedness, 152
Chaos theoreticians, 226–227
Chase Bank, 201, 250, 256, 268, 283, 296, 310
Chase Manhattan Bank, 35, 123
Chase National Bank, 78
Check-cashing shops, 293
Check processing, 249–263, 310
Chemical Bank, 35, 184, 201, 275, 296
Chernow, Ron, 164
Chesterton, G.K., 156
Chevy Chase Bank, 292
Chicago Board of Trade, 8–9, 12

Chicago Board of Trade Clearing Corporation, 124
Chicago Mercantile Exchange, 118, 133–135, 209–210, 212
Chile, 83
CHIPS system, 212–214, 261
Chrysler Corporation, 185
Churchill, Winston, 61–62, 81
Citibank, 5, 126, 174, 184, 239, 269, 275
Citicorp, 78, 159, 283
Citigroup, 283
Civil Aeronautics Board (CAB), 52
Civil rights movement, 286, 288
Clarke, Robert, 49
Clayton Act of 1914, 32
Clearinghouses, 146, 148, 212–215
Cleveland, Harold van B., 174
Clifford, Clark, 112, 237
Clinton, Bill, 44, 48, 58, 201, 208, 216, 319
Clinton, Hillary, 58, 208
CMO market, 222–223
Coinage Act of 1965, 74
Commodity Futures Trading Commission, 134
Community Development Financial Institutions, 297–298
Community Reinvestment Act of 1977, 285, 288–292, 294, 296, 297–298, 303
Conference of State Bank Supervisors, 46–47, 129, 271–272
Connolly, Paul M., 252
Conover, Todd, 124
Considine, Jill, 212
Consumer price inflation, 220, 221
Contemporaneous accounting, 197
Continental Illinois Bank, 49, 115, 123–127, 129, 130, 271, 290
Continuous Linked Settlement (CLS), 261–262
Cooke, Peter, 278
Cook Islands, 240
Coolidge, Calvin, 25
Coombs, Charles, 175, 227, 229–230
Coopers & Lybrand, 117
Corrigan, E. Gerald, 21, 112, 118, 137, 145, 273, 281–282
Council of Economic Advisers, 91, 175, 186, 206
Coyne, Joe, 125

CRA. *See* Community Reinvestment Act of 1977
Credit-Anstalt, 227
Credit cards, 251, 310
Credit controls, 195–196
Credit Suisse First Boston, 268
Crocker Bank, 38
Crockett, Andrew, 16
Crosse, Howard B., 174
Cumming, Christine, 282, 317–318
Currency board, 95–96
Currie, Lauchlin, 158
Curtiss, F.H., 145–146

Daiwa Bank, 238
Dall, Bob, 172
D'Amato, Alphonse, 47
Danmarks Nationalbank, 5
D'Arista, Jane, 157
Data Exchange Standards Association, 263
Davies, Howard, 39, 51, 315
Daylight overdrafts, 213, 214, 255
Deane, Marjorie, 57
Debt deflation, 104–105, 110, 155–156
Defense Mobilization, 91
De Gaulle, Charles, 181
Demand deposits, 42, 168, 170, 174, 248
Deming, Fred, 198–199
Depository Institutions Deregulation and Monetary Control Act of 1980, 40, 196, 218
Designated Order Turnaround (DOT) system, 133, 135
Deutsche Bank, 5–7, 29, 239, 268
Dillon, Douglas, 175
Director, Aaron, 77
Discount Corporation of America, 174
Discrimination, 286–289, 294–295
Dole, Robert, 208
Dornbusch, Rudiger, 96
Douglas, Lewis, 159
Douglas, Paul, 77, 90–91
Downey, Thomas, 85
Dresdner Bank, 5, 65
Drexel Burnham, 42, 206
Dukakis, Michael, 219
Dulles, Eleanor Lansing, 80
Dunne, Gerald T., 40–41, 66–67
Dymski, Gary A., 287

Eccles, Marriner, 25, 32–33, 79, 81–82, 84–90, 95, 158, 160–162, 167, 188, 207
Ecuador, 96
Edge, Walter, 234
EDIFACT group, 262
Eichler, Ned, 177
Eisenhower, Dwight D., 89–90, 166, 230
Electronic payments, 251–263, 282, 292–294, 310
El Salvador, 96
Ely, Bert, 121
Emergency Banking Act of 1933, 159, 160
Emminger, Otmar, 181, 192
Engels, Friedrich, 3
Equal Credit Opportunity Act, 291, 294
Estonia, 96
Eurobank, 173
Euro currency, 29–30, 40, 72, 173, 182, 183, 193, 232, 235, 239
European-American Bank, 122, 239
European Central Bank (ECB), 5, 13, 16, 29–30, 40, 72, 83, 236, 255
European Monetary Institute, 16
European Parliament, 29
European Payments Union, 228, 229
Evans, M.R., 88, 89
Evolution of U.S. Finance, The (D'Arista), 157
Exchange Stabilization Fund, 109, 227
Exter, John, 174
Ezekiel, Mordecai, 158

Fay, Stephen, 109, 113, 119
Federal Advisory Council (FAC), 67–68, 161
Federal Bank Commission, proposed, 39
Federal Banking Agency (FBA), 40, 43
Federal Deposit Insurance Corporation (FDIC), 37–39, 75, 120–122, 124–132, 220, 234, 271, 289, 290
Federal Deposit Insurance Corporation Improvement Act (FDICIA), 43, 274, 290
Federal Financial Institutions Examination Council, 277
Federal Home Loan Bank Board, 52, 217, 277

Federal Home Loan Bank of San Francisco, 177, 218
Federal Home Loan Bank system, 177, 217, 218
Federal Home Loan Mortgage Corporation (Freddie Mac), 178–179, 277
Federal National Mortgage Association (Fannie Mae), 178–179, 277
Federal Open Market Committee (FOMC), 10, 15, 18, 19, 84, 86, 88, 90–92, 127, 144–145, 159, 168, 192, 193, 199, 210–211, 223, 224–225, 235, 236
Federal Reserve Act of 1913, 66, 68, 70, 74, 108, 146, 148, 149, 234, 305
amendments to (1935), 70, 94
Federal Reserve Automation System (FRAS), 255
Federal Reserve Bank of Atlanta, 127, 305
Federal Reserve Bank of Boston, 305
Federal Reserve Bank of Chicago, 8, 9, 33, 124, 127, 128, 135, 144, 252
Federal Reserve Bank of Dallas, 128
Federal Reserve Bank of Kansas City, 305, 313
Federal Reserve Bank of Minneapolis, 254
Federal Reserve Bank of New York, 5, 81, 107, 108, 111, 144, 154–155, 160, 161, 166, 183, 184, 192, 229, 237, 266–268, 279, 283, 294
Federal Reserve Bank of Philadelphia, 25
Federal Reserve Bank of Richmond, 255, 259
Federal Reserve Bank of San Francisco, 144, 254, 257
Federal Reserve Notes, 72–75
Federal Reserve System
Burns's chairmanship, 79, 93, 96–97, 144, 166, 182–184, 186–187, 189, 198, 224, 230, 236, 303
Clinton administration and, 208, 216
Community Reinvestment Act (CRA) ratings and, 285, 288–292, 294, 296, 297
Eccles's chairmanship, 25, 32–33, 79, 81–82, 84, 95, 158, 161–162, 188
Federal Open Market Committee (FOMC), 10, 15, 18, 19, 84, 86, 88,

90–92, 127, 144–145, 159, 168, 192, 193, 199, 210–211, 223, 224–225, 235, 236
Fed Funds, 170–174, 176, 178, 188, 193, 194, 219, 222–225
Great Depression and, 143, 154–162
Greenspan's chairmanship, 10–15, 18, 19, 22, 26, 51, 58, 79, 180, 204–210, 215–216, 218–225, 236, 309, 313–314, 316–317, 319–322
internationally, 226–246
Johnson administration and, 175–176
Kennedy administration and, 175
Martin's chairmanship, 77, 79, 83, 92, 164–169, 172, 175–176, 179, 181–183, 188, 227, 303
McCabe's chairmanship, 87–90, 188
member banks, 68–78
Miller's chairmanship, 187, 188, 192
Nixon administration and, 183–184
October 15, 1998 intervention, 10–12, 51, 180, 224–225, 316–317
October 1987 market crash, 133, 136–137, 209–211
Office of the Comptroller and, 30–36
open market operations, 144, 145, 152–153
payments system, 247–263, 310
the poor and, 285–298
public disclosure in banking and, 19–20
Reagan administration and, 198–204
1990–91 recession, 219–221
reorganization of, 76–79
reserve requirements, 23–24, 147, 149, 152, 153, 171–174, 189, 193, 197
SEC and, 51–52
staff, 303–305, 307
supervision and examination functions, 28–34, 37, 40, 45, 48–52, 264–284, 302, 322
Volcker's chairmanship, 11, 41, 58, 124, 127–128, 192–195, 197–204, 210, 230–231, 235, 236, 303–304
Federal Savings and Loan Insurance Corporation (FSLIC), 177, 217, 218
Federal Trade Commission (FTC), 52, 294–296, 302
Fed Funds, 170–174, 176, 178, 188, 193, 194, 219, 222–225

FedWire, 73, 134, 173, 210, 213, 214, 249, 251, 254–257, 261
Fender, Ingo, 22
Ferguson, Roger, 262–263, 304
Financial Accounting Standards Board, 49
Financial Holding Company (FHC), 50, 51
Financial Institutions Reform, Recovery and Enforcement Act (FIRREA), 43, 132
Financial Services Authority (United Kingdom), 30
Financial Services Information Technology Secretariat, 262
Financial Services Policy Committee, 276
Financial Stability Forum, 240
Financial Standards Assessment Program, 240
Finch, Phil, 256
Fink, Matt, 44–45
First American Bank, 237
First Fidelity Bank of New Jersey, 239
First National Bank of Chicago, 227, 288
First National Bank of Keystone, Virginia, 49
First National City Bank of New York, 36, 78, 173
First Republic Bank, 128, 129
First Union Bank, 239
Fisher, Irving, 104, 155
Fisher, Peter, 236, 308
Floating exchange rates, 199, 234
Folkerts-Landau, David, 6–7
Ford, Bill, 127
Ford, Gerald, 130, 206, 230
Foreign Bank Supervision Enhancement Act of 1991, 237
Fowler, Henry, 175
Franchise tax, 74–75
Frank, Barney, 305
Frank, Jerome, 158
Franklin National Bank of New York, 38–39, 121–122
Freedom of Information Act, 292
Friedman, Milton, 13, 94, 104, 152, 166, 189–191, 193, 195, 197, 221
Friedman, Thomas, 14

Fringe banks, 113–114
Frost, David, 301–302, 322
Furash, Ed, 266, 272, 310
Furash & Company, 214
Futures contracts, 8–9, 12, 133–134, 137

Garn–St. Germain Act of 1982, 37, 40–41, 126
Garvin, George, 170
Garwood, Griff, 292
General Accounting Office (GAO), 69, 75–76, 123, 238, 253, 276, 292, 295, 307
General Electric Capital, 257–258
George, Eddie, 112, 117
German Reichsbank, 65–66
Giannini, A.P., 85
Gibraltar, 240
Gibson, Dunn & Crutcher, 50
Gilbert, Milton, 16, 229
Gilbert, William Schwenck, 289
Gillray, James, 60
Gingrich, Newt, 208
Glass, Carter, 67, 68, 78, 145, 161
Glass-Steagall Act of 1933, 34, 35, 40, 67, 68, 78, 157, 159, 168, 302
Glauber, Robert, 207, 211
Gold, 13, 56, 57, 73, 74, 81, 115, 150, 151, 155, 160, 181–182, 185, 193, 206, 226–229, 314
Gold and the Dollar Crisis (Triffin), 228–229
Goldman, Sachs, 5, 117, 118, 184, 208, 269
Gold Settlement Fund, 73
Goldsmith, Oliver, 156
Golembe, Carter, 51, 121, 267–268
Gonzalez, Henry, 129, 202–203
Goodhart, Charles, 58, 64, 314
Goodman, George J.W. ("Adam Smith"), 185
Gould, George, 207
Government Sponsored Enterprises, 178
Gramley, Lyle E., 253
Gramlich, Edward M., 180
Gramm, Phil, 297
Gramm-Leach-Bliley Act of 1999, 28, 37, 45–47, 49–52, 207, 297, 302, 306, 307
Grand Canyon State Bank, 290

Granite Capital, 223
Grant, James, 107
Great Depression, 74, 81, 102, 143, 154–162, 196, 198
Great Society, 38
Greenbacks, 66, 73
Greenspan, Alan, 6, 13–15, 18, 19, 22, 26, 41, 58, 79, 80, 101, 267, 268, 308–309. *See also* Federal Reserve System
    background of, 206
    as chairman of Council of Economic Advisers, 186
    on electronic ventures, 260–261
    on fair lending, 295–296
    October 15, 1998 intervention, 10–12, 51, 180, 224–225, 316–317
    October 1987 market crash and, 136, 209–210
    physical appearance of, 205
    Rubin, relationship with, 49–50, 208
    S&Ls and, 218–219
    on world financial crisis of 1997–98, 105–106
Greider, William, 58, 169, 181, 183, 200
Group of Thirty, 5, 8, 111, 233, 281
Gutfreund, John, 267, 268
Guttentag, Jack M., 104
Gyohten, Toyoo, 194, 203

Hackley, Howard H., 249
Hamilton, Alexander, 66
Hamming, Richard, 318–319
Hanke, Steve, 95
Harrison, George, 154, 155
Harris Trust, 135, 137
Harrod, Roy, 153–154
Hart, Albert, 77
Hawke, John B., Jr. ("Jerry"), 48, 306
Hayes, Alfred, 227
Hedge funds, 7, 12, 222–223, 266–269
Heimann, John, 31, 94, 278, 281, 283, 312
Heinz, John, 202
Heller, H. Robert, 110
Heller, Walter, 175
Herstatt crisis of 1974, 103, 233
Hitler, Adolf, 62
Hoehn, James, 131
Hoffmeyer, Erik, 25–26

Holding companies, 34–37, 41, 43, 303
Holmes, Oliver Wendell, Jr., 101
Holt, John, 319
Home equity loans, 26
Homer, Sidney, 179
Hong Kong dollar, 96
Hong Kong Shanghai (HSBC), 31, 239
Hoover, Herbert, 25, 77, 78, 156
Hopkins, Harry, 158
House Banking Committee, 46, 47, 71, 94, 106, 128–129, 143, 147, 202–203, 207
House Commerce Committee, 46
Housing and Urban Development, Department of (HUD), 295–296
Housing starts, 178
Hubbard, Elbert, 28
Huertas, Thomas E., 174
Hume, David, 190
Humphrey, David, 252
Humphrey-Hawkins Act of 1978, 13, 94, 187
Hunt brothers, 215
Hussein, Saddam, 9

IBM Corporation, 194
Indonesian banking system, 95, 311
Industrial Bank of Japan, 5
Inflation, 10, 13, 40, 58, 75, 86, 181, 186–198, 204, 219–221, 320, 321
Information technology, 20–21, 97, 320, 321
Initial public offerings, 8
Institute of International Bankers, 40
Interagency Country Exposure Committee (ICEC), 234–235
Interest equalization tax, 232
Interest rates, 10, 11, 15, 21–23, 26, 29, 75, 154, 156–158, 167–172, 178–180, 182, 184, 187–189, 191–197, 201, 204, 224, 225, 231, 236, 312–314, 320–321
International Banking Act of 1978, 234, 235
International Banking Facility (IBF), 235
International Monetary Fund (IMF), 4–8, 18, 83, 102, 109, 111, 188, 192, 228, 229, 234, 240, 242, 311
Internet purchases, 261

Interstate Commerce Commission (ICC), 52
Intraday loans, 213–214
Investment Company Institute, 44
Iran, 191
Isaac, William, 49, 124, 125, 127, 128, 271, 272
Italy, 150, 233
It's a Wonderful Life (movie), 109

Japan, 7, 13, 17, 107, 136, 162–163, 217, 231, 238, 309, 313, 315, 317, 320
Japanese Government Bond (JGB), 117
Jersey, 233, 240
Jett, Joe, 222–223
Johnson, Lyndon B., 38, 74, 75, 144, 166, 175–176
Johnson, Manuel, 203, 217, 218, 304
Johnson, Samuel, 150–151
J.P. Morgan, 5, 107, 124, 169–173, 242, 268, 278, 285
Junk bonds, 42
Justice, Department of, 291–292

Kamin, Steven, 221
Kaufman, George, 274
Kaufman, Henry, 18, 24–26, 179, 268, 316
Keating, Charles, 41, 219
Keehn, Silas, 127–128, 135
Kennedy, John F., 35, 87*n*, 166, 175, 227
Kennedy, Joseph, 87*n*
Keogh, James, 113
Keynes, John Maynard, 22, 57, 81, 155, 157, 158, 314
Kidder Peabody, 134, 222–223
Kindleberger, Charles, 72, 108
Kipling, Rudyard, 75
Knight, Frank, 77
Kohl, Helmut, 232
Komansky, David, 4
Korean War, 83, 86
Krause, Susan, 18, 241
Kregel, Jan, 10, 318
Krugman, Paul, 22

Lacker, Jeffrey M., 258
LaFalce, John, 129, 218
Lagged accounting, 197
Lambsdorff, Otto von, 232

Lamfalussy, Alexandre, 16, 103, 212, 214, 309
Lamont, Thomas W., 81
Lance, Bert, 112, 237
Large, Sir Andrew, 240–241, 308
Large Complex Banking Organizations (LCBOs), 239, 275, 280
Larosière, Jacques de, 199, 202, 234
LaSalle Bank, 239
Lastra, Rosa, 316
Latuhamallo, Adolf, 247
Law, John, 64
Leach, Jim, 45–47, 306n
Leach, Ralph, 172–174
Leeson, Nicholas, 116–118
Leffingwell, Russell, 154
Lend-lease programs, 173
Lewis, Michael, 267
Liar's Poker (Lewis), 267
Liberty Bonds, 152
Lichtenstein, 240
Limbaugh, Rush, 208–209
Lincoln, Abraham, 73
Lincoln Savings & Loan, 219
Lindsey, Larry, 156, 285, 296, 304
Liquidity trap, 157, 314, 315
Litan, Robert, 270
Lombard Street (Bagehot), 103
London Metals Exchange, 215
Long Term Capital Management (LTCM), 7, 11, 138–139, 215, 238, 266–269
Lowenstein, Roger, 268
Ludwig, Eugene, 44–46, 48, 49, 296, 306
Luxembourg, 233

Maastricht Treaty of 1991, 13
Maisel, Sherman, 164–166, 184, 188–189, 193
Malkin, Larry, 194
Mann, Maurice, 210
Mantel, Brian, 260
Manufacturers Hanover Bank, 122
Marine Midland Trust Company, 31
Marshall Plan, 173, 228, 229
Martin, Preston, 180, 199–200, 304
Martin, William McChesney, Jr., 77, 79, 83, 90–93, 164–169, 172, 175–176, 179, 181–183, 188, 190, 207, 227, 303
Marx, Karl, 103–104, 109, 314

Mattei, Ivan E., 306
Mattingly, Virgil, 303
McAdoo, William G., 69, 71
McCabe, Thomas, 87–90, 165, 188
McCulloch, Hugh, 30
McCullough, David, 84
McDonough, William, 8, 239, 255, 268, 269, 278, 308
McFadden Act of 1927, 34, 286
McGovern, George, 183
McKenna, William, 218
Medlin, John, 36
Melamed, Leo, 212
Mellon, Andrew, 25, 156, 157
Melton, William C., 193
Mencken, H.L., 223
Mercantile Bank of St. Louis, 35
Meriwether, John, 267, 268
Merrill Lynch, 5, 41, 117–119, 126, 132
Mexico, 17, 83, 101, 109, 208–209, 235
Meyer, Eugene, 156–157, 159
Meyer, Laurence H., 40, 296, 307
Michigan National Bank, 123
MICR (magnetic ink character recognition), 250
Mieno, Yasushi, 313
Milken, Michael, 42
Miller, Adolf, 157
Miller, G. William, 187, 188, 192–195
Mills, Ogden, 157
Minsky, Hyman, 10, 264, 269, 270, 317
Mitchell, George, 166, 189, 193, 213
Monetary Control Act of 1980, 253
Monley, Donald P., 214
Moore, George, 36, 78, 82, 159
Moral hazard, 131, 311
Morgan Stanley, 5, 117, 234, 269, 282
Morris, Frank, 304
Mortgage loans, 42, 156, 178–179, 222
Moscow, Michael, 9
Moussa, Mike, 283
Moynihan, Patrick, 206
Mulford, David, 202–203
Mullins, David, 211
Munnell, Alicia, 294
Mussolini, Benito, 81

NAIRU (Non-Accelerating Inflation Rate of Unemployment), 197
Napoleon Bonaparte, 64

Narodny Bank, 173
National Automated Clearing House Association, 257
National Bank Act, 73
National Bank Examiners, 269
National City Bank of New York, 227
National Commission on Housing, 178, 200
National Commission on Social Security Reform, 206
National currencies, end of, 29
National debt, 151, 183
National Examination Database, 279
NationsBank of North Carolina, 44, 280
Netherlands Antilles, 233
New Deal, 73, 121, 158–161, 178
New York Clearing House, 212–214, 255, 256, 261
New York Commodity Exchange ("Comex"), 115, 215
New York Stock Exchange, 66, 133, 135–136, 165, 166
New York Times, The, 14, 58, 268, 319
New Zealand, 83
Nixon, Richard M., 38, 90, 93, 144, 166, 183, 184, 186, 193, 195
Nixon for President Committee, 206
Norman, Montagu, 61–62, 81, 154, 226

O'Brien, Sir Leslie, 63, 113
O'Donoghue, R.B., 254
O'Driscoll, Gerald, 307
Office of Management and Budget (OMB), 75, 272
Office of the Comptroller of the Currency (OCC), 29–36, 39, 43–46, 48–50, 234, 240, 270–273, 275, 279, 289, 296, 306*n*
Oil prices, 113, 186–187, 191–192, 198, 201, 230
Open Market Investment Committee, 153, 155
Open Market Policy Conference, 155–157
Oppenheimer, Robert, 318–319
Organization for Economic Cooperation and Development (OECD), 17, 240, 277
Osborne, Bruce, 135

Paine, Thomas, 56, 59
PaineWebber, 134
Pakistanis, 112, 237
Palmer, Joe H., 281
Panics, 66, 103, 104, 108, 109, 118, 133, 136–137, 209–212
Papadimitriou, Dimitri, 287
Pardee, Scott, 236
Paribas, 268
Parris, Stan, 128–129
Partee, Charles, 15, 20
Patman, Wright, 143–144, 169
Patrikis, Ernest, 233, 237, 276
Patterson, Oakley, 82
Paul, Ron, 206
Payments system, 247–263, 282, 292–294, 310
Peel Act of 1844, 103, 106, 109
Penalty rates of interest, 109, 111
Penn Central Railroad, 184–185
Penn Square Bank, 123, 127
Pension funds, 137
People's Bank of China, 83
Perkins, James, 159
Philips curve, 197
Phillips, Ronnie J., 287
Piccozzi, Jake, 250
Plaza Agreement, 201
Poor, the, 285–298
Pope, Alexander, 14
Populists, 66
Pre-Commitment Approach (PCA), 282
Premier Bank of Wytheville, Virginia, 292
President's Working Group, 278–279
Pringle, Robin, 57
Proxmire, William, 39, 203, 288
Prussian State Bank, 65
Pulley, Lawrence, 252
Purpose credit, 79

Q theory of investment, 221–222
Quinn, Brian, 111, 112, 117

Radcliffe Commission, 94–95
Rand, Ayn, 206
Randolph, John, 15
Reagan, Ronald, 41, 178, 199, 200, 203–205, 278

Real bills doctrine, 148–150, 153, 190
Real Time Gross Settlement systems, 255, 310
Recessions, 149, 187, 195–196, 209, 219–221
Redlining, 286, 288
Reed, John, 269, 283, 308, 317
Regan, Donald, 41, 126, 199, 200
Repurchase agreements, 70, 178, 193
Rhodes, Eugene Manlove, 28
Richardson, Gordon, 113–114
Riegel, Don, 43
Risk-adjusted capital standards, 17
Rivlin, Alice, 262, 304
Robb, Victoria, 119
Robertson, A. Willis, 35
Robertson, J.L., 39, 304
Robertson, Julian, 7
Rockefeller Foundation, 5, 223
Rogers, Donald, 37
Roosa, Robert V., 175, 198, 202
Roosevelt, Franklin D., 25, 33, 73, 77, 84, 109, 159–161, 190, 227
Root, Elihu, 68–69
Rossant, Murray, 92
Rubin, Robert, 4, 47, 48–50, 101, 201, 208, 281
Ruding, Onno, 303
Russia, 6, 7, 11, 22, 203, 282, 283, 311, 315
Ryback, William, 40

Safire, William, 14
Saint-Phalle, Thibaut de, 36, 235
Sanford, Charles, 137
Santander, 239
Sarbanes, Paul, 138
S&L industry, 41, 127, 131, 132, 177–178, 200, 217–220, 277
Saxon, John, 35, 44, 171–172
Sayers, R.S., 62, 81, 188, 191
Say's Law, 190
Schacht, Hjalmar, 62
Schapiro, Mary, 118
Schmidt, Helmut, 192
Schultz, Fred, 199
Schultze, Charles, 193, 194
Schumpeter, Joseph, 301, 318
Schwartz, Anna J., 102, 104
Seattle First Bank, 123–124

Seay, George J., 72
Secretary of the treasury, 68–69
Secrets of the Temple (Greider), 58, 200
Securities and Exchange Commission (SEC), 28–29, 45, 46, 49–52, 235, 280, 304, 305
Securities and Investment Board (United Kingdom), 115
Securities Exchange Act of 1934, 32
Security Pacific Bank, 272–273
Seeger, Martha, 130
Seidman, L. William, 121, 128–130, 133, 186, 217, 219, 220, 230
Seignorage, 56, 80
Senate Banking Committee, 35, 43, 47, 94, 202
Shah of Iran, 191
Shared National Credit program, 279
Sheffield Bank, 247
Sheng, Andrew, 102–103, 105, 110, 131
Shull, Bernard, 131
Shultz, George, 230
Siebert, Muriel, 31
Silver dollar, 66
Simon, William, 186, 230, 233
Simons, Henry, 77
Sindona, Michele, 38, 122
Singapore International Monetary Exchange (SIMEX), 116, 118
Singapore Monetary Authority, 117–119
Skadden Arps, 242
"Smith, Adam" (George J.W. Goodman), 185
Smith, H. Arnholdt, 38
Snyder, John, 86–92, 165
Social Security Administration, 294
Société Général, 268
Society for Worldwide Interbank Financial Telecommunications (SWIFT), 254
Solomon, Tony, 199
Somers, A.A., 220
Soros, George, 6, 167
South Korea, 17, 83, 107, 242, 277, 311
SouthTrust, 272
Soviet Union, 173, 203
Special Drawing Rights, 109
Spillenkothen, Richard, 279
Sprague, Irvine, 124, 126, 127
Sprague, O.M.W., 108

Sprinkel, Beryl, 198–200
Sproul, Allan, 67, 86–87, 90, 92, 143, 166
Stagflation, 185, 186, 321
State-chartered banks, 31, 32, 34, 35, 38, 43–45, 71, 149
State Savings & Loan, 177
Steelman, John, 91
Stein, Howard, 137
Sternlight, Peter, 211, 236
Stockman, David, 198
Strong, Benjamin, 25, 72, 81, 96, 120, 151, 153, 154, 155, 226
Structured Early Intervention and Resolution (SEIR), 274
Subcommittee on Credit, Reserves, and Risk Management (SCRIM), 276
Subordinated notes, 307
Suharto, President, 95
Sultan of Brunei, 117
Sumitomo Bank, 215
Summers, Bruce, 255–256
Summers, Lawrence H., 48, 50, 105, 240
Swedish Riksbank, 58–59
Switzerland, 65

Taft, Robert, 88
Task Group on Regulation of Financial Services, 40
Texas Commerce Bank, 201
Thailand, 109, 241, 242, 311
Thatcher, Margaret, 186
Thomas, Kenneth H., 285, 290–292, 298
Thornton, Henry, 60
Timberlake, R.H., 106
Time deposits, 168, 175
Tisch, Larry, 38
Tobin, James, 175, 221–222
Todd, Walker, 133
Transparency, 15–19, 223–224, 308, 309, 311
Treasury, Department of the, 7, 31, 38, 41–43, 57, 75, 76, 86–92, 151–152, 202, 207, 208, 226, 227, 233
Triffin, Robert, 228–229
Truman, Edwin, 208
Truman, Harry, 83, 84, 87–92, 144, 175, 237
Truth-in-Lending Act of 1969, 52
Tugwell, Rex, 158

Turner, Philip, 221
Twohig, Peggy, 294, 302

Unemployment, 197, 198, 288
Union Bank of Switzerland (UBS), 174, 238, 268
United Nations Conference on Trade and Development (UNCTAD), 9–10
United States National Bank of San Diego, 38
Unit trusts, 115

Value-at-Risk model, 282–284
Van 't dack, Jozef, 221
Vatican, 233
Vault cash, as reserve, 147
Venture capitalists, 179
Victory Bonds, 152
Vietnam War, 38, 75, 176, 181
Vinson, Fred, 89
Volcker, Paul, 5–7, 11, 41, 58, 101, 124, 127–128, 130, 192–195, 197–205, 210, 230–231, 235–237, 303–304
Voluntary Credit Restraint Program, 82

Waage, Tom, 122, 184, 250
Wachovia Bank of North Carolina, 36
Wage and price controls, 86, 186
Wallace, Henry, 77
Wallich, Henry, 303
Wall Street Journal, 13
War Powers Act, 184
Washington, George, 60
Washington Post, The, 14, 156
Waters, Maxime, 296
Webster, Daniel, 15
Weinberg, John A., 259
Weintraub, Bill, 193
Weld, White, 202
Wells Fargo Bank, 35, 254
Wentzler, Nancy A., 266
When Genius Failed (Lowenstein), 268
"Whip Inflation Now" campaign, 130
White, George, 250
White, William, 16
White, William R., 109, 312
Whitehead, John, 204
Whitney, Alan, 125
Whitney, Richard, 165

Wille, Frank, 130
Willis, H. Parker, 68, 145
Willis, Mark, 296
Wilson, Harold, 233
Wilson, Woodrow, 67, 69
Woljinower, Albert, 18
Woodin, Will, 159
Woods, George, 164
Woodward, Bob, 208

World Bank, 4–8, 159, 165, 192, 240
World War I, 72, 151–152, 227
World War II, 82, 83, 167, 173, 227, 229
Wray, L. Randall, 287
Wriston, Walter, 96–97, 174, 186

Yellen, Janet, 304
Yeo, Ed, 199, 233
Yom Kippur War (1973), 186